Digital Technologies in Behavior Science

Digital Technologies in Behavior Science is the first book of its kind to highlight innovative and cutting-edge work in the theory and application of digital technologies in behavior science.

Bringing together the work of experts in the field, this edited book showcases current and future trends in the use of digital technologies in the behavioral sciences. The chapters outline the important historical, theoretical, and conceptual background for this timely field, looking at practical applications in varied settings. The book is divided into five sections and explores history and systems in behavior science, machine learning and artificial intelligence, the process and research, digital platforms, and health and human applications.

This timely book will be essential reading for graduate and advanced undergraduate students of behavioral science, behavior analysis, and psychology. It will also be highly relevant for professional behavior analysts and all those interested in the future of behavior science.

Darlene E. Crone-Todd is Professor Emeritus in the Department of Psychology at Salem State University, USA.

Donald A. Hantula is Associate Professor in the Department of Psychology and Neuroscience, College of Liberal Arts, Temple University, USA.

T. V. Joe Layng is Adjunct Professor of Behavior Analysis, Endicott College, USA. He is also Cofounder and Partner of Generategy, an educational software company whose products are based on generative instruction principles.

Behavior Science: Theory, Research and Practice
Series Editor: The Association for Behavior Analysis International

Applied Behavior Science in Organizations
Consilience of Historical and Emerging Trends in Organizational Behavior Management
Edited by Ramona A. Houmanfar, Mitch Fryling & Mark P. Alavosius

A Programming Contingency Analysis of Mental Health
By Israel Goldiamond

Acceptance and Commitment for Behavior Analysts
A Practice Guide from Theory to Treatment
Edited by Mark R. Dixon, Steven C. Hayes and Jordan Belisle

Women in Behavior Science
Observations of Life Inside and Outside of the Academy
Edited by Ruth Anne Rehfeldt, Traci Cihon and Erin Rasmussen

Digital Technologies in Behavior Science
Theoretical and Practical Applications
Edited by Donald A. Hantula, Darlene E. Crone-Todd and T. V. Joe Layng

For more information about this series, please visit: www.routledge.com/Behavior-Science/book-series/ABAI

Digital Technologies in Behavior Science

Theoretical and Practical Applications

Edited by Darlene E. Crone-Todd, Donald A. Hantula, and T. V. Joe Layng

Routledge
Taylor & Francis Group
NEW YORK AND LONDON

Designed cover image: Cover illustration: Martin Burch, Association for Behavior Analysis International.

First published 2026
by Routledge
605 Third Avenue, New York, NY 10158

and by Routledge
4 Park Square, Milton Park, Abingdon, Oxon, OX14 4RN

Routledge is an imprint of the Taylor & Francis Group, an informa business

ISBN: 978-1-032-46217-2 (hbk)
ISBN: 978-1-032-46211-0 (pbk)
ISBN: 978-1-003-38060-3 (ebk)

DOI: 10.4324/9781003380603

Typeset in Optima
by Apex CoVantage, LLC

Contents

List of Contributors *vii*
Preface *ix*
Acknowledgments *xiii*

SECTION 1
Foundations of Digital Technology and Behavior Science 1

1 Technology and Computer Programming in Behavior Analysis: Historical Trends and Guidance for Behavior Analysts 3
SHAWN PATRICK GILROY

2 Complex Systems Theory in Behavior Analysis 17
J. J. MCDOWELL

3 Behavioral Science in the Fourth Industrial Revolution 30
ELIZABETH GARRISON, LINDSAY OUELLETTE, AND JARED B. DANIEL

SECTION 2
Machine Learning, AI, and Predictive Models in Behavior Science 41

4 Machine Learning to Support Decision-Making in Behavior Science: Current Research and Future Directions 43
MARC J. LANOVAZ AND PHILIPPE LEROUX

5 Reinforcement Learning in Behavior Science and Artificial Intelligence 54
DAVID J. COX, LAURA WEIL, JOSHUA FARROW, ADRIENNE M. JENNINGS, CARLOS SANTOS, AND JACOB SOSINE

6 Extending Neural Network Predictions of Human Behaviors 69
CHRIS NINNESS, CHRISTINE BERGAN, LEE MASON, AND SHARON NINNESS

SECTION 3
Tools and Technologies for Research and Applications 81

7 **An Updated and Simplified Version of a Low-Cost Arduino-Visual Basic Interface for Operant Research** 83
ROGELIO ESCOBAR, RODRIGO BENAVIDES, AND BRISSA GUTIÉRREZ

8 **Simulation-Based Assessment and Training** 94
ELLIE KAZEMI, BRIANNA HERRERA, MATTHEW S. DAVIES, ADISA PTAH, ERIC MCCOY, AND VICTOR RAMIREZ

9 **Using Virtual Reality within Behavior Analysis Practice** 106
ANA ESCALANTE

10 **Behavioral and Digital Technologies in the Treatment of Substance Use Disorder** 116
JESSE DALLERY AND BETHANY R. RAIFF

11 **Developing AI Personas for Use in Behavior Analytic Training: A Case Study of an Autism Parent** 126
ANNA M. LINNEHAN

Index *141*

Contributors

Rodrigo Benavides, National Autonomous University of Mexico, Mexico

Christine Bergan, Behavioral Software Systems

David J. Cox, Endicott College, USA, and RethinkFirst

Jesse Dallery, University of Florida, USA

Jared B. Daniel, Temple University, USA

Matthew S. Davies, California State University, Northridge, USA

Ana Escalante, BehaviorMe, Inc.

Rogelio Escobar, National Autonomous University of Mexico, Mexico

Joshua Farrow, Paragon Autism Services

Elizabeth Garrison, Temple University, USA

Shawn Patrick Gilroy, Louisiana State University, USA

Brissa Gutiérrez, National Autonomous University of Mexico, Mexico

Brianna Herrera, California State University, Northridge, USA

Adrienne M. Jennings, Daemen University, USA

Ellie Kazemi, California State University, Northridge, USA

Marc J. Lanovaz, École de psychoéducation, Université de Montréal, Canada, and Centre de recherche de l'Institut universitaire en santé mentale de Montréal, Canada

Philippe Leroux, École de psychoéducation, Université de Montréal, Canada, and Centre de recherche de l'Institut universitaire en santé mentale de Montréal, Canada

Anna M. Linnehan, Institute for Applied Behavioral Science, Endicott College, USA

Lee Mason, Child Study Center, Cook Children's Health Care System and Burnett School of Medicine, Texas Christian University, USA

Eric McCoy, California State University, Northridge, USA

J. J. McDowell, Department of Psychology, Emory University, USA

Chris Ninness, Behavioral Software Systems, USA

Sharon Ninness, East Texas A&M University, USA

Lindsay Ouellette, Temple University, USA

Adisa Ptah, California State University, Northridge, USA

Bethany R. Raiff, Rowan University, USA

Victor Ramirez, California State University, Northridge, USA

Carlos Santos, Endicott College, USA

Jacob Sosine, RethinkFirst, USA

Laura Weil, Endicott College, USA

Preface

Dear Reader,

In 2026, a book about digital technologies may seem ironic, or perhaps oxymoronic. Are deep dives into our digital tools, their applications, and implications for behavior science relevant in an age of TikTok, memes, blog posts, social media, quick communications, and rapid change? We, and the authors in this volume, see great value in taking some time to read and reflect on the promises and potential perils of our digital existence. This volume is not standing atop history, looking backward and yelling "stop!" It is also not an elucidation of a technotopia panacea.

To be sure that we are all on the same page, we should take a moment to consider what is meant by "digital technology." In English, the modifier often precedes the object being modified, so we will consider the object, *technology*, first. What is technology? Computer scientist Alan Kay defined *technology* as anything invented after you were born, but perhaps a more formal and fitting definition is from David Kipnis (1991), who defines technology as using systematic procedures to produce intended effects. In Kipnis's view, technology is not a thing, but it is a process. *Digital* refers to electronic devices and systems that process and transmit data in binary (0/1) form (Brynjolfsson & McAfee, 2014). These issues are more than semantic. As Negroponte (1995) observes, the critical difference between technology as a thing and technology as a digital process is the difference between atoms and bits. If you are reading this book in printed form, you are engaging with atoms, but if you are reading this book in an e-format, you are engaging with bits.

Take a moment to consider the implications. For one, distributing this printed book involves manipulating atoms to create paper pages and the cover. Transmitting the book to you involves warehouses and the transportation and delivery of these arranged atoms. By contrast, an e-book requires none of this. It can be transmitted to thousands of readers instantly with the click of a mouse and copied easily. It is just a bunch of bits. As we move from an entirely physical world to one of both atoms and bits, certainly some things are gained, but some things are lost.

This book emerged out of the editors' long-standing interests in the intersections among behavior science, technology, later digital technologies, and artificial intelligence. Our conversations at related scientific meetings and through email correspondence span over three decades. As the world emerged from the global pandemic, a shift seemingly occurred in the extent to which people use digital technology. Virtual work and virtual teams became normalized; communication technologies such as BlueJeans, Google Meet, and Zoom seemed to pop up overnight without fading away; and long-held beliefs about time, place, and work were shattered. But it should be noted that all these technologies were developed and in use in the 20th century. Although they may seem to magically appear out of the ether, technologies are not developed and implemented overnight; as Ebbinghaus (1908/1910) observed about psychology, any technology has a long past but a short history.

We created this book with the goal of inviting a diverse group of contributors who could bring to the table a variety of topics and discuss their relevance, challenges, and key questions. This volume is not intended to be definitive or exhaustive. Instead, it is intended to be illustrative and heuristic. Certainly, many topics and applications are left out, as any one book is limited in terms of the number of atoms, bits, or both. Any omission does not imply unimportance; chapters were written based on the authors' current interests and work. Indeed, many topics near and dear to the editor's hearts and brains, such as digital personalized systems of instruction, artificial intelligence (AI) performance assistants, social robotics, virtual teamwork, neurodiversity in digital workplaces, automated systems for gradual changes in rehabilitative or sports movement, and so many more topics, were not included. Perhaps they can be covered in a follow-up volume? We hope that one or more of these chapters sparks readers to explore how various digital technologies can extend their work. It is our belief that any technology can be used wisely or not and that behavioral science is an important player in evaluating the use of any technology and how the use impacts behavior. It should be noted that the behavioral data collected also shape the technology.

Our intended audience for the book is anyone who has an interest in these topics. Scientists and the intellectually curious in applied fields will find within these pages cutting-edge information and updates on the use of digital technology in behavioral science. These topics will be equally interesting to well-prepared undergraduate students, graduate students, researchers, and practitioners.

We collectively express our own hope for the future with this book in that it provides a sampling of the ways in which digital technologies can be used to advance research and help individuals make behavioral changes that are important to them in terms of their own values and goals. To this end, the contents of the book include many socially relevant topics.

The book is organized into three main sections. First, the section titled "Foundations of Digital Technology and Behavior Science" includes three chapters. Gilroy leads the book with a chapter devoted to a historical overview of the use of technology in both experimental and applied behavior analysis, current trends, and guidance for the future. An important reminder about mentoring, collaboration, and training is relevant across time and space. The second chapter, by J. J. McDowell, describes simple versus complex systems and how modern theory development assumes complex systems are operating within organisms. However, testing of a complex system theory such as the evolutionary theory of behavioral dynamics (ETBD; McDowell, 2013, 2019) suggests that the complex behavior of systems emerges based on lower-level rules. The importance of such a theory is that it can also be used to test artificial organisms in their own right and compare these systems to humans or other organisms. Rounding out this section is a chapter by Garrison, Ouellette, and Daniel, who provide an examination of the ways in which the fourth industrial revolution (4IR; Schwab, 2016) is requiring a careful consideration of how we define our relationship with digital technology and work. Increasing use of AI and other systems is disruptive, and there are many challenges related to leadership, education and training, and workforce adaptation. They argue that behavior science can play a key role in terms of our expertise in learning environments and performance systems, as well as creating environments to foster well-being.

The second section, "Machine Learning, AI, and Predictive Models in Behavior Science," includes three chapters devoted to these topics. Lanovaz and Leroux (Chapter 4) provide an overview of how machine learning operates in terms of the use of programmed algorithms to more effectively "read" data – i.e., identify and interpret patterns. While there is great promise for the technology to be used, they point out that behavior analysts have been slow to adopt it. As such, they provide a helpful primer with the goal of providing examples of applications, challenges, and future directions (see also Lanovaz & Turgeon, 2020). Chapter 5, by Cox, Weil, Farrow, Jennings, Santos, and Sosine, discusses how the historical study of basic concepts like reinforcement and punishment in previous centuries allowed for an important understanding of the function of the behavior of organisms within their environments (see Cox, 2025 for further extensions). They describe the history of this work, as well as the extension to testing how artificial intelligence agents may be considered organisms to study in their own right and how researchers can move their research ahead by using artificial agents to test theories, compare their performance to humans or other species, and otherwise advance knowledge. We should note that reinforcement learning (Sutton & Barto, 1998) is the basis of modern robotics. Rounding out this section, Ninness, Bergan, Mason, and Ninness provide an overview of the ways in which deep neural networks (DNNs) are relevant in terms of the rapidly accelerating pace of machine learning to emulate human behavior. This digital technology can provide important and helpful clinical applications and has implications for humanity. These three chapters provide cutting-edge and timely reminders that the future is here and is creating an environment of opportunity. Will we use that opportunity wisely for the betterment of all?

The third section, "Tools and Technologies for Research and Applications," provides practical examples of how to use digital technology for beneficial purposes. Escobar, Benavides, and Gutiérrez (Chapter 7) provide an overview of an economical digital interface to run operant chambers. This is key when funding is scarce for basic research and is desirable in any case. Kazemi, Herrera, Davies, Ptah, McCoy, and Ramirez (Chapter 8) describe how behavioral skills training (BST; Miltenberger, 2016) of behavior analysts can be more efficiently accomplished using technologies such as virtual reality, robotics, and AI simulations. Such systems allow for real-time data collection, feedback, and progress. Escalante (Chapter 9) focuses on the use of VR simulations for clinical research and practice itself, with key reminders about the importance of staying true to both the science and the application of behavior analysis. Dallery and Raif (Chapter 10) then move to the important public health issue of addiction. Their overview of reinforcement-based clinical approaches as aided and assisted using digital technology (Stitzer & Petry, 2022) is an example of the way in which approaches evolve and lead the way to the future. Finally, Linnehan (Chapter 11) describes a unique case study on the use of AI to create a persona of a parent of an individual diagnosed with autism. The chapter describes the evolution of the persona based on prompts and outputs and how it can be used (for example) to train behavior analysts to more effectively interact with parents in these types of situations.

In all, the chapters included in this book have a common theme: What has come before has been an example of technology developed and applied to help solve basic research and applied/clinical questions that are important to us. These chapters also challenge us to reassess our current practices and knowledge in their wake. The experimental side of the field has long been at the forefront of developing and using various research technologies (Lattal, 2008); however, the applied side has been much more recalcitrant to do so (Pennypacker, 2017). Using new digital technologies requires learning new skills; for example, programming skills are required to take advantage of the interface described by Escobar, Benavides, and Gutiérrez, and Cox (2025) points out that AI is math, and math skills are required for effective and ethical use of AI. If a mathematical background is not emphasized in applied training, as Marr (2017) suggests, then this may prove a stumbling block for many on the applied side who want to use AI. As the technology progresses, so too should the training of those in the relevant fields. The current state of the field is a mix: those who fully adopt, those who do so in a more hesitant way (awaiting results), and those who have not yet adopted technology. As the new adage goes: AI will not replace you, but you are likely to be replaced by someone with expertise who also knows how to use AI. Digital technologies are here, just as the printing press was many centuries ago. To ignore that would be a mistake, and to use it unwisely would be a mistake too. However, harnessing the power of digital technology to benefit humanity would be a great advance.

Darlene E. Crone-Todd, Donald A. Hantula,
and T. V. Joe Layng

References

Brynjolfsson, E., & McAfee, A. (2014). *The second machine age: Work, progress, and prosperity in a time of brilliant technologies*. W. W. Norton & Company.

Cox, D. J. (2025). Ethical behavior analysis in the age of artificial intelligence (AI): The importance of understanding model building while formal AI literacy curricula are developed. *Perspectives on Behavior Science*. https://doi.org/10.1007/s40614-025-00459-z

Ebbinghaus, H. (1910). *A summary of psychology* (M. Meyer, Trans.). Veit. (Original work published 1908)

Kay, A., as cited in Tapscott, D. (1998). *Growing up digital: The rise of the net generation* (p. 47). McGraw-Hill.

Kipnis, D. (1991). The technological perspective. *Psychological Science, 2*(2), 62–69.

Lanovaz, M. J., & Turgeon, S. (2020). Tutorial: Applying machine learning in behavioral research. *Perspectives on Behavior Science, 43*(4), 697–723. https://doi.org/10.1007/s40614-020-00253-y

Lattal, K. A. (2008). JEAB at 50: Coevolution of research and technology. *Journal of the Experimental Analysis of Behavior, 89*(3), 287–305.

Marr, M. J. (2017). The future of behavior analysis: Foxes and hedgehogs revisited. *Behavior Analyst, 40*, 197–207.

McDowell, J. J. (2013). A quantitative evolutionary theory of adaptive behavior dynamics. *Psychological Review, 120*(4), 731–750. https://doi.org/10.1037/a0034244

McDowell, J. J. (2019). On the current status of the evolutionary theory of behavior dynamics. *Journal of the Experimental Analysis of Behavior, 111*(1), 130–145. https://doi.org/10.1002/jeab.495

Miltenberger, R. G. (2016). Behavioral skills training. In *Behavior modification: Principles and procedures* (6th ed.). Cengage Learning.

Negroponte, N. (1995). *Being digital*. Alfred A. Knopf.

Pennypacker, H. S. (2017). Where are all the behavior analysts coming from? *Behavior Analyst, 40*, 183–185.

Schwab, K. (2016). *The fourth industrial revolution*. Crown Business.

Stitzer, M. L., & Petry, N. M. (2022). Digital contingency management in the treatment of substance use disorders: A systematic review. *Journal of Substance Abuse Treatment, 136*, 108663. https://doi.org/10.1016/j.jsat.2022.108663

Sutton, R. S., & Barto, A. G. (1998). *Introduction to reinforcement learning*. MIT Press.

Acknowledgments

We would like to express our appreciation to the authors who contributed their time and expertise to contribute the chapters that made this book possible. The three of us are also grateful for the collaborative and collegial nature of working together on this project. We thank Taylor & Francis, the publisher, for their patient guidance throughout the process, and the Association for Behavior Analysis International (ABAI) for the privilege of including this book in its series.

Darlene E. Crone-Todd
Donald A. Hantula
T. V. Joe Layng

Section 1

Foundations of Digital Technology and Behavior Science

1 Technology and Computer Programming in Behavior Analysis

Historical Trends and Guidance for Behavior Analysts

Shawn Patrick Gilroy

Introduction

The behavior of human and nonhuman animals is a phenomenon that has been studied for millennia. Factors believed to shape and sustain behavior have been debated by scholars and researchers across various domains, including philosophy, law, education, behavioral science, and more (e.g., religion). With regard to the study of human behavior, specifically, most have elected to look inward in search of factors that govern human choice and behavior.

Behaviorism emerged as a perspective on the behavior of organisms in stark contrast to contemporary psychological perspectives. Novel in its time, this account viewed specific behavioral phenomena (i.e., individual responses) as elements warranting study and not simply as a proxy for some broad inferred trait or latent factor (e.g., self-efficacy). Departing from accounts of the mind, human will, and other inferred causes for behavior at the time, this perspective prompted further inquiry into various contextual factors, which were seldom emphasized at the time. Specifically, the emphasis here was on measuring responses over time and examining relationships between these responses and various features present in the environment. The emphasis on *precisely* measuring responses over time in behaviorism prompted expansions in both the types of questions researched as well as the methods used to answer those questions (see Skinner, 1956, for a reflection on the topic). Over the past century, through various waves of behaviorism (e.g., methodological behaviorism, behavior analysis), the perspective and methodology have grown to include increasingly complex responses (e.g., anxiety; Friman et al., 1998) and behavior taking place across extended intervals (e.g., molar models of response allocation; Baum, 2002). The emphasis on precisely and repeatedly capturing responses over time prompted the development of various novel tools (e.g., apparatuses, software) to meet these needs. Specifically, tools were developed to study behavior when the act of directly observing these responses was either infeasible or otherwise introduced a confound or barrier to undertaking the research (see Escobar, 2014, for an excellent account of this technology in behaviorism).

Excellent reviews of technology in both historical and contemporary behavior analysis have already been produced (see Catania, 2002, for another account of technology in operant research), and in lieu of revisiting that history, this chapter instead focuses on a history of computer programming in behavior analysis and provides recommendations for those with an interest in acquiring repertoire related to modern technology and behavior analysis. A short history of behavior analysts developing hardware and software is presented here to provide the reader with a context for current trends in behavior analytic software ventures as well as to contextualize recommendations for learners and the field at large.

DOI: 10.4324/9781003380603-2

Early Technology in Behavior Analysis

Research in behavior analysis, like all fields, was facilitated by the tools and methods available at the time. Reflecting back upon various advances in behavior analytic theory and research, many are linked to tools and methods novel at the time (see Lattal, 2008, for a reflection on the topic). Perhaps the most iconic example of such is B. F. Skinner's introduction of the components that comprised the operant chamber (e.g., Skinner, 1932). It warrants noting that apparatuses at the time were already sufficient to record various responses in behavioral experiments (e.g., Thorndike's "Problem Box"; see Thorndike, 1911), but the technology adapted by Skinner was novel with regard to the *questions* it was designed to answer. For example, Skinner's research questions around this time focused more on rates of behavior in relation to specific environmental events (e.g., consequences) over time, whereas most others were examining responses in terms of fixed, immediate contexts and blocks of trials or series (see Iversen, 1992). Much of Skinner's early work explored what would become operant conditioning as a process complementary to reflexive conditioning – a prevailing account of learning at the time. The development of the operant chamber is relevant to the history of technology in behavior analysis because it marked an early point when behavioral scientists leveraged the technology available to them at the time to develop apparatuses and facilitate new avenues for behavioral research (for a related discussion, see Weiss, 1969).

The operant chamber was the product of combining several mechanical components and utilizing them to serve a novel purpose. Specifically, kinetic energy captured as a result of the organism performing the response (e.g., depressing a lever or key) was transferred mechanically, via some type of transducer, to some mechanism designed to record an event (e.g., a mark upon paper). Skinner's instrumentation captured response *rates* by translating relevant events (e.g., lever press, food delivery) onto a modified kymograph that allowed for a visual inspection of behavior across units of time. The kymograph, a device used to mechanically transfer a signal to a spinning drum via some drawing instrument (i.e., akin to the printing of some receipt), was repurposed to function as what we now consider the cumulative recorder (see Lattal, 2004, for additional history on the cumulative recorder).

The constant speed of the spinning drum permitted a means of examining responses in terms of units of time (e.g., responding, deliveries per hour). The introduction of a mechanical means of recording behavior rates (e.g., behavior per unit of time) supported two features that were highly relevant to operant research – rates of responding as a central metric and a focus on visually depicting rates in behavioral experiments. The development of this technology, as well as the openness and transparency of its design and construction, supported the wave of operant research that would follow and established visual analysis as a defining strategy for behavior analytic research and practice (see Sidman, 1960, for early discussions).

Advancing Technology and Behavior Analysis

The field of behavior analysis has changed considerably since the introduction of technology supporting a focus on rates and the inspection of how ecological events influenced those rates. Although practicing behavior analysts and contemporary behavioral scientists are unlikely to use such early technology in their work, a short history of expansions upon the design is provided to establish a context for trends in behavior analytic research incorporating modern computing.

The operant chamber (and other associated tools) provided a starting point from which novel tools and questions would follow, and various operant scientists would build from this functionality in various ways (Lattal, 2004). The initial design, a purely mechanical instrument, was eventually modified and used vacuum tube technology as an alternative to mechanically managing and recording the states and signals for an experiment. For example, the state in an experiment might refer to whether some sound or visual stimulus (e.g., a light) was present and signaled the availability of a reinforcer contingent on some type of response. Likewise, a relevant signal might be the occurrence or nonoccurrence of a response on the part of an organism (e.g., prompting the record of a unit of responding to some media). The move from purely mechanical components offered various benefits (e.g., size, safety), accommodated more complex designs (i.e., more complex state management), and could capture a broader range of responses. For example, earlier mechanical devices often functioned by transmitting the *force* of a response (e.g., pressing a lever, depressing a plate), and a certain degree of force was necessary to emit a signal mechanically. Functionally, this limited the types of responses that could be measured in behavioral experiments at that point in time.

Another significant shift was the introduction of solid-state components (e.g., relays) as well as the associated hardware controlling or being controlled by them. Following increases in the accessibility and affordability of solid-state components was the onset of the electronic era and the sunsetting of the mechanical era. Solid-state components differed from earlier components in that states and signals could be stored and/or mutated via electronics (e.g., a computer or controller could manage state through electronic cycles or voltage). Apart from providing improved control, reliability, and portability, the move to an electronic system allowed scientists to more easily interface with other forms of electronic devices (e.g., telephones, analytical computing devices). For example, states and signals in behavioral experiments could be programmed and monitored using computers, and responses could be recorded on various forms of electronic media (see Polson, 1973, for a relevant example of a state change language). However, it warrants noting that most computers around this period were neither affordable nor accessible for personal use and instead were specialized for burdensome calculations (e.g., statistics), and general computers and programming opportunities would be limited to larger research labs and projects for some time.[1]

Computers and Computer Programming in Behavior Analysis

The availability of computer hardware in North America can be traced back as early as the 1940s/1950s; however, "off-the-shelf" personal computers and other related components were seldom affordable or accessible to most until around the 1970s/1980s. The increased affordability and access to these tools allowed for these tools to be used in ways beyond their traditional purposes (e.g., calculations). During this period of growth and technological development, the field of behavior analysis saw a tremendous increase in the use of computers to both design/manage experiments and explore basic behavioral processes.

The rapid introduction of computers in behavioral experiments marked an inflection point for behavior analysis, wherein *software* and the programming of experimental states started to become more relevant than the act of building and maintaining custom hardware (i.e., general hardware existed, but it needed to be specifically *programmed* to perform experiments). For example, it was common at the time for computer devices to feature various input/output ports (e.g., serial, parallel ports), and these were used to transmit and receive information from peripheral devices (e.g., racks of relays, storage media). Researchers with sufficient training and experience could program computers to manage and record experimental states using one of the various programming languages available at the time (e.g., C, BASIC, Fortran). Unsurprisingly, various commercial products emerged during this period to provide general software development kits that simplified the programming of behavioral experiments (e.g., Med Associates). That is, these commercial offerings supported research by providing a layer of abstraction to behavioral scientists such that less boilerplate was necessary to design basic experiments (e.g., sending/detecting signals, recording signals to memory). The Med State Notation Language introduced by Med Associates, a language modeled from the state-based style common in early behavioral research, exists even today and is used in the MED-PC behavioral control software (for a historical review, see Escobar, 2014). A simple example of state management in MED-PC, with credit to the source author(s), is provided in the appendix.

Throughout the 1980s and 1990s, behavior analytic researchers and trainees frequently designed the software necessary to run basic experiments, with various instances being published in behavior analytic outlets (e.g., BASIC; see Hantula, 1991). The Visual Basic (VB) language, a derivative of the BASIC programming language, was released in 1991, and the simplicity of this language would eventually contribute to substantial adoption in behavior analysis (see Dixon & MacLin, 2003, for a text specific to VB and behavior analysis). Although the VB language is no longer actively supported or maintained by developers (i.e., support for the language officially ended in 2008) and has been replaced by the broader .NET ecosystem, some legacy applications designed using VB remain in circulation and are used by behavior analysts even now (e.g., BDataPro; Bullock et al., 2017).

Contemporary Computer Programming in Behavior Analysis

There is a rich, long history of behavior analysts designing and building apparatuses to research principles governing human and nonhuman behavior. This tradition originated from a basic science culture that existed in nonhuman animal research labs that continued into the digital age, with basic behavior analytic researchers being the earliest consumers and developers of behavior analytic software. Although computer programming has never been considered a central feature of behavior analytic practice or research, this existing repertoire likely emerged and had been maintained due to students having access to training experiences and mentorship associated with the building, maintaining, and modification of basic science experiments (e.g., managing chambers, experimental state).

In a general recollection of graduate training in behavioral science during this period of rapid technological sophistication, Catania (2002) noted that his training experiences and mentorship related to constructing and managing mechanical components translated quite well to managing state using electronic components and engaging in computer programming. However, these opportunities and experiences remained largely restricted to labs more representative of the experimental analysis of behavior (EAB, e.g., basic research), and we have seen far fewer opportunities for labs representative of applied behavior analysis (ABA, e.g., research in real-world contexts).

Programming in the Experimental Analysis of Behavior

Students and researchers working in the experimental analysis of behavior have, by and large, maintained their traditions of using computers and computer programming to facilitate basic research. Indeed, the MED-PC suite of tools and devices remains in use by students and researchers in behavior analysis even today.[2] Current graduate students and trainees in behavior analysis working in the experimental analysis of behavior continue to have access to opportunities to engage in computer programming, access to mentorship related to programming (i.e., MED-PC, Med State Notation), and access to labs with the resources to perform these skills in structured contexts.

Unsurprisingly, labs and researchers with an established training pipeline that included computer programming made considerable contributions in terms of published software as well as contributed to the range of hardware supported. For example, behavior analysts working in the experimental analysis of behavior have contributed to the design of and support for less commonly used, but more affordable, components (e.g., Escobar & Santillán, 2017) and have even provided plans for 3D printing critical components related to basic behavioral science methodologies (see Escobar et al., 2022).

Regarding software design, which is related but distinct from the utilization and incorporation of hardware components, there has been substantial growth in the range of tools available to support researchers in the experimental analysis of behavior. For example, EAB research in recent years has seen an increased interest in, and consumption of, practices consistent with open science aspirations (e.g., Gilroy & Kaplan, 2019) as well as an increased emphasis on the use and extension of open-source software (e.g., R Core Team, 2021). In just the past decade, behavior analytic researchers in the experimental analysis of behavior have produced various peer-reviewed open-source tools such as the beezdemand R package (Kaplan, 2018), the Discounting Model Selector (Gilroy et al., 2017), and the Demand Curve Analyzer (Gilroy et al., 2018). Consistent with historical trends in the experimental analysis of behavior, trainees and researchers within this tradition have continued the trend of eagerly leveraging technology to extend basic research, with noteworthy growth in terms of the adoption of open-source tools to perform more modern and robust analytical strategies (e.g., Young, 2018b). Specifically, there is considerable growth in the use of modern programming languages such as R, Python, and C/C++ to this end.

Programming in Applied Behavior Analysis

Although both the experimental and applied arms of behavior analysis explore and apply the same basic principles of behavior, a distinction is drawn here to highlight the ways that iterations of technology differentially influenced basic and applied research in behavior analysis. Most notably, the two arms of behavior analysis often explore different questions (e.g., basic vs. applied questions) and take place in different contexts (e.g., laboratory vs. real-world settings). Said a bit more directly, researchers in the experimental analysis of behavior had greater latitude to overcome the shortcomings of prevailing technology that was historically limited in terms of its portability, versatility, or affordability when first introduced (e.g., labs could be built to accommodate such technology). For researchers in applied contexts, early work with computers and computer programming was limited by the scarce resources (e.g., space, financial constraints) of the applied settings in which that research typically took place (e.g., homes, schools). Naturally, for these reasons, the adoption and extension of modern technologies in applied behavior analysis did not keep pace with the experimental analysis of behavior.

Increases in the affordability and portability of multimedia devices (e.g., tablets, smartphones, wearables) eventually mitigated several of the historical barriers to leveraging modern technology in applied behavior analytic research and practice. For example, the introduction of commercial apps on affordable touchscreen devices led to a tremendous shift in the modalities used for teaching social-communicative behavior for pre- and minimally vocal learners (e.g., Lorah et al., 2015). Similarly, various applied research teams successfully partnered with industry to inform the development of apps and frameworks facilitated through these devices to support initiatives such as diabetes management (e.g., Raiff & Dallery, 2010) and smoking cessation (e.g., Raiff et al., 2018).

Despite the growing use of technology in research and practice within applied behavior analysis, most training models in this tradition did not afford the same opportunities for experiences and mentorship related to computer programming. As a result, fewer software contributions are reflected in the applied behavior analytic literature, relatively speaking. Most prominent among these is the BDataPro data collection program (Bullock et al., 2017), a program written in VB 6.0 and still used by behavior analysts in various settings. This program was designed to capture rates of behavior in unique applied settings (e.g., severe and potentially life-threatening behavior) where there is both a wide range of responses being investigated and highly specialized schedule arrangements being evaluated. Relatedly, others have also designed software to support various aspects of applied research when using single-case experimental designs, such as graphical interfaces for facilitating research synthesis for single-case designs (Bulté & Onghena, 2013) and rendering plots for single-case designs (Gilroy, 2021/2023).

There is presently an upward trend in the design and dissemination of software (e.g., scripts, executables) with the goal of supporting various aspects of applied behavior analytic research and practice. However, despite growth over the past two decades, it warrants noting that many of these contributions tend to be narrow in scope and focus predominantly on streamlining practical applications of applied research and practice (e.g., tutorials for creating figures, programmatically constructing phase change lines) rather than expanding applications of the science (e.g., novel methods of designing curriculum, personalized systems of instruction). More specifically, these contributions are nearly exclusively either VB macros used in conjunction with spreadsheet software, interfaces built using VB to automate the creation of spreadsheets (e.g., outputting event data to a file), or scripts used to summarize the results of multiple spreadsheets (e.g., score for interrater reliability). Although these contributions have clear value to busy clinicians, especially in clinical and practical circumstances where the dependencies on such tools are common, limited adoption of more modern frameworks and languages has constrained the types of methods, tools, and supports that have been generated in this area (e.g., access to modern quantitative tools).

Supporting Computer Programming in Behavior Analysis

Research and practice in behavior analysis are heavily influenced by technology, and, overall, there is an ongoing trend toward adopting more modern technologies in research and practice. A short review of mainline behavior analytic research venues reveals a growing interest in improving the application of statistics and applying more contemporary statistical methods (see Young, 2018a, for a relevant discussion), in translating emerging technological media such as augmented/virtual reality (e.g., Neely et al., 2022), in exploring applications of machine learning (e.g., Plötz et al., 2012), and in other game-based extensions involving technology (see Morford et al., 2014, for a commentary).

For behavior analytic trainees and early career researchers with limited access to mentors with expertise in computer science, various online and in-person special interest groups (SIGs) have emerged to assist professional learners in their search for training and mentorship.

Apart from informational resources and occasional technical guidance, the emergence of these SIGs has served to highlight a distinct subset of behavior analytic researchers and practitioners with skills and/or interests related to the integration of behavior analysis and computer science. These groups generally provide support and guidance regarding available resources (e.g., availability of assets, tools), opportunities for training (e.g., coursework and mentorship), and general guidance related to computer programming (e.g., debugging and general technical support). Although the growth of these communities is a positive indicator of interest in computer science and behavior analysis, the growing demand for support in these groups highlights the limited amount of guidance available to learners seeking to develop and incorporate programming into their behavior analytic research and practice (e.g., standards, recommendations, examples). For these reasons, a number of recommendations and general standards are presented here.

Suggested Practices and Expansions

For both reviewers and consumers of behavior analytic research, we can expect to see an increasing representation of software contributions in behavior analytic venues. In response to this ongoing trend, the literature would benefit from the development of a minimum set of standards and expectations for software contributions. The specific goals of this would be to enhance the usability, reliability, compatibility, and accessibility of peer-reviewed behavior analytic contributions. Although the introduction of additional demands on the peer-review process is seldom desired, a set of agreed-upon standards would enhance this process for software contributions in several ways. First, behavior analytic reviewers and authors have varying degrees of familiarity with software development, and a transparent set of guidelines would help minimize a lack of clarity in terms of what constitutes a complete and validated offering suitable to behavior analytic research and/or practice. Second, conventions in software design change frequently, and even reviewers with prior training in computer science may not be current with contemporary practices related to development. Third, a set of expectations would provide a basis from which potential authors can form goals and tests for their projects and do so prior to initiating the peer-review process. A complete list of tests and standards related to software development in behavior analysis is beyond the scope of this chapter, but a collection of highly relevant practices is discussed in the sections that follow.

User Testing, Unit Testing, and End-to-End Testing

Computer scientists have established various practices and workflows with the goal of identifying which processes lead to more reliable and streamlined development. In a test-driven development (TDD) approach, this process begins by specifying the fundamental tests (i.e., objectives) that the project must pass to be considered complete. Specifically, a set of predetermined tests is developed before the software is written (i.e., similar to a task analysis), and this predetermined process is valuable for several reasons. First, a TDD approach encourages the developer to write no more code than is necessary to accomplish the core objectives (i.e., less opportunity for issues), requires the developer to develop and commit code in a fashion that is incremental and testable in terms of incremental units (e.g., one new commit should address a failed/failing test), and prompts the developer to focus on consistently accomplishing the ultimate goals of the product (i.e., tests should be run repeatedly to ensure consistency and reliability).

For research outlets that regularly review and publish software offerings, packages must be submitted and pass various software checks (e.g., builds across ecosystems, run embedded tests across ecosystems) before that software can even begin the peer-review process (e.g., the *Journal of Statistical Software*). Although no behavior analytic venues perform such checks, all packages designed for the R Statistical Framework[3] and hosted via the Comprehensive R Archive Network (CRAN) must pass these checks before the network agrees to host the package. The lack of a baseline expectation regarding testing is problematic for a few reasons. First, unit tests are a first-line safeguard against code that may not reliably accomplish what it is designed to perform. Although complete coverage is seldom necessary, the presence of unit testing serves as evidence that the author(s) took steps to scrutinize the reliability and validity of the methods designed to accomplish a certain purpose (e.g., reliably estimate a certain quantity in a certain fashion). In the case of tools that could directly influence decision-making made by clinicians, errors in this context have the potential to negatively affect standard of care (e.g., erroneous calculation of interval counts, timings, etc.). Similarly, tools that do not perform consistently *between* operating systems have the potential to interfere with the delivery of effective services (e.g., web-based tools rendering differently for different systems). Second, in addition to unit tests, user and end-to-end (E2E) tests provide a modern means of testing and simulating user behavior with the interfaces. For example, such tests can simulate the behavior of the software under various constraints, such as users with varying screen sizes, internet bandwidth, and browsers. This form of testing helps provide evidence that the human-computer interface functions reliably and consistently for users across systems and situations. For example, systems vary considerably in terms of resources (e.g., learners from rural settings and internet connectivity), and E2E testing allows the developer to specifically test and evaluate the software for use under limited resource conditions.

Modern tools and packages go through rigorous, continuous testing (i.e., CI/CD) to ensure that products function reliably on a range of devices (e.g., multiple operating systems, screen sizes) and under a range of different conditions (e.g., weak internet signal, limited computational capabilities), both for their initial releases as well as following updates and changes. Given that behavior analytic software has direct links to research, as well as the delivery of a certain standard of care, the standards for behavior analytic software should, in actuality, *be greater* than for some form of software with less of a risk for harm. For these reasons (and others), work submitted for publication in behavior analytic venues should include at least some evidence that such testing has been performed and that it passes basic usability tests before being disseminated broadly for consumption by other behavior analysts.

Accessibility and Compliance with the Americans with Disabilities Act

Software released for public use should work across the full range of modern systems (e.g., operating systems), under various conditions (e.g., varying screen sizes, internet capabilities), and for the full range of intended users. The intended user of the software may encounter the interface with some form of disability that influences their ability to engage with the interface in the same manner as the developers would (e.g., limited/no vision, difficulty operating mouse/pointing device). Indeed, many users may interact with software through the support of assistive technology (AT). Modern software development readily acknowledges these needs and the support of AT (e.g., screen readers), and these considerations take place in the design of the interface. Various patterns and standards exist, and for web-based tools and systems using comparable markup, the Accessible Rich Internet Applications (ARIA) framework is a standardized pattern that standardizes markup in a way to support interaction with screen readers and other forms of AT.[4] The ARIA framework is a well-documented example of accessibility support, and comparable implementations exist for various languages and frameworks as well (e.g., role and context markup in Qt C++ widgets).[5]

Such frameworks function by embedding tags within components that assist in conveying the context of the interface and the expected behavior of the software through the AT. For example, users may need support from AT to effectively navigate between pages/states, to determine what types of information are expected for a given field, and to navigate between fields (e.g., tab ordering). Modern frameworks and components come equipped with tools that continuously evaluate for accessibility coverage in a manner that is consistent with unit/E2E testing practices. Such tools assist in assessing poor/ambiguous coverage and providing recommendations consistent with modern standards. As a baseline standard for published works in behavior analytic venues, a requirement of evidence that the software presented is accessible would serve to benefit a wide range of users and would be more consistent with behavior analytic values related to social validity and equity.

Documentation, Licensing, and Support

Apart from the source code and tools that comprise a software product, various other aspects are equally critical to consider. For open-source contributions in particular, the availability of documentation, terms for licensing, and various other details related to support are required if others are to meaningfully use and extend the software. First and foremost, published software should have human-readable documentation to accompany the release. Using published R packages as an example, packages released on CRAN must include a minimum standard level of documentation; otherwise, submissions are dismissed outright with review.[6] Likewise, submissions for peer review in behavior analytic venues should also insist upon a baseline minimum standard for documentation so that current and future users can understand the underlying structure and function.

Licensing is perhaps the most critical aspect of work, whether published or archived on the internet. Specifically, licensing dictates the terms by which users can use the software and leverage the source material provided to derive new works or embed said software in larger products. As a behavior analyst working with open-source software, I offer the following advice: Assume the author (whomever they are) has not surrendered the rights to that work unless they explicitly state such. That said, works that provide source code are not technically open source unless they license that code with a respective license (see https://opensource.org/licenses/ for a list of common open-source licenses and respective terms). Additionally, certain licenses carry stipulations that may require certain actions of those releasing derivative works. For example, the icon General Public License (Version 3.0) and other related "copy-left" licenses require that derivative terms adopt the same license as well as furnish the necessary assets needed to build against to generate the final binaries (see terms of specific variants). For computer programs submitted to review in behavior analytic venues, there should be a minimum baseline expectation that a license is specified in the source code archived to clearly outline the rights passed on to end users with respect to source code and relevant binaries.

As a final aspect relevant to the publication of software in clinical journals, behavior analysts submitting this work should articulate the level and duration of support available to users of the software. As often seen with commercial software and development kits, these products provide a specified window and level of support (e.g., consultation, technical support).

This is particularly critical for software that may be used as an element of behavior analytic practice and research, given that users may not wish to include a particular form of software in that work if the platform is no longer supported or maintained. Like issues related to accessibility and testing, the availability of support is particularly important should some piece of software be involved in routine clinical activities or in extended research applications.

Guidance for Behavior Analysts with an Interest in Programming

Most readers of this chapter are either behavior analysts interested in learning how to program or behavior analysts looking to expand their computer programming repertoires. As a behavior analyst in computer programming, I have outlined several suggestions to guide other behavior analysts on a similar path (i.e., what to focus on and prioritize).

When deciding which language/framework to learn, I suggest distinguishing between whether the function of this pursuit is 1) for personal growth and/or general interest or 2) for enhancing some aspect of your clinical practice or research program. If the former, the traditional behavior analytic response to this personal goal would be to respect the choice of the learner and to support them in effectively following their reinforcers. Indeed, most veteran programmers would likely admit to spending more than a few weekends learning the intricacies of obscure tools and programming languages (I can note learning to reverse engineer and compile Fortran 90 being a relevant personal example). However, if the goal of learning computer programming is to ultimately support an area of your clinical practice and generate publishable research, the emphasis is then placed on the end users, and the languages/frameworks to learn would be those that best equip the analyst to accomplish the goals of the program and support the widest range of users. For those on this path, specifically, several resources are listed in the following.

Modern Frameworks and Tooling

Computer science and programming are rapidly evolving domains and modern languages, and learners in computer science are presented with a choice between more complex modern tools and simpler, more dated tools. This choice here mirrors the classic decision structure in the delay discounting paradigm – a choice between a lesser but more immediate prospect and a more substantial prospect that incurs some delay in realizing that benefit. Many behavior analysts at such a crossroads are faced with such a choice, often evaluating a quicker path resting on dated but familiar practices (e.g., Visual Basic) and another longer path that involves learning the many skills necessary to produce a consistent, scalable, and accessible product for a wide range of users.

I generally encourage the choice to pursue a modern approach and discourage using dated practices and having to make up for the lack of modern features for a number of reasons. First, behavior analysts who plan for the generalization of skills and approaches that are either deprecated or no longer supported have limited generality. Any repertoire should be practiced such that it remains pragmatic and useful at all times (e.g., clinical, research purposes) and taught in such a way that it has broad generality across applications (e.g., behavior analysis, computer science). Whether to support personal learning or learning for others, narrowly taught and practiced skills are less likely to substantially aid the learner across a range of different environments and contexts.

Second, behavior analysts are committed to taking steps to maximize social validity in both research and practice. When considering how to implement a particular form of software or develop software to meet some clinical need, behavior analysts are bound by professional ethics to account for whether their practices may (unintentionally or not) restrict the range of users who can access and benefit from the services. Given that behavior analysts serve a diverse range of consumers, plans for research and practice must consider the full range of learners expected to interface with their work and adjust accordingly.

Third, behavior analytic practices emphasize replicability in the development and validation of tools and practices. Indeed, replicability is a defining feature of behavior analytic research and distinguishes the field from others in behavioral science. To set such a high bar in human and nonhuman research and not in the development and evaluation of tools is not in keeping with historical standards for behavior analytic research. In computer science, the reliability and validity of software are revealed through rigorous, repeated testing, and various forms of continuous testing (e.g., unit, E2E) are viewed as indicators of mature offerings.

Last, modern tooling is typically accompanied by various features that support the development process and assist developers in keeping up with changing standards. For example, modern languages and frameworks typically offer first-party support in the form of linting (i.e., enforce an understandable style, convention, pattern), unit/E2E testing (e.g., plugins for code coverage), integrations with tools that assess whether interfaces meet standards for accessibility (e.g., Lighthouse, accessibility audits), and support to address modern safety concerns (e.g., potential exploits for dependencies). Furthermore, modern approaches now include powerful features such as null/type safety and borrow checking (i.e., Rust), which further enhance the stability of projects in the short and long term.

Mentorship, Collaboration, and Training

Acquiring a robust repertoire for computer programming is not a trivial goal and is not one that will be accomplished alone. Even with high-level languages (e.g., Python, C#), which do not require the user to master low-level programming details (e.g., manually allocating, tracking, and releasing memory), many conventions and patterns are abstract and will require years of practice and refinement before the programmer becomes fluent with a given language or platform. Students and early career professionals seeking to establish and refine their programming repertoires should identify appropriate mentors who can advise them in forming their training plans, establishing specific goals, and identifying the resources necessary to help them meet those goals.

Formal coursework and training are equally critical in this regard, and no substitute exists for formal training and instruction in computer science. Fortunately, there has never been a better time in which to access and consume coursework in computer science, and many refined options exist via the internet, many at no cost to the end user. For example, the Massachusetts Institute of Technology (MIT) provides various introductory-level computer programming courses at no cost to the learner through its CourseWare offerings (MIT OpenCourseWare). This resource, specifically, offers free introductions to languages such as C/C++, Python, and Java.

Last, various communities exist on the internet, and engaging with open-source projects is an inherently social event. That said, I would encourage early programmers to identify online communities related to their clinical/research interests (e.g., open-source communities related to Alternative and Augmentative Communication system development) and seek out potential collaborators in these communities. Generally, most individual open-source developers contribute their work in the hopes that others find it useful, and such interactions with developers likely reinforce and maintain their work in a given area.

Appendix: Example MED-PC Source Code

```
                  \ Inputs ***************************
^headIN = 3       \ IR head entry detector
^LLever2 = 1      \ left lever press
^RLever2 = 2      \ right lever press

                  \ Outputs ***************************
^leftlever = 1
^rightlever = 2
^dipper = 3       \ On Liquid Dipper
^house = 7        \ houselight
^blueCS = 9       \ Blue CS light (for Pavlovian)
^LightLeft = 4    \ stimulus lights above Left Lever
^LightRight = 5   \ stimulus lights above Right Lever

                  \ CONSTANTS************************
^DipDuration = 5 \dipper up duration (sec)

S.S.2,            \INITIALIZE

s1,
         #start:~initANL926;~;~SetRack (MG, 2);~;
         ~SetAmp (MG,BOX, 90);~;
         ~SetRF (MG,BOX, 10);~;~SetFreq (MG,BOX, 2500);~;
         ON^House; ON^blueCS; - >s3


[Abbreviated for Space]

Snippet from https://github.com/NautiyalLab/OperantPrograms-MEDPC
```

Notes

1 Although broad access to general purpose computing was limited at the time, Lattal (2008) recalled that published works in the *Journal of the Experimental Analysis of Behavior* including computerized components began as early as the 1960s.
2 MED-PC originally provided offerings based on the Assembly language but later provided a more general abstraction based upon conventions in BASIC. The move to conventions in BASIC simplified programming by abstracting out many boilerplate programming requirements.
3 Certain frameworks, such as the Comprehensive R Archive Network (CRAN), require R packages to pass a set of tests before software is eligible to be made available to users.
4 For additional documentation on ARIA, see Mozilla Developer Network, "ARIA," https://developer.mozilla.org/en-US/docs/Web/Accessibility/ARIA.
5 For a non-web-based example of AT markup, see QT Group, "Accessibility for QWidget Applications," https://doc.qt.io/qt-5/accessible-qwidget.html.
6 Additional information related to standards for documentation, examples, and vignettes in R packages is provided at Comprehensive R Archive Network, "Get started with roxygen2," https://cran.r-project.org/web/packages/roxygen2/vignettes/roxygen2.html.

References

Baum, W. M. (2002). From molecular to molar: A paradigm shift in behavior analysis. *Journal of the Experimental Analysis of Behavior, 78*(1), 95–116. https://doi.org/10.1901/jeab.2002.78-95

Bullock, C. E., Fisher, W. W., & Hagopian, L. P. (2017). Description and validation of a computerized behavioral data program: "BDataPro". *The Behavior Analyst, 40*(1), 275–285. link.springer.com. https://doi.org/10.1007/s40614-016-0079-0

Bulté, I., & Onghena, P. (2013). The single-case data analysis package: Analysing single-case experiments with R software. *Journal of Modern Applied Statistical Methods, 12*(2).

Catania, A. C. (2002). The watershed years of 1958–1962 in the Harvard Pigeon lab. *Journal of The Experimental Analysis of Behavior, 77*(3), 327–345. CMEDM.

Dixon, M. R., & MacLin, O. H. (2003). *Visual basic for behavioral psychologists*. Context Press.

Escobar, R. (2014). From relays to microcontrollers: The adoption of technology in operant research. *Revista Mexicana de Análisis de La Conducta, 40*(2), 127–153. https://doi.org/10.5514/rmac.v40.i2.63673

Escobar, R., Gutiérrez, B., & Benavides, R. (2022). 3D-printed operant chambers for rats: Design, assembly, and innovations. *Behavioural Processes, 199*, 104647. https://doi.org/10.1016/j.beproc.2022.104647

Escobar, R., & Santillán, N. (2017). New technologies applied to operant research: Inexpensive photocells for the Arduino-visual basic interface. *Mexican Journal of Behavior Analysis, 43*(2), Article 2. https://doi.org/10.5514/rmac.v43.i2.62315

Friman, P. C., Hayes, S. C., & Wilson, K. G. (1998). Why behavior analysts should study emotion: The example of anxiety. *Journal of Applied Behavior Analysis, 31*(1), 137–156. https://doi.org/10.1901/jaba.1998.31-137

Gilroy, S. P. (2023). *Faux XL charting in R (fxl)* [HTML]. https://github.com/miyamot0/fxl (Original work published 2021)

Gilroy, S. P., Franck, C. T., & Hantula, D. A. (2017). The discounting model selector: Statistical software for delay discounting applications: Discounting model selector. *Journal of the Experimental Analysis of Behavior, 107*(3), 388–401. https://doi.org/10.1002/jeab.257

Gilroy, S. P., & Kaplan, B. A. (2019). Furthering open science in behavior analysis: An introduction and tutorial for using GitHub in research. *Perspectives on Behavior Science, 42*(3), 565–581. https://doi.org/10.1007/s40614-019-00202-5

Gilroy, S. P., Kaplan, B. A., Reed, D. D., Koffarnus, M. N., & Hantula, D. A. (2018). The demand curve analyzer: Behavioral economic software for applied research. *Journal of the Experimental Analysis of Behavior, 110*(3), 553–568. https://doi.org/10.1002/jeab.479

Hantula, D. A. (1991). A simple BASIC program to generate values for variable-interval schedules of reinforcement. *Journal of Applied Behavior Analysis, 24*(4), 799–801. https://doi.org/10.1901/jaba.1991.24-799

Iversen, I. H. (1992). Skinner's early research: From reflexology to operant conditioning. *American Psychologist, 47*(11), 1318.

Kaplan, B. A. (2018). *Beezdemand: R package containing functions to help aid in analyzing behavioral economic demand curve data* [Computer software]. GitHub.

Lattal, K. A. (2004). Steps and pips in the history of the cumulative recorder. *Journal of the Experimental Analysis of Behavior, 82*(3), 329–355. https://doi.org/10.1901/jeab.2004.82-329

Lattal, K. A. (2008). JEAB at 50: Coevolution of research and technology. *Journal of the Experimental Analysis of Behavior, 89*(1), 129–135. https://doi.org/10.1901/jeab.2008.89-129

Lorah, E. R., Parnell, A., Whitby, P. S., & Hantula, D. (2015). A systematic review of tablet computers and portable media players as speech generating devices for individuals with autism spectrum disorder. *Journal of Autism and Developmental Disorders, 45*(12), 3792–3804. https://doi.org/10.1007/s10803-014-2314-4

Morford, Z. H., Witts, B. N., Killingsworth, K. J., & Alavosius, M. P. (2014). Gamification: The intersection between behavior analysis and game design technologies. *The Behavior Analyst, 37*(1), 25–40. https://doi.org/10.1007/s40614-014-0006-1

Neely, L., Carnett, A., Quarles, J., MacNaul, H., Park, S.-W., Oyama, S., Chen, G. (Qian), Desai, K., & Najafirad, P. (2022). The case for integrated advanced technology in applied behavior analysis. *Advances in Neurodevelopmental Disorders*. https://doi.org/10.1007/s41252-022-00309-y

Plötz, T., Hammerla, N. Y., Rozga, A., Reavis, A., Call, N., & Abowd, G. D. (2012). Automatic assessment of problem behavior in individuals with developmental disabilities. *Proceedings of the 2012 ACM Conference on Ubiquitous Computing*, 391–400. https://doi.org/10.1145/2370216.2370276

Polson, P. G. (1973). SCAT: Design criteria and software. *Behavior Research Methods & Instrumentation*, *5*(2), 241–244. https://doi.org/10.3758/BF03200173

R Core Team. (2021). *R: A language and environment for statistical computing* [Manual]. https://www.R-project.org/

Raiff, B. R., & Dallery, J. (2010). Internet-based contingency management to improve adherence with blood glucose testing recommendations for teens with type 1 diabetes. *Journal of Applied Behavior Analysis*, *43*(3), 487–491. https://doi.org/10.1901/jaba.2010.43-487

Raiff, B. R., Fortugno, N., Scherlis, D. R., & Rapoza, D. (2018). A mobile game to support smoking cessation: Prototype assessment. *JMIR Serious Games*, *6*(2), e11. https://doi.org/10.2196/games.9599

Sidman, M. (1960). *Tactics of scientific research: Evaluating experimental data in psychology* (pp. x, 428). Basic Books.

Skinner, B. F. (1932). On the rate of formation of a conditioned reflex. *The Journal of General Psychology*, *7*(2), 274–286.

Skinner, B. F. (1956). A case history in scientific method. *American Psychologist*, *11*(5), 221–233. https://doi.org/10.1037/h0047662

Thorndike, E. (1911). *Animal intelligence*. Macmillan.

Weiss, B. (1969). Instrumentation for operant behavior research. *American Psychologist*, *24*(3), 255–258. https://doi.org/10.1037/h0028410

Young, M. E. (2018a). A place for statistics in behavior analysis. *Behavior Analysis: Research and Practice*, *18*(2), 193.

Young, M. E. (2018b). Discounting: A practical guide to multilevel analysis of choice data. *The Journal of the Experimental Analysis of Behavior*, *109*(2), 293–312. https://doi.org/10.1002/jeab.316

2 Complex Systems Theory in Behavior Analysis

J. J. McDowell

Complex systems consist of elements that follow simple rules. Following the rules produces higher-level emergent outcomes, which are said to be self-organizing because their structure is determined by the operation of the low-level rules. An important feature of these systems is that the outcomes are not, and cannot be, built into the low-level rules. In addition, the outcomes cannot be predicted by examining the rules, nor can they be deduced mathematically from them. To obtain the emergent outcomes, the rules must be allowed to operate.

An example of a complex system is a murmuration of starlings (Bunyard-Wild, 2013). When in flight, the flock of birds changes shape, density, speed, and direction in astonishing ways. These phenomena are not likely to be caused by external forces operating on the flock as a whole. Instead, they are probably the result of each bird following simple rules, such as "remain equidistant from the six nearest birds" (Ballerini et al., 2008). In other words, the operation of the rules causes the flock to self-organize into various shapes, densities, speeds, and directions.

The rules the elements of a complex system follow constitute a theory of how the system operates. The theory can be tested by generating emergent outcomes and then comparing these outcomes to data from the natural world. To the extent that the emergent outcomes accurately describe the data, the theory is supported.

Complex systems theories are a relatively recent development in science, dating from about the 1970s (Vemuri, 1978). Work on the theories was significantly advanced by the founding of the Santa Fe Institute in 1984, the establishing mission of which was to promulgate research on complex systems. Traditional theoretical approaches in science (for example, astronomy and mechanics) date back to at least Aristotle, and hence to around 400 BCE (McDowell, 1988). As is well known, these approaches were further developed by Ptolemy, Copernicus, Kepler, and Newton over the next two millennia. They came to focus on sensible properties of phenomena, for example, distance, mass, velocity, and time, and on mathematical relations among these properties. The history of the traditional theoretical approaches in science is described in detail by McDowell (1988). An important feature of complex systems *theories* is that they eschew the traditional focus on sensible properties of phenomena and their mathematical relations. Instead, the phenomena and their interrelations are *consequences* of the theory, that is, they are consequences of the rules the elements of the system follow. In traditional theories, the sensible properties of interest are selected in advance; in complex systems theories, properties of interest are extracted from the emergent outcomes the theories produce. These may, and usually do, include properties that are described by traditional theories, but they typically include a host of additional properties exhibited by the emergent outcomes.

DOI: 10.4324/9781003380603-3

Complex Systems Theories in the Physical and Social Sciences

Mitchell (2009) reviewed the development of complex systems theories in the physical and social sciences. Her review includes complex systems that implement evolutionary rules (e.g., Holland, 1995, 1998; Fogel, 1998; Muro et al., 2011) and cellular automaton rules (Wolfram, 2002) and complex systems that generate biological (Bentley, 2001) and social (Miller & Page, 2007) phenomena. Mitchell's objective was to develop a unified science of complexity that could be applied to all phenomena, but this objective was not realized (McDowell, 2013a). In contrast to Mitchell's deliberate approach, Stephen Wolfram (2002) baldly asserted that all phenomena in the universe are likely to be explainable by the operation of a particular class of complex systems known as cellular automata. Needless to say, this remains to be demonstrated (McDowell & Popa, 2009). Cellular automata were invented in the 1940s by Stanislaw Ulam and John von Neumann at the Los Alamos National Laboratory (McDowell & Popa, 2009; von Neumann & Burks, 1966). These finite state machines provide a good example of how complex systems operate, and some of their emergent outcomes have been compared to the adaptive behavior of live organisms. For these reasons, the operation of cellular automata is described briefly here.

The simplest cellular automaton begins with a row of squares, or cells, each of which is colored black (represented by the integer 1) or white (represented by the integer 0). The cellular automaton generates subsequent rows of cells by considering the color of each target cell's left and right neighbors in the current row. Clearly, there are four neighbor conditions: both neighbors black, both white, left black and right white, and left white and right black. These conditions are shown in Table 2.1 in the standard order used for generating cellular automaton outcomes. There are four neighbor conditions when the target cell in the current row is white (0s in the second column of the table) and four when the target cell is black (1s in the second column of the table). The rightmost column of the table shows the color of the target cell in the subsequent row, given the color and neighbor condition of the target cell in the current row. This column can be set to any sequence of 1s and 0s. Evidently, there are 2^8 possible sequences, yielding 256 two-state, nearest-neighbor cellular automata. Cellular automaton rules are named by taking the binary number that appears in the rightmost column, starting at the bottom and reading up. This binary number is then converted to a base-10 integer. The binary number in Table 2.1 is 01101110, which translates to the decimal integer, 110. Hence Table 2.1 specifies Rule 110.

Table 2.1 Example of Cellular Automaton Rules

Neighbor Condition			
Left	*Target*	*Right*	*Next Target*
0	0	0	0
0	0	1	1
0	1	0	1
0	1	1	1
1	0	0	0
1	0	1	1
1	1	0	1
1	1	1	0

The operation of Rule 110 is shown in Figure 2.1. It begins with an initial row of 256 cells at the top of the left panel, colored black or white at random. The second row is produced by applying the rules in Table 2.1 to the cells in the initial row, the third row is produced by applying the rules to the cells in the second row, and so on down the panel. The first and last cells of each row are neighbors. The operation of the automaton continues down the panel, then on to the top row of the center panel, and finally on to the third panel. There are 295 rows in each panel. The emergent outcome shown in the figure begins with an explosion of activity at the top of the left panel. This soon coalesces into identifiable structures, such as the apparent spirals and various straight lines that appear in all panels. As shown in the figure, these structures often collide, producing changes in direction and sometimes new structures.

The organized complexity of the emergent outcome shown in Figure 2.1 is astonishing given the utter simplicity of the rules that generate it. Nothing in Table 2.1 gives any indication that this outcome can be generated by Rule 110. Note also that the operation of the automaton could have started with a different initial row, for example, with cells colored alternately black or white. What outcome would that generate? The rules would have to be allowed to operate to find out. Even more remarkable than the complex structure shown in the figure is the proof by Matthew Cook (2004) that, given specific initial conditions, Rule 110 is capable of universal computation. That is, it can carry out any mathematical calculation whatsoever, including logical operations such as AND, NOR, and XOR (McDowell & Popa, 2009). Examples of cellular automata carrying out mathematical calculations are given by McDowell (2013b, pp. 353ff) and McDowell and Popa (2009, pp. 345ff.).

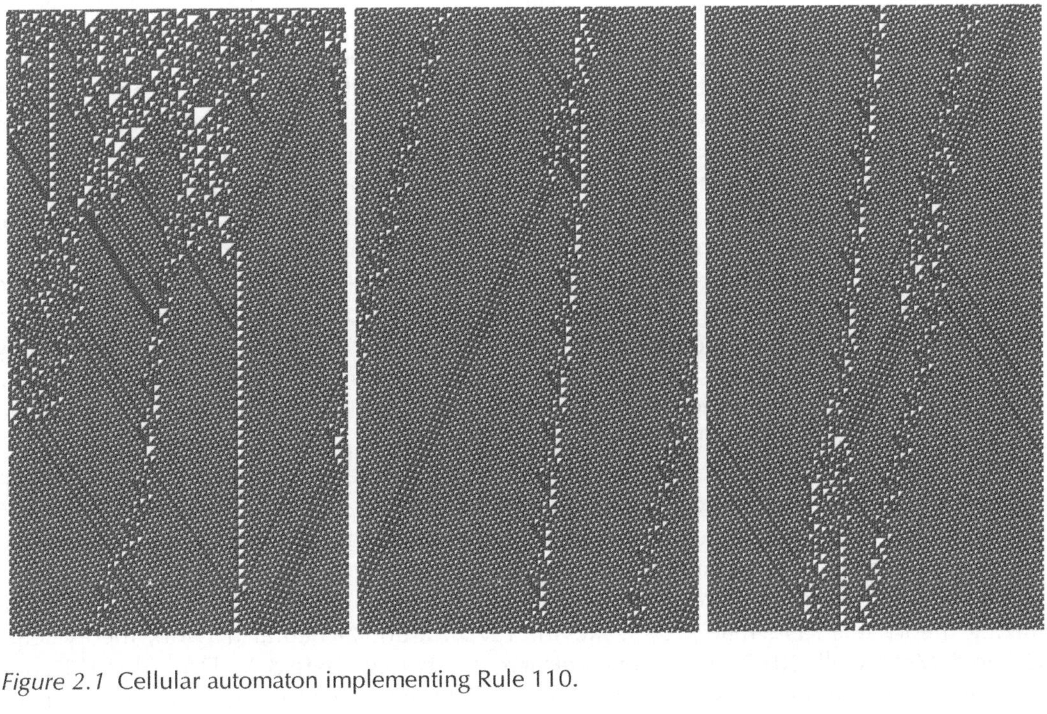

Figure 2.1 Cellular automaton implementing Rule 110.

Briefly Developed Complex Systems Theories in Behavior Analysis

Several behavior-analytic theories that are consistent with the basic premise of complex systems theories have appeared in the literature. The basic premise, of course, is that formal rules may generate emergent outcomes that describe natural phenomena. Interestingly, complex systems theories began appearing in behavior analysis about the same time they began appearing in the physical and social sciences.

The earliest behavior-analytic theory that was consistent with the basic premise of complex systems theory was Shimp's (1966) theory of momentary maximizing. This theory entails only one rule, which applies to probabilistically reinforced responding and to responding on concurrently available alternatives. The rule is that every response occurs on the alternative with the higher/highest probability of reinforcement at the moment of emission. Shimp found that in some situations, this momentary maximizing rule produced emergent behavior that conformed to Herrnstein's (1961) matching law (McDowell, 2013c).

A second theory consistent with the basic premise of complex systems theory is the neural network theory of Donahoe and his colleagues (Donahoe et al., 1993; Donahoe & Palmer, 1994). Their networks entail relatively simple rules that govern the connection weights between artificial neurons.

> These artificial neural networks have been shown to generate higher-order phenomena, such as the acquisition and extinction of Pavlovian conditional responses (CRs), the faster reacquisition of a previously conditioned CR following its extinction, and the blocking of control of a CR by part of a compound conditional stimulus.
>
> (McDowell & Popa, 2009, p. 351)

A third relatively simple complex systems theory in behavior analysis is Catania's (2005) theory of the operant reserve, which is an extension of Skinner's (1938) reflex reserve theory. Catania's theory consists of two rules, one that depleted the reserve when responding occurred and one that replenished it when reinforcement occurred. The principal emergent outcomes of this theory were cumulative records of responding. Catania reported that many of these outcomes were similar to the cumulative records produced by live organisms working on random-ratio schedules, random-interval schedules, a few additional schedules, and extinction.

A fourth complex systems theory in behavior analysis was developed by McDowell and Popa (2009). It used cellular automata to generate emergent outcomes that could be compared to live-organism behavior. They showed that columnar mappings of Rule 22 (rightmost column in the rules table [Table 2.1] reading 01101000 from top to bottom) and Rule 30 (rightmost column reading 01111000 from top to bottom) could be used to generate cumulative records of responding that resembled those produced by live organisms. They also showed that various rates of responding could be generated by columnar mappings of Rule 152 (rightmost column in the rules table reading 00011001 from top to bottom) and that these rates conformed to Herrnstein's (1970) hyperbola.

Note that for all of these theories, the phenomena of interest do not appear in the theories themselves. Instead, the phenomena of interest, for example, cumulative records, response and reinforcement rates, and their quantitative relationships, are extracted from the outcomes produced by the operation of the theory's rules.

The theories described here have not escaped criticism. Specifically, momentary maximizing theory (e.g., Heyman, 1979; Nevin, 1979), artificial neural network theory (e.g., Calvin & McDowell, 2015, 2016), reflex reserve theory (e.g., Berg & McDowell, 2011), and cellular automaton theory (McDowell & Popa, 2009) have been found wanting in various ways. Some of these articles also include suggestions for improving the theories and developing them further.

The Evolutionary Theory of Behavior Dynamics

A fifth complex systems theory in behavior analysis is the evolutionary theory of behavior dynamics (ETBD). This theory was originally proposed by McDowell (2004) and has been developed further and tested extensively since then. It is the most highly developed complex systems theory in behavior analysis. It is also the most widely applied and thoroughly tested complex systems theory. The rules of the ETBD and their operation are described briefly in the present section. In the following section, evidence supporting the theory is reviewed.

The ETBD creates artificial organisms (AOs) that are made up of populations of potential behaviors, each of which is defined by a decimal integer and the 10-digit binary representation of that integer. The decimal integer is referred to as the behavior's phenotype; the binary representation of the integer is referred to as the behavior's genotype. In all studies of the ETBD to date, the range of possible phenotypes extends from 0 through 1023. Collections of phenotypes may form target response classes for an AO. For example, the 40 integers from 471 through 511 might represent different ways of operating an operandum in an experimental chamber. An AO behaves by emitting one behavior at random from its population of potential behaviors at each tick of time. This produces a stream of behaviors that can be studied just as if it were the behavior of a live organism. The basic rules of the theory consist of a genetic algorithm that causes an AO's population of potential behaviors to evolve under the selection pressure of reinforcement from the environment. Background (i.e., nontarget) reinforcement (McDowell & Klapes, 2020) and punishment (McDowell & Klapes, 2019) have also been implemented in the theory.

The ETBD consists of rules of emission, selection, recombination, mutation, and punishment. The emission rule, noted prior, states that one behavior is emitted from an AO's population of potential behaviors at each tick of time. If the emitted behavior is reinforced, or if it goes unreinforced, then the AO's existing population of potential behaviors is replaced with a new population. The new population is constructed by choosing pairs of what might be referred to as parent behaviors from the existing population. If the emitted behavior was reinforced, then the pairs of parent behaviors are chosen according to the theory's selection rule. This rule specifies that parent behaviors are chosen on the basis of their fitness, which is a function of the difference between the integer value of the possible parent behavior and the integer value of the behavior that was reinforced. The smaller the difference, the fitter the behavior. According to the selection rule, fitter behaviors are more likely to become parents than less fit behaviors. McDowell (2017) has provided a straightforward explanation of how this rule operates, including how reinforcer magnitude is related to selection strength. If the emitted behavior was not reinforced, then pairs of parent behaviors are chosen at random from the existing population.

Once pairs of parent behaviors have been chosen, either by the operation of the selection rule or at random, they are recombined to form what might be referred to as child behaviors. Recall that each parent behavior consists of a 10-digit bit string, which is the binary representation of its integer value. A child behavior can be constructed by building a new 10-digit bit string, where the bit at each location in the string is the same as the bit in that location in either the father's or the mother's bit string with equal probability. It turns out that the integer values of the resulting child behaviors are like the integer values of the parent behaviors, which is to say that the child behaviors resemble their parents. If parent behaviors were chosen based on their similarity to the emitted behavior (which occurs when an emitted behavior is reinforced), then the new population of child behaviors aggregates more or less closely around the integer value of the just-emitted behavior. This means that a behavior in that range is more likely to be emitted in the next time tick. This is the effect of reinforcement on the population of potential behaviors.

Once a new population of potential behaviors is constructed, it is subjected to mutation. This is accomplished by flipping a random bit from 0 to 1 or from 1 to 0 in a percentage of the population's bit strings. The percentage of behaviors subjected to mutation is referred to as the mutation rate. It is important to understand that mutation is a necessary feature of the evolutionary algorithm. If mutation is not implemented, then behaviors tend to aggregate and remain at various arbitrary locations in the range of phenotypes (McDowell, 2004). Following mutation, a new behavior is emitted at random from the population of potential behaviors. If the newly emitted behavior is reinforced or goes unreinforced, then the cycle of selection, recombination, and mutation repeats.

If an emitted behavior is punished rather than being reinforced or going unreinforced, then the cycle of selection, recombination, and mutation does not occur. Instead, the theory's forced-mutation punishment rule operates (McDowell & Klapes, 2019). According to this rule, each behavior in the target class may undergo mutation implemented by the flip of a random bit in its bit string. The probability that a behavior will undergo mutation depends on the context of reinforcement in which the punishment occurs. If the environment is rich, that is, if the target behavior is frequently reinforced, then the probability of punishment is lower than if the environment is lean. In other words, punishment is less effective in a rich environment than a lean one. Note that punishment may cause a behavior to leave a target class, in which case the probability that a behavior from that class will be emitted in the next tick of time is reduced.

Reinforcement for background behaviors, which are behaviors that do not belong to a target class, can be arranged in the same way that reinforcement for target behaviors is arranged. If a background behavior is reinforced, then pairs of parent behaviors are chosen based on their fitness with respect to the background phenotype that was reinforced. These parent behaviors then recombine to form child behaviors, and the new population of potential behaviors undergoes mutation. Arranging background reinforcement makes an AO's environment more naturalistic. Note that reinforced background behaviors compete with target responding. This is because when a background behavior is reinforced, selection with respect to that behavior may pull behaviors out of a target class.

Detailed accounts of the rules of the evolutionary theory are given in McDowell (2013d, 2017, 2019), McDowell and Arashanapalli (2021), and McDowell and Klapes (2019, 2020). Readers interested in experimenting with a software program that implements the theory can download executable files from https://www.dropbox.com/scl/fi/2fye0lsd6f1vaypyi5kau/ETBD_Executable.zip?rlkey=3mwl4sxfdckwcj8zue606yqmn&e=1&dl=0. A guide to running the code is provided by Klapes (2022).

Evidence Supporting the Evolutionary Theory of Behavior Dynamics

Single and Concurrent Interval Schedules

Steady-State Properties

Some of the emergent outcomes generated by AOs animated by the evolutionary theory when responding on random-interval (RI) schedules (Equation 1) and concurrent RI RI schedules (Equations 2 and 3) are the following quantitative relations:

$$B = \frac{kR}{R + c}, \tag{1}$$

$$\frac{B_1}{B_2} = b\left(\frac{R_1}{R_2}\right)^a, \tag{2}$$

and

$$\frac{B_1}{B_2} = b\left(\frac{R_1}{R_2}\right)^{aR}\left(\frac{M_1}{M_2}\right)^{aM}, \tag{3}$$

where *B* and *R* represent average rates of responding and reinforcement respectively, *M* represents the magnitude of reinforcement, the numerical subscripts refer to the two response alternatives of a concurrent schedule, and the other quantities in the equations are free parameters. When fitted to average AO response and reinforcement rates, these equations account for large percentages of variance without leaving residual trends (McDowell, 2004; McDowell et al., 2008, 2012). It follows that these quantitative relations are emergent outcomes of the evolutionary dynamics implemented by the ETBD.

These equations are familiar to behavior analysts, of course. Equation 1 is the single-alternative hyperbola, Equation 2 is the generalized matching law, and Equation 3 is the concatenated generalized matching law. These equations are known to accurately describe the behavior of many species working on variable interval (VI) and concurrent VI VI schedules (Cording et al., 2011; Baum, 1974, 1979; de Villiers, 1977; Herrnstein, 1970; McDowell et al., 2012). The parameters in the equations also behave the same way for AOs as for live organisms (McDowell, 2004; McDowell et al., 2008, 2012). It follows that the ETBD can be considered a theoretical foundation for these well-known equations, which were originally developed empirically.

Dynamic Properties

AOs working on single RI schedules produce cumulative records and interresponse-time distributions that are similar to those produced by live organisms working on VI schedules (Kulubekova & McDowell, 2008; McDowell, 2013b). In addition, AOs working on concurrent RI RI schedules show changeover patterns and responsivity to changeover delays that are the same as those shown by live organisms working on concurrent VI VI schedules (McDowell et al., 2008, 2012).

In a more complicated experimental environment, Kulubekova and McDowell (2013) and Li et al. (2018) studied AO behavior on concurrent interval schedules presented sequentially in each session without associated discriminative stimuli. These were replications of Davison and Baum's (2000) experiments with pigeons. The AOs showed gradual moment-by-moment development of preference that depended on the difference between the interval schedules in the two components. In addition, details of reinforcer-by-reinforcer switching between alternatives depended on which alternative had been previously reinforced. These results were the same as those reported by Davison and Baum for pigeons.

Concurrent Ratio Schedules

McDowell and Klapes (2018) found that AOs working on concurrent random-ratio (RR) schedules with unequal ratios in the components developed exclusive preference for the alternative with the smaller ratio. If the ratios were equal, then the AOs developed exclusive preference for one or the other alternative. These findings are the same as those reported for live organisms working on variable-ratio (VR) schedules (McDowell & Klapes, 2018).

Background Reinforcement

Herrnstein (1970) derived Equation 1 for single-alternative responding from the original matching law. But as is well known, the original matching law has been superseded by the generalized matching law (Equation 2). McDowell (1986, 2005) derived the following single-alternative equation from the generalized matching law:

$$B = \frac{kR^a}{R^a + c}. \tag{4}$$

Evidently, this single-alternative equation supersedes Equation 1. Note that Equation 4 reduces to Equation 1 when $a = 1$. McDowell and Klapes (2020) studied the behavior of AOs working on single RI schedules in the presence of background reinforcement. They found that when Equation 4 was fitted to their behavior, the parameters of the fitted equation varied with properties of background reinforcement just as they do in most live-organism experiments. Specifically, as the rate of background reinforcement increased, k, which is the asymptote of the equation, remained constant; a, which represents the sensitivity of behavior to target reinforcement, decreased; and c increased, which means that the equation approached its asymptote more slowly.

Punishment

Superimposed on Concurrent Interval Schedules of Reinforcement

McDowell and Klapes (2019) studied AO behavior on concurrent RI schedules when punishment was superimposed on one component. They found that behavior in the punished component decreased in frequency while behavior in the unpunished component increased in frequency. They also found that when equal scheduled rates of punishment were superimposed on the two components, preference (i.e., the exponent in Equation 2) increased over the baseline no-punishment condition. Finally, McDowell and Klapes found that preference did not change when the superimposed punishment rates were proportional to the scheduled reinforcement rates. These findings were the same as those reported for live organisms (McDowell & Klapes, 2019).

Superimposed on Single Interval Schedules of Reinforcement

McDowell et al. (2023) studied the behavior of AOs working on RI schedules of reinforcement with superimposed RI and RR schedules of punishment and also with no superimposed punishment. These were replications of Bradshaw et al.'s (1977, 1978, 1979) experiments with human participants. McDowell et al. found that AO responding was well described by the ordinary hyperbola (Equation 1, prior) in all conditions. They also found that the asymptote of the fitted hyperbola was the same when RI punishment was superimposed as when no punishment was superimposed but that it was lower when RR punishment was superimposed. In addition, they found that the fitted hyperbola's *c*-parameter was larger (indicating a slower approach to asymptote) for both punishment conditions compared to the no-punishment condition. Finally, they found that response suppression under punishment was greater at lower than at higher reinforcement rates. These results were identical to those Bradshaw et al. reported for their human participants.

Resurgence

Falligant, Klapes, et al. (2022) studied the resurgence of AO behavior during extinction. They reported findings that were the same as those reported for live organisms. Hagopian and Falligant (2023) noted that similar agreement between AO and live-organism behavior has also been reported for other modes of resurgence (Falligant, Hagopian, et al., 2022; Klapes et al., 2023).

Additional Support

Some additional, often highly technical, evidence supporting the evolutionary theory has been noted by McDowell (2023, p. 128).

Discussion of Empirical Support

It is clear that empirical support for the ETBD is extensive and varied. It is important to note that the details of the ETBD's algorithm were the same in all tests of the theory, that is, the algorithm was not tweaked in any way to obtain specific outcomes.

Empirical support for the ETBD exceeds that for any other complex systems theory in behavior analysis, as well as for any traditional theory in the discipline, such as matching theory (McDowell, 2021, 2023; McDowell & Calvin, 2015; McDowell & Klapes, 2018; Popa & McDowell, 2010). As a consequence, one might say that the ETBD is the most successful behavior-analytic theory to date.

General Discussion

Several second-stage predictions of the evolutionary theory have been developed and explored (McDowell, 2023, p. 128). A second-stage prediction is a prediction of a phenomenon that has not yet been observed (von Neumann & Morgenstern, 2007). Such predictions provide important, and powerful, opportunities to disconfirm a theory (Popper, 1965).

The applicability of the evolutionary theory to the evaluation, diagnosis, and treatment of clinical problems has been discussed in detail (McDowell, 2023). These problems include attention-deficit/hyperactivity disorder (ADHD), automatically reinforced self-injurious behavior (Morris & Lucia, 2023; Morris & McDowell, 2021), and severe challenging behavior (Hagopian & Falligant, 2023). For example, AOs with ADHD can be created by arranging high mutation rates. These AOs exhibit behavior that is similar to that of humans with ADHD, and they respond to treatment just as humans do (McDowell, 2023; Popa, 2013).

The material interpretation of the ETBD has been discussed at length (e.g., McDowell, 2013b, 2023). The rules of the theory are probably best considered as supervening on the biological operation of the brain. This means that while the brain's material operation and the ETBD's formal operation may differ, they give the same answers.

AO Behavior as Artificial Intelligence

Let us consider intelligence to be the apparent ability to acquire and demonstrate knowledge and skills. A general definition of *artificial* intelligence (AI) is "intelligence . . . demonstrated by machines, as opposed to intelligence displayed by humans or by other animals" (Artificial Intelligence, 2023, May 17). A general definition like this is probably best because the field of AI includes many research areas that deal with different phenomena, such as machine learning in general, reinforcement learning in particular, pattern recognition, and large language models, as in today's popular chatbots.

According to this general definition, the adaptive behavior of AOs animated by the evolutionary theory constitutes artificial intelligence. The AOs can distinguish among the beneficial, harmful, and neutral consequences of their past behavior and adjust their future behavior accordingly. The AOs can also detect changes in the environment and modify their adjustment to the changed environment as necessary.

There are some important differences between the AI of AOs and the AI exhibited by some other mechanisms. Consider, for example, reinforcement learning and pattern recognition. These types of AI usually entail neural networks that require extensive training to enable them to exhibit the desired intelligent behavior. In supervised training, the networks are given examples of behaviors or patterns, and a human trainer then indicates whether a particular example is acceptable or not. Following this training, the networks can identify new instances of behaviors or patterns as acceptable or not acceptable. Large language models also require training on substantial amounts of text to statistically identify which words go together best. In contrast, AOs animated by the evolutionary theory require no prior training to exhibit intelligent behavior. The user must identify positive and negative consequences and specify their magnitudes, but then the AO learns to behave as it encounters these consequences in the environment. This difference also means that when outcomes change, the networks and the large language model must be retrained. But this is not necessary for the AOs. New consequences and magnitudes can be specified, but then the AO learns on its own as it interacts with the new environment. A final difference is that the AI of reinforcement learning typically maximizes reinforcement. But biological organisms do not necessarily maximize (e.g., Heyman, 1979; Nevin, 1979), and neither does the AI exhibited by AOs. One advantage of nonmaximization is that ranges of behaviors that do not produce reinforcement are available to detect changes that may occur in the environment.

An interesting area for future research is the possibility of combining the AI of AO behavior with other AI areas, such as general language models. One objective of this work could be to produce mechanical agents that both converse intelligently and behave adaptively, including with respect to social consequences from humans interacting with them.

Author Note

I thank Bryan Klapes, Cyrus Chi, and Ryan Higgenbotham for their helpful comments on an earlier version of this chapter. I also thank Steven Riley for his informative discussions of artificial intelligence.

References

Artificial Intelligence. (2023, May 17). In Wikipedia. https://en.wikipedia.org/wiki/Artificial_intelligence#:~:text=Artificial%20intelligence%20(AI)%20is%20intelligence,generalize%2C%20and%20to%20infer%20meaning.

Ballerini, M., Cabibbo, N., Candelier, R., Cavagna, A., Cisbani, E., Giardina, I., Lecomte, V., Orlandi, A., Parisi, G., Procaccini, A., Viale, M., & Zdravkovic, V. (2008). Interaction ruling animal collective behavior depends on topological rather than metric distance: Evidence from a filed study. *Proceedings of the National Academy of Sciences of the United States of America, 105*, 1232–1237. https://doi.org/10.1073/pnas.0711437105

Baum, W. M. (1974). On two types of deviation from the matching law: Bias and undermatching. *Journal of the Experimental Analysis of Behavior, 22*, 231–242.

Baum, W. M. (1979). Matching, undermatching, and overmatching in studies of choice. *Journal of the Experimental Analysis of Behavior, 32*, 269–281.

Bentley, P. J. (2001). *Digital biology*. Simon & Schuster.

Berg, J. P., & McDowell, J. J. (2011). Quantitative, steady-state properties of Catania's computational model of the operant reserve. *Behavioural Processes, 87*, 71–83.

Bradshaw, C. M., Szabadi, E., & Bevan, P. (1977). Effect of punishment on human variable-interval performance. *Journal of the Experimental Analysis of Behavior, 27*, 275–279. https://doi.org/10.1901/jeab.1977.27-275

Bradshaw, C. M., Szabadi, E., & Bevan, P. (1978). Effect of variable-interval punishment on the behavior of humans in variable-interval schedules of monetary reinforcement. *Journal of the Experimental Analysis of Behavior, 29*, 161–166. https://doi.org/10.1901/jeab.1978.29-161

Bradshaw, C. M., Szabadi, E., & Bevan, P. (1979). The effect of punishment on free-operant choice behavior in humans. *Journal of the Experimental Analysis of Behavior, 31*, 71–81. https://doi.org/10.1901/jeab.1979.31-71

Bunyard-Wild, P. (2013). *Gretna green starling murmurations*. Retrieved June 18, 2023, from https://www.youtube.com/watch?v=M1Q-EbX6dso

Calvin, N. T., & McDowell, J. J. (2015). Unified-theory-of-reinforcement neural networks do not simulate the blocking effect. *Behavioural Processes, 120*, 54–63.

Calvin, O. L., & McDowell, J. J. (2016). Extending unified-theory-of-reinforcement neural networks to steady-state operant behavior. *Behavioural Processes, 127*, 52–61.

Catania, A. C. (2005). The operant reserve: A computer simulation in (accelerated) real time. *Behavioural Processes, 69*, 257–278.

Cook, M. (2004). Universality in elementary cellular automata. *Complex Systems, 15*, 1–40.

Cording, J. R., McLean, A. P., & Grace, R. C. (2011). Testing the linearity and independence assumptions of the generalized matching law for reinforcer magnitude: A residual meta-analysis. *Behavioural Processes, 87*, 64–70.

Davison, M., & Baum, W. M. (2000). Choice in a variable environment: Every reinforcer counts. *Journal of the Experimental Analysis of Behavior, 74*, 1–24. https://doi.org/10.1901/jeab.2000.74-1

de Villiers, P. A. (1977). Choice in concurrent schedules and a quantitative formulation of the law of effect. In W. K. Honig & J. E. R. Staddon (Eds.), *Handbook of operant behavior* (pp. 233–287). Prentice-Hall.

Donahoe, J. W., Burgos, J. E., & Palmer, D. C. (1993). A selectionist approach to reinforcement. *Journal of the Experimental Analysis of Behavior, 60*, 17–40.

Donahoe, J. W., & Palmer, D. C. (1994). *Learning and complex behavior*. Allyn & Bacon.

Falligant, J. M., Hagopian, L., Laureano, B., & Klapes, B. (2022). Examining resurgence and repetition with the evolutionary theory of behavior dynamics. *Behavioural Processes, 203*, Article 104776. https://doi.org/10.1016/j.beproc.2022.104776

Falligant, J. M., Klapes, B., & Hagopian, L. P. (2022). Modeling resurgence with an evolutionary theory of behavior dynamics. *Behavioural Processes, 197*, 1–9. https://doi.org/10.1016/j.beproc.2022.104623

Fogel, D. B. (Ed.). (1998). *Evolutionary computation: The fossil record*. IEEE Press.

Hagopian, L. P., & Falligant, J. M. (2023). Application of the evolutionary theory of behavior dynamics to severe challenging behavior. *Journal of Applied Behavior Analysis, 56*(4), 729–744.

Herrnstein, R. J. (1961). Relative and absolute strength of response as a function of frequency of reinforcement. *Journal of the Experimental Analysis of Behavior, 4*, 267–272.

Herrnstein, R. J. (1970). On the law of effect. *Journal of the Experimental Analysis of Behavior, 13*, 243–266.

Heyman, G. M. (1979). A Markov model description of changeover probabilities on concurrent variable-interval schedules. *Journal of the Experimental Analysis of Behavior, 31*, 41–51.

Holland, J. H. (1995). *Hidden order*. Perseus Books.

Holland, J. H. (1998). *Emergence*. Perseus Books.

Klapes, B. (2022, May 30). Performing simulated experiments using an evolutionary theory of behavior dynamics: A tutorial. In B. Laureano (Chair), *Modeling severe problem behavior and treatment effects using artificial organisms: A new frontier* [Conference symposium] 48th Association for Behavior Analysis International Annual Convention, Boston, MA. https://www.researchgate.net/publication/360950785_Performing_Simulated_Experiments_Using_an_Evolutionary_Theory_of_Behavior_Dynamics_A_Tutorial

Klapes, B., Falligant, J. M., & Hagopian, L. P. (2023). Modeling and quantifying resurgence in the evolutionary theory of behavior dynamics. *Behavioural Processes, 208*, Article 104860. https://doi.org/10.1016/j.beproc.2023.104860

Kulubekova, S., & McDowell, J. J. (2008). A computational model of selection by consequences: Log survivor plots. *Behavioural Processes, 78*, 291–296.

Kulubekova, S., & McDowell, J. J. (2013). Computational model of selection by consequences: Patterns of preference change on concurrent schedules. *Journal of the Experimental Analysis of Behavior, 100*, 147-164.

Li, D., Elliffe, D., & Hautus, M. J. (2018). A multivariate assessment of the rapidly changing procedure with McDowell's evolutionary theory of behavior dynamics. *Journal of the Experimental Analysis of Behavior, 110*, 336–365. https://doi.org/10.1002/jeab.478

McDowell, J. J. (1988). Behavior analysis: The third branch of Aristotle's physics. *Journal of the Experimental Analysis of Behavior, 50*, 297–304. https://doi.org/10.1901/jeab.1988.50-297

McDowell, J. J. (1986). On the falsifiability of matching theory. *Journal of the Experimental Analysis of Behavior, 45*, 63–74. https://doi.org/10.1901/jeab.1986.45-63

McDowell, J. J. (2004). A computational model of selection by consequences. *Journal of the Experimental Analysis of Behavior, 81*, 297–317. https://doi.org/10.1901/jeab.2004.81-297

McDowell, J. J. (2005). On the classic and modern theories of matching. *Journal of the Experimental Analysis of Behavior, 84*, 111–127. https://doi.org/10.1901/jeab.2005.59–04

McDowell, J. J. (2013a). Calculi of complexity: How phenomena emerge from rules. A review of *Complexity: A guided tour* by Melanie Mitchell. *Journal of the Experimental Analysis of Behavior, 99*, 234–244. https://doi.org/10.1002/jeab.16

McDowell, J. J. (2013b). Representations of complexity: How nature appears in our theories. *The Behavior Analyst, 36*, 345–359.

McDowell, J. J. (2013c). On the theoretical and empirical status of the matching law and matching theory. *Psychological Bulletin, 139*, 1000–1028. https://doi.org/10.1037/a0029924

McDowell, J. J. (2013d). A quantitative evolutionary theory of adaptive behavior dynamics. *Psychological Review, 120*, 731–750. https://doi.org/10.1037/a0034244

McDowell, J. J. (2017). The effect of reinforcement, and the roles of mutation rate and selection pressure, in an evolutionary theory of behavior dynamics. *The Behavior Analyst, 40*(1), 75–82. https://doi.org/10.1007/s40614-017-0094-9

McDowell, J. J. (2019). On the current status of the evolutionary theory of behavior dynamics. *Journal of the Experimental Analysis of Behavior, 111*, 130–145. https://doi.org/10.1002/jeab.495

McDowell, J. J. (2021). Empirical matching, matching theory, and an evolutionary theory of behavior dynamics in clinical application. *Perspectives on Behavior Science, 44*, 561–580. https://doi.org/10.1007/s40614-021-00296-w

McDowell, J. J. (2023). Creating and studying the behavior of artificial organisms animated by an evolutionary theory of behavior dynamics. *Perspectives on Behavior Science, 46*, 119–136. https://doi.org/10.1007/s40614-023-00366-1

McDowell, J. J., & Arashanapalli, S. (2021). Evolutionary theory prediction: Response rate on single schedules as a joint function of reinforcement rate and reinforcer magnitude. *Journal of the Experimental Analysis of Behavior, 116*, 225–242. https://doi.org/10.1002/jeab.710

McDowell, J. J., & Calvin, N. T. (2015). Against matching theory: Predictions of an evolutionary theory of behavior dynamics. *Behavioural Processes, 114*, 14–25. https://doi.org/10.1016/j.beproc.2015.02.007

McDowell, J. J., Caron, M. L., Kulubekova, S., & Berg, J. P. (2008). A computational theory of selection by consequences applied to concurrent schedules. *Journal of the Experimental Analysis of Behavior, 90*, 387–403. https://doi.org/10.1901/jeab.2008.90-387.

McDowell, J. J., & Klapes, B. (2018). An evolutionary theory of behavior dynamics applied to concurrent ratio schedules. *Journal of the Experimental Analysis of Behavior, 110*, 323-335. -https://doi.org/10.1002/jeab.468

McDowell, J. J., & Klapes, B. (2019). An implementation of punishment in the evolutionary theory of behavior dynamics. *Journal of the Experimental Analysis of Behavior, 112*, 128-143.

McDowell, J. J., & Klapes, B. (2020). All behavior is choice: Revisiting an evolutionary theory's account of behavior on single schedules. *Journal of the Experimental Analysis of Behavior, 114*, 430–446. https://doi.org/10.1002/jeab.630

McDowell, J. J., Klapes, B., & Arashanapalli, S. (2023). A test of the evolutionary theory's account of punishment superimposed on single-alternative schedules. *Journal of the Experimental Analysis of Behavior, 119*, 117–128. https://doi.org/10.1002/jeab.811

McDowell, J. J., & Popa, A. (2009). Beyond continuous mathematics and traditional scientific analysis: Understanding and mining Wolfram's *A New Kind of Science*. *Behavioural Processes, 81*, 343–352. https://doi.org/10.1016/j.beproc.2009.01.012.

McDowell, J. J., Popa, A., & Calvin, N. T. (2012). Selection dynamics in joint matching to rate and magnitude of reinforcement. *Journal of the Experimental Analysis of Behavior, 98*, 199–212. https://doi.org/10.1901/jeab.2012.98-199

Miller, J. H., & Page, S. E. (2007). *Complex adaptive systems: An introduction to computational models of social life*. Princeton University Press.

Mitchell, M. (2009). *Complexity: A guided tour*. Oxford University Press.

Morris, S. L., & Lucia, S. M. (2023). Applying the evolutionary theory of behavior dynamics to model the subtypes of automatically reinforced self-injurious behavior. *Journal of Applied Behavior Analysis, 56*(2), 442–457. https://doi.org/10.1002/jaba.982

Morris, S. L., & McDowell, J. J. (2021). Modeling subtypes of automatically reinforced self-injurious behavior with the evolutionary theory of behavior dynamics. *Perspectives on Behavior Science, 44*, 581–603. https://doi.org/10.1007/s40614-021-00297-9

Muro, C., Escobedo, R., Spector, L., & Coppinger, R. P. (2011). Wolf-pack (Canis lupus) hunting strategies emerge from simple rules in computational simulations. *Behavioural Processes, 88*(3), 192–197. https://doi.org/10.1016/j.beproc.2011.09.006

Nevin, J. A. (1979). Overall matching versus momentary maximizing: Nevin (1969) revisited. *Journal of Experimental Psychology: Animal Behavior Processes, 5*, 300–306.

Popa, A. (2013). *The evolutionary theory of behavior dynamics: Complexity, Darwinism, and the emergence of high-level phenotypes* [Doctoral dissertation, Emory University]. http://pid.emory.edu/ark:/25593/f8hw4

Popa, A., & McDowell, J. J. (2010). The effect of Hamming distances in a computational model of selection by consequences. *Behavioural Processes, 84*, 428–434.

Popper, K. (1965). *Conjectures and refutations: The growth of scientific knowledge*. Harper.

Shimp, C. (1966). Probabilistically reinforced choice behavior in pigeons. *Journal of the Experimental Analysis of Behavior, 9*, 443–455.

Skinner, B. F. (1938). *The behavior of organisms: An experimental analysis*. Appleton Century Crofts.

Vemuri, V. (1978). *Modeling of complex systems: An introduction*. Academic Press.

von Neumann, J., & Burks, A. W. (1966). *Theory of self-reproducing automata*. University of Illinois Press.

von Neumann, J., & Morgenstern, O. (2007). *Theory of games and economic behavior*. Princeton University Press. (Original work published 1944)

Wolfram, S. (2002). *A new kind of science*. Wolfram Media.

3 Behavioral Science in the Fourth Industrial Revolution

Elizabeth Garrison, Lindsay Ouellette, and Jared B. Daniel

Introduction

Disruption has long been an integral part of changing and shaping the world we live in today. In particular, industrial revolutions (IRs) are the most significant disruptions in the development of society. Water and steam power resulted in mass production during the first industrial revolution. During this time, we also see the development of cities as people flocked to urban environments in pursuit of better socioeconomic opportunities (Reichental, 2023; Avis, 2022). The second IR (2IR) centered around the invention of electricity and the combustible engine, which transformed communication and transportation. The third IR (3IR) taught us about digitalization and how computers process information. Commonly known as the information age, the 3IR connected people over the internet and digitally transformed the world. It also created an environment with the conditions to set the stage for a fourth industrial revolution (4IR) (Reichental, 2023; Avis, 2022).

The idea of Industry 4.0 was developed by German engineers in 2011 (Pfeiffer, 2017) to describe the integration of new technologies such as the Internet of Things (IoT), artificial intelligence, robotics, and algorithms (Reichental, 2023). However, Klaus Schwab, head of the World Economic Forum, coined and popularized the 4IR in 2016 (Schulze, 2019). The 4IR builds upon the 3IR by bridging the gap between physical and digital spaces (Ross & Maynard, 2021) to create a "vast ecosystem of interconnected, complex and dynamic interaction between humans and the built environment from a single space to a city scale" (Ross & Maynard, 2021, p. 159).

Schwab (2016) identifies a vital distinction that characterizes the 4IR: velocity, scope, and systems impact. In the 4IR, innovation is moving at an exponential rather than a linear pace compared to past IRs. Connection and access to knowledge will be at the fingertips of billions of people, and these technologies will vastly impact how we live life, from our physical bodies to the products we consume to the buildings we inhabit. To provide a more vivid perspective on the rapid pace of innovation in the 4IR, it took 75 years for the telephone to reach 100 million users, Instagram accomplished the same feat in just 2 years, and the interactive mobile game Pokémon Go achieved this milestone in a mere month (Schulze, 2019).

While we are still very much in the early stages of the 4IR, it is critical to understand the intricacies of its gains and risks and the role of cyber-physical systems. One area of significant disruption is in the future of work, spanning across the individual and organizational levels. This chapter first guides the reader through the concepts of skill disruption in the 4IR and the challenges that leaders will face in the 4IR. Next, we provide strategies for supporting transitions to the 4IR through synthesizing behavior science and AI-driven performance management systems and redefining the value of work in the 4IR. We conclude with a call to action for behavior scientists during this transition to the fourth industrial revolution.

DOI: 10.4324/9781003380603-4

Skill Disruption in the Fourth Industrial Revolution

Skill disruption in the 4IR appears inevitable as automation, AI, and robots begin to replace routine, repetitive tasks (Reichental, 2023). Knowledge and skill will evolve for workers in the 4IR as they focus on more collaborative approaches (i.e., working with AI, robots, and virtual assistants). As work becomes more cyber-physical, clusters of knowledge and skills, referred to as regional knowledge (Bernstein, 2000), will be required of future employees and are expected to place a premium on complex cognitive capabilities in problem-solving, teamwork, emotional intelligence, adaptability, and innovation and flexibility (Avis, 2022).

Addressing skill disruption within the 4IR is essential. Technological advancements in AI have led to workplace disruption by automating tasks with cloud computing, advanced robotics, and AI chatbots (Ghislieri et al., 2018; Brynjolfsson et al., 2023). We have also seen a shift in workplace settings, where social media and augmented and virtual reality create new spaces for future workers to learn and work. The Burning Glass Institute analyzed millions of job postings from 2016 to 2021 and, using data from what they term "The Great Disruption," found that most jobs had some form of skill disruption, with more jobs requiring skills in digital technology (Sigelman et al., 2022). As workplace tasks become automated and workplace settings digitized, future workers will be expected to quickly learn new technological skills to interact with digital systems or risk losing employment.

In the last 30 years, we have adapted to and relied on computers and technology to assist with our work. The COVID-19 pandemic brought a mandatory shift to remote work that challenged many workplaces to consider their technological capital – with the transition from the physical workspace, video technology, virtual assistants, remote network access, and automated systems allowed people to work from anywhere (Ross & Maynard, 2021). Following the pandemic, remote work continues to be prominent as 58% of the Americans surveyed through McKinsey and Company's American Opportunity Survey report working from home at least one day per week (Dua et al., 2022), despite recent initiatives to get workers back in brick-and-mortar offices.

Industries such as service and hospitality, medical and healthcare, logistics, and warehousing are expected to see the highest levels of disruption with the advent of robotics and automation (Vyas, 2022). Automation found within AI and robotic systems has replaced humans in tasks such as packing and shipping processes found in warehouses, and AI chatbots have replaced customer service representatives. Self-driving and autonomous vehicle systems, once running, have the potential to replace logistics careers such as rideshare and delivery services. Within these industries, it will be imperative for future workers to learn new skills as they collaborate with AI and prepare for new types of employment.

With the advent of the "gig economy," more workers have taken on self-employment or side jobs to supplement their income from their primary place of employment. In the 4IR, remote work capabilities could set the stage to create a new stereotypical work environment of work from anywhere and at any time (Akaev et al., 2019; Silvestrini Vieira Alves, 2020), causing the gig economy to rise (Starr-Glass, 2019; Eichhorst et al., 2017; Mpofu & Nicolaides, 2019). Crowdsourcing platforms such as Amazon's Mechanical Turk, Upwork, and Fiverr have changed how gig workers find work. The digital nature of these platforms requires that workers remain up to date with technological trends and continuously develop their skills to stand out in a pool of workers competing for the same job. Furthermore, working within these platforms requires developing soft skills like communication, time management, and project management (Sigelman et al., 2022). In the 4IR, individuals should prioritize developing competencies such as active learning, creativity, digital literacy, information technology proficiency, knowledge-sharing abilities, complex problem-solving skills, spontaneity, inventiveness, persistence, flexibility, proactive anticipation, emotional intelligence, and expertise in science, technology, engineering, and mathematics (STEM) fields (Maimina et al., 2019; Piątkowski, 2020; Furstenau et al., 2020). Employees will need to learn multiple skills to succeed in the 4IR rather than focus on a singular skill set, as these are no longer static within the digital workplace. "Upskilling" or "reskilling" is the process of learning new technological skills (Fung, 2020; Fung & Hosseini, 2023; Haverland et al., 2023). Upskilling involves learning new skills related to one's current job, whereas reskilling refers to learning new skills or jobs. For instance, a retail worker might reskill by learning a new programming language, such as Java or Python, to start a new career in cybersecurity. In upskilling, a call center representative whose job gets automated with chatbots will learn new programming skills to manage chatbots. There will be a constant need for upskilling and deskilling to support digitalization and interdisciplinary skills in the workplace in the 4IR. This will require a proactive approach to continuous learning at the individual and organizational levels (Avis, 2022).

Challenges for Leaders in the Fourth Industrial Revolution

In the 4IR, the rise of remote work brought opportunities and challenges during the global pandemic. During this time, the concept of "work-life balance" became even more widespread, leading to the rise of the "Great Resignation" and "Quiet Quitting." As people began to challenge the conventional eight-hour workday in pursuit of more control over their work and personal lives, the emergence of the metaverse, a blend of virtual reality and digital interaction, presents an intriguing opportunity for redefining workplace interactions and environments (Kniffin et al., 2021; Formica & Sfodera, 2022; Ning et al., 2023). Essentially, the metaverse could redefine traditional workspaces by preserving organizational culture while providing employees with more work-life balance. The speed at which innovation accelerates and disruption unfolds in the 4IR can be difficult to grasp or foresee fully. These driving factors consistently bring surprises, even for the most well-connected and informed leaders, and it will be critical for leaders to reassess constantly (Schwab, 2016). Bughin and Hazan (2017) highlight the increasing importance of adaptability, suggesting that firms that are agile and willing to pivot quickly will thrive amidst uncertainty. Leaders are now responsible for operational and financial decisions and the broader ethical implications of those decisions.

As the 4IR shifts toward more collaboration and integrated systems of AI, ethics becomes a core issue for leadership. Many questions arise, such as what AI should be able to do independently versus what must be deferred to a human (Reichental, 2023). When it comes to shared responsibility, who gets the last say (Inthorn et al., 2015)? Who is responsible when something goes wrong? The infusion of emerging technologies into the workplace creates legal gaps as laws grapple to keep pace with the rapid evolution of technology (O'Sullivan et al., 2018). AI lacks culpability, and the responsibility for technical problems does not automatically fall on the worker (Attia et al., 2018). As technology advances, ethical considerations become increasingly crucial.

The Society for Industrial and Organizational Psychology (SIOP) is the professional association for industrial and organizational psychology. SIOP is the 14th division under the American Psychological Association (APA). Therefore, it adheres to the APA code of ethics and conduct principles of Beneficence and Nonmaleficence, Fidelity and Responsibility, Integrity, Justice, and Respect for People's Rights and Dignity (American Psychological Association, 2023a). While ethical principles do not provide clear rules, they promote self-reflection, dialogue, and conversation, which are the heart of responsible and ethical practice (Nakkula & Ravich, 1998). This also allows leaders to develop systems tailored to their organizational needs. While there are more questions than answers, leaders are encouraged to grapple with these questions to prepare us for a future when the 4IR is more apparent in the workplace and to have the ability to shape that evolution.

AI-Driven Performance Management Systems

In everyday conversations, the term "artificial intelligence" (or "AI") occurs frequently. One area where it is notable is in employment, especially as businesses capitalize on AI. Examples of business capitalization in 2023 include the integration of IBM's Watson with business solutions and the partnership developed between Microsoft and OpenAI's ChatGPT. Between 2016 and 2030, the transition in the workforce to AI automation is expected to replace 400 million jobs, and smart technology, AI, robotics, and algorithms (STARA) were estimated to eliminate 33% of occupations by this year (2025; see Frey & Osborn, 2013; Bhargava et al., 2021; Manyika & Sneader, 2018; Bort, 2014; Lynch, 2015; Frey & Osborn, 2013; Thibodeau, 2014). While STARA and digital work environments have been in the workplace for decades, the rapid pace of change within the 4IR prompts comments on how people interact with AI (Schwab, 2016; Ghislieri et al., 2018). With this exponential change, future workers will need to gain new technological and soft skills, demonstrating flexibility to meet the demands of the changing workplace.

Another notable area in which the term "AI" occurs frequently is in management. With the integration of AI in management systems growing since the 3IR, the rapid pace of change within the 4IR is prompting comments on how managers will utilize and promote cyber-physical systems (Schwab, 2016; Ghislieri et al., 2018) to perform various operations such as production, logistics, and office management (Oosthuizen, 2022). For example, performance feedback evaluations are often based on an annual review. Consistent and frequent feedback delivery is an effective way to create meaningful organizational change, and integrating AI-driven performance management systems makes such a system possible. These systems analyze employee activities, provide real-time feedback, and offer actionable insights, ensuring that employees receive timely recognition and guidance, leading to improved productivity.

Often based on annual reviews, traditional performance evaluations must be updated and more effective (Daniels, 2009). With AI-driven performance management systems, continuous feedback becomes feasible. These systems analyze employee activities, provide real-time feedback, and offer actionable insights, ensuring that employees receive timely recognition and guidance, leading to improved productivity. An AI performance management system integrates well with Daniels and Bailey's (2014) performance management process within the following example, as shown in Figure 3.1:

1. Computer vision systems observe behavioral pinpoints in real time within the workplace.
2. Measurement systems continuously collect data through AI multimodal systems.
3. Systems deliver feedback and reinforcement where, once the pinpoint is observed or not observed, it can trigger a response from the system to the worker.
4. The worker responds following feedback from the system.
5. Managers review and evaluate data collected on worker performance daily after receiving prompts from the AI system, updating goals and learning objectives based on data collected within the digital workplace.

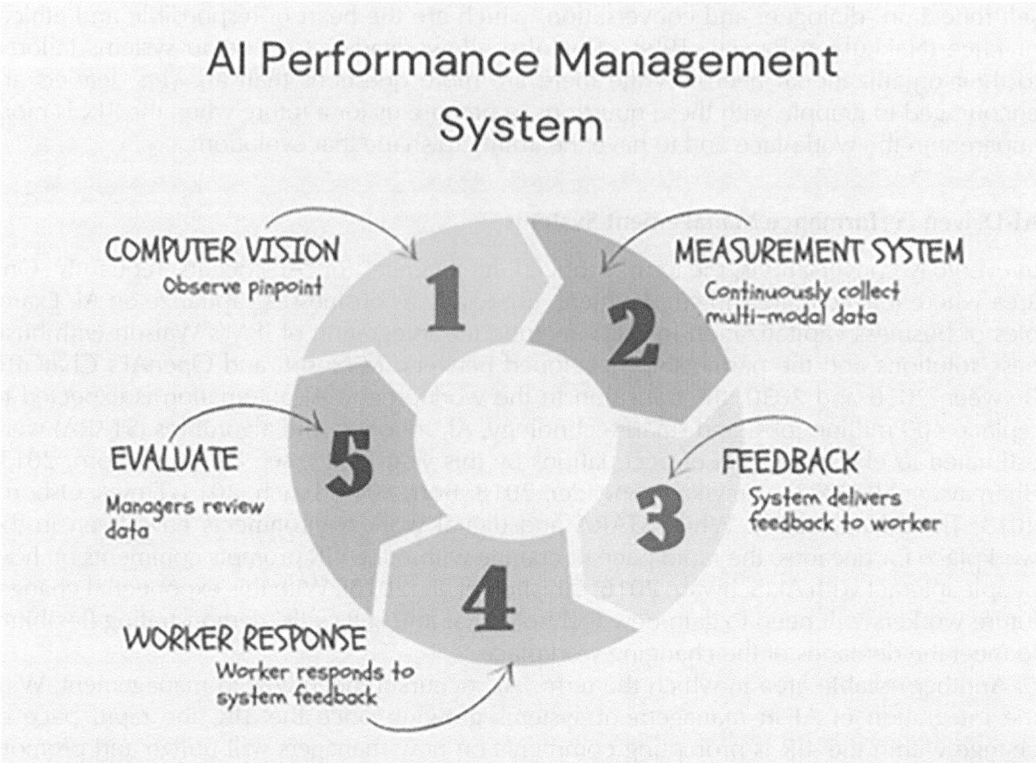

Figure 3.1 AI performance management system process map based on Daniels and Bailey's (2014) performance management system.

It is important to note that within this AI system, the colloquial phrase "garbage in, garbage out" is critical regarding data management. Managers will need to be trained in data evaluation and communication with AI systems as part of this process, thus upskilling their role (Ghislieri et al., 2018). One example of creating an AI system combined with humans in the loop is through performance scorecards using real-time feedback systems (Abernathy, 2014). Within traditional performance scorecard systems, managers monitor individual employee performance pinpoints daily or weekly, spending hours collecting data and reviewing feedback with employees. With technological advances within a digital workplace, AI systems can assist managers in creating performance scorecard systems, where AI data collection systems monitor individualized performance goals. With these systems, daily (or even hourly) feedback prompts the employee's next response(s). Within these systems, there is also the capacity to provide employees with immediate incentives for their performance in the digital workplace.

With the pioneering work of Thomas Gilbert and Aubrey Daniels and the *Journal of Organizational Behavior Management* (*JOBM*) founding in 1977, behavior scientists have provided consultation in performance management for decades. The field of behavior science also excels in designing instructional programs and establishing learning settings, positioning it to efficiently assist future workers in acquiring new skills. However, as practitioners who play a key role in the behavioral dynamics of workplace environments, there is

Table 3.1 Relevant Keyword Searches within the *Journal of Organizational Behavior Management*

Keyword or Phrase	*Topics of Discussion in Articles*	*Number of Article Mentions in JOBM*
Artificial intelligence (AI)	Virtual reality training; web-based behavioral training	4
Robotics	Accident prevention	1
Algorithms	Coding; work efficiency; quality assurance; job training	5
Smart technology	Human performance technology; data collection; professional development; productivity; task clarification; feedback delivery; prompting; assessments	9
Digital workplace	Data collection; manufacturing systems; assessments; gamification; feedback delivery	8
Total articles		**27**
Total articles searched 2013–2023		**263**

a large gap in the behavioral science literature/practices/research on the advent and impact of STARA in organizations. Searching for these keywords in the *JOBM* from 2013 to 2023 yielded only 19 articles out of 263 (Table 3.1). In addition, when searching for the words "digital workplace" in the *JOBM* literature, it was found that only 3% of articles (8 out of 263 articles) included content involving workplaces in digital environments. This indicates that behavior scientists may need more preparation to answer the call to address such issues.

Personalized Learning Systems with Humans in the Loop

Continuous learning is essential as the job market becomes more competitive and technological change accelerates. By using machine learning algorithms combined with principles of behavior science, companies can personalize training modules to suit individual preferences, career goals, and learning pace, making the training process more efficient and relevant to the worker. In this shift away from traditional, one-size-fits-all learning approaches toward personalized learning and development systems, workers can access learning modules reminiscent of Keller's Personalized Systems of Instruction (Keller, 1968). AI large language models (LLMs), such as ChatGPT, replace human proctors within these individualized instruction systems. The integration of LLMs in training modules offers numerous advantages. First, they deliver instantaneous feedback, cater to individual queries, and adjust content delivery based on the learner's progress. However, these advancements come with potential pitfalls. Relying solely on LLMs could lead to biases, oversimplifications, or misinterpretations. The AI system might only sometimes understand specific industry jargon or cultural considerations. Hence, a "human in the loop" approach becomes indispensable. The term "human in the loop" refers to an AI system where a human oversees an AI system's data inputs and response output (Kumar et al., 2019; Wu et al., 2022) and does not allow the AI system to work independently without oversight.

Requiring a "human in the loop" ensures that the information provided in personalized learning and development systems is accurate and appropriate. For instance, human oversight is necessary when the content touches on sensitive topics or safety is a priority, such as healthcare, construction, or law enforcement. This dual approach, which merges the computational power of AI with human oversight, offers an efficient and balanced learning experience to the worker in the digital workplace.

In addition to using LLMs within personalized learning systems, the development of new technology within virtual and augmented reality provides flexible environments for digital workers to learn. With the use of behavior skills training, in conjunction with these virtual and augmented realities, workers learn in environments that are closely related to or resemble the workplace without needing to leave their homes (Clay et al., 2021; Chiang et al., 2022; Chang et al., 2023). Virtual and augmented reality platforms provide real-time haptic feedback (Caporaso et al., 2022). This feedback can be tailored to the individual learner when combined with AI algorithms. For instance, if a worker makes a mistake in the virtual environment, the system can immediately pinpoint the error and, using haptics, provide immediate corrective feedback and suggest additional resources or training modules. Over time, these AI systems can also track a learner's progress, identifying strengths and areas for improvement. This is especially beneficial in sectors where hands-on training might be dangerous, costly, or logistically challenging. For example, a worker in the construction industry, using virtual reality, can simulate walking through a construction site, identifying potential hazards, and learning best practices for safety – all without the risks of a real-world setting. In the medical field, surgeons can practice complex procedures in augmented reality before performing them on actual patients, reducing the chances of error through practice. Though some argue that advanced robotics may replace aspects of some of these tasks in the future, human workers will still need training to provide human-machine collaboration and oversight to these worksites (Ma et al., 2022).

Redefining Meaning and Value of Work: Employee Well-Being and Health

Most people's sense of self is closely tied to their workforce participation and their careers (Cerf & Matz, 2022, p. 425). Hantula (2015) describes the value of high job satisfaction and how it permeates into the realms of family and community, contributing significantly to work-life balance and overall life contentment. This underscores the perils linked to low job satisfaction, such as burnout and depression. It also underscores their potential to spill over and negatively impact personal well-being, relationships, and community engagement (Hantula, 2015). However, if leaders maintain human-centric integration of cyber-physical systems, the 4IR could pave the way for a more meaningful life-altering time between work and leisure (Schwab, 2016). An example is the current experimentation of the four-day workweek in various organizations and countries (Veal, 2023).

After World War I, economic prosperity and opportunity became equated with ability and achievement (a.k.a. the "American dream") (Churchwell, 2018). In the 21st century, it is still expected that if people work hard enough, they can be as rich as Bill Gates (Museum of Science, Boston, 2016). Today, that ethos has developed into a cultural phenomenon known as the "glamourization of busyness," influenced by escalating work demands and the pursuit of productivity and achievement. Despite the common association of busyness with elevated social status and achievement, it is crucial to acknowledge the simultaneous prevalence of a mental health crisis, with two out of five adults reporting symptoms of anxiety and depression (Vahratian et al., 2021). Moreover, the US Surgeon General has officially recognized loneliness as a public health crisis (US Surgeon General, 2023). Gilbert (2007) wrote about hard work, sacrifice, and self-denial as cloaked virtues of work ethic and revealed that living by this mindset ultimately breeds "sloth, wastefulness, inefficiency, inflation, and incompetence." Instead, Gilbert supported a model where the value of achievement is greater than the behavioral expense. This model resulted in the acquisition of leisure, providing both the time and opportunity to pursue other endeavors. As the adage goes, no one ever finds themselves on their deathbed wishing they had worked more.

The 4IR may be reframed as a gain in "human leisure time" instead of perceiving technological progress as a loss of human employment opportunities. This emerging perspective places behavioral scientists at the forefront of a pivotal movement. They can redefine the meaning of work, incorporating well-being and health as primary objectives. This approach emerges from understanding the detrimental psychological effects of an overworked lifestyle (Bellezza et al., 2016). With the potential that 4IR brings, there is a promising horizon where the work structure accentuates well-being over mere productivity. For instance, as the separation between professional and personal life becomes increasingly indistinct due to the pervasive nature of technology, behavioral science can guide the formulation of work-life balance initiatives. These initiatives can empower employees to delineate boundaries, take more breaks, and pursue passions outside their work domain.

Applying reinforcement systems, where behaviors linked to mental well-being are acknowledged and reinforced, also plays a pivotal role. Examples include incentivizing regular break intervals, participating in holistic wellness programs, or engaging in activities that alleviate stress. It is important to note that despite the rapid technological progression of the 4IR, human connection remains irreplaceable. Here, behavioral science can also promote social integration through team-building endeavors, establishing peer support circles, and setting up mentorship systems within the workplace. Such initiatives enhance social bonds and act as buffers against the isolation that technological immersion may induce.

Conclusion

Overall, the 4IR has ushered unprecedented change into the workplace, particularly in skill disruption and leadership challenges. Cyber-physical system spaces, powered by the 3IR's artificial intelligence, are at the heart of this transformation, which can revolutionize performance management systems and necessitate a profound reevaluation of the meaning and value of work. As we stand at this crossroads, there is an increased emphasis on prioritizing employee well-being and health, ensuring that human work remains at the core of all endeavors as technology advances.

Behavior scientists are pivotal in navigating this shift to the 4IR. It is vital for behavior scientists to continuously update their skill sets to understand and anticipate the behavioral implications of new technologies. Furthermore, they should support the development of AI-enabled performance management systems and interventions that assist leaders in managing the complexities and challenges associated with rapid technological change. Additionally, integrating their professional skills and advocating for and designing training programs that emphasize the well-being of employees is crucial.

To the community of behavior scientists, the fourth industrial revolution is not merely a phase of technological advancement but a call to reassert the importance of human behavior in an increasingly automated world. We can bridge the gap between rapid technological growth and the human need for purpose and well-being. Embrace the challenge, collaborate across disciplines, and lead the way in ensuring that humanity's essence is preserved and nurtured amidst all the change. The future awaits.

References

Abernathy, W. B. (2014). Beyond the Skinner box: The design and management of organization-wide performance systems. *Journal of Organizational Behavior Management, 34*(4), 235–254.

Akaev, A., Rudskoi, A., Sarygulov, A., & Sokolov, V. (2019). A new era of machinery: Will the accumulation of capital grow and labor intensity decrease? *Social Evolution & History, 18*(1), 67–93. https://doi.org/10.30884/seh/2019.01.04

American Psychological Association. (2023a). *Ethical principles of psychologists and code of conduct.* https://www.apa.org/ethics/code/index

American Psychological Association. (2023b). *Society for industrial and organizational psychology.* https://www.apa.org/about/division/div14

Attia, M., Hossny, M., Nahavandi, S., Dalvand, M., & Asadi, H. (2018). Toward trusted autonomous surgical robots. In *2018 IEEE international conference on systems, man, and cybernetics* (pp. 4083–4088). IEEE. https://doi.org/10.1109/SMC.1018.00692

Avis, J. A. (2022). Thinking about the future: The fourth industrial revolution, capitalism, waged labour, and anti-work. In M. Malloch, L. G. Cairns, K. Evans, & B. N. O'Connor (Eds.), *The Sage handbook of learning at work* (pp. 497–511). Sage.

Bellezza, S., Paharia, N., & Keinan, A. (2016). Why Americans are so impressed by busyness. *Harvard Business Review*. https://hbr.org/2016/12/research-why-americans-are-so-impressed-by-busyness

Bernstein, B. (2000). *Pedagogy, symbolic control and identity*. Rowman & Littlefield.

Bhargava, A., Bester, M., & Bolton, L. (2021). Employees' perceptions of the implementation of robotics, artificial intelligence, and automation (RAIA) on job satisfaction, job security, and employability. *Journal of Technology in Behavioral Science, 6*, 106–113. https://doi.org/10.1007/s41347-020-00153-8

Bort, J. (2014). Bill Gates: People don't realize how many jobs will soon be replaced by software bots. *Business Insider*. http://www.businessinsider.com.au/bill-gates-bots-are-taking-away-jobs-2014-s-2013

Brynjolfsson, E., Li, D., & Raymond, L. R. (2023). *Generative AI at work* (No. w31161). National Bureau of Economic Research.

Bughin, J., & Hazan, E. (2017). The new spring of artificial intelligence: A few early economies. *VoxEU.org, 21*.

Caporaso, T., Grazioso, S., & Di Gironimo, G. (2022). Development of an integrated virtual reality system with wearable sensors for ergonomic evaluation of human-robot cooperative workplaces. *Sensors, 22*(6), 2413.

Cerf, M., & Matz, S. (2022). Where the future might take us. In S. Matz (Ed.), *The psychology of technology: Social science research in the age of big data* (pp. 421–430). American Psychological Association. https://doi.org/10.1037/0000290-013.

Chang, A. A., Kazemi, E., Esmaeili, V., & Davies, M. S. (2023). The effectiveness of virtual reality training: A systematic review. *Journal of Organizational Behavior Management*, 1–19.

Chiang, F. K., Shang, X., & Qiao, L. (2022). Augmented reality in vocational training: A systematic review of research and applications. *Computers in Human Behavior, 129*, 107125.

Churchwell, S. (2018). *Behold, America: The entangled history of America first and the American dream*. Hachette Book Group.

Clay, C. J., Schmitz, B. A., Balakrishnan, B., Hopfenblatt, J. P., Evans, A., & Kahng, S. (2021). Feasibility of virtual reality behavior skills training for preservice clinicians. *Journal of Applied Behavior Analysis, 54*(2), 547–565.

Daniels, A. C. (2009). *Oops! 13 management practices that waste time and money (and what to do instead)*. Performance Management Publications.

Daniels, A. C., & Bailey, J. S. (2014). *Performance management: Changing behavior that drives organizational effectiveness* (5th ed., pp. 1–344). Performance Management Publications.

Dua, A., Ellingrud, K., Kirschner, P., Kwok, A., Luby, R., Palter, R., & Pemberton, S. (2022). *Americans are embracing flexible work – and they want more of it.* McKinsey & Company.

Eichhorst, W., Hinte, H., Rinne, U., & Tobsch, V. (2017). How big is the gig? Assessing the preliminary evidence on the effects of digitalization on the labor market. *Management Revue, 28*(3), 298–318. http://www.jstor.org/stable/26381578

Formica, S., & Sfodera, F. (2022). The great resignation and quiet quitting paradigm shifts: An overview of current situation and future research directions. *Journal of Hospitality Marketing & Management, 31*(8), 899–907.

Frey, C. B., & Osborne, M. A. (2013). *The future of employment: How susceptible are jobs to computerisation?* http://www.oxfordmartin.ox.ac.uk/downloads/academic/The_Future_of_Employment.pdf

Fung, M. (2020). Developing a robust system for upskilling and reskilling the workforce: Lessons from the skills future movement in Singapore. In B. Panth & R. Maclean (Eds.), *Anticipating and preparing for emerging skills and jobs* (pp. 321–327). Springer.

Fung, M., & Hosseini, S. (2023). Reimagining education and workforce preparation in support of the UN's sustainable development Goals. In D. Araya & P. Marber (Eds.), *Augmented education in the global age: Artificial intelligence and the future of learning and work* (pp. 30–47). Taylor & Francis.

Furstenau, L. B., Sott, M., Kipper, L., Machado, Ê., Lopez-Robles, J., Dohan, M., Cobo, M., Zahid, A., Abbasi, Q., & Imran, M. (2020). Link between sustainability and Industry 4.0: Trends, challenges and new perspectives. *IEEE Access, 8*, 1. 10.1109/ACCESS.2020.3012812

Ghislieri, C., Molino, M., & Cortese, C. G. (2018). Work and organizational psychology looks at the fourth industrial revolution: How to support workers and organizations? *Frontiers in Psychology, 9*, 2365.

Gilbert, T. (2007). *Human competence: Engineering worthy performance*. Pheiffer.

Hantula, D. (2015). Job satisfaction: The management tool and leadership responsibility. *Journal of Organizational Behavior Management, 35*, 81–94. https://doi.org/10.10180/01608061.2015.1031430

Haverland, S., Halkias, D., & Diaz, J. (2023). *Critical success factors for reskilling and upskilling engineer leaders in customized executive education programs: An integrative literature review* (SSRN 4434273). SSRN.

Inthorn, J., Tabacchi, M., & Seising, R. (2015). Having the final say: Machine support of ethical decisions of doctors. In S. Peter van Rysewyk & M. Pontier (Eds.), *Machine medical ethics* (pp. 181–206). Springer International Publishing.

Keller, F. S. (1968). Good-bye teacher. *Journal of Applied Behavior Analysis, 1*, 79–89.

Kniffin, K. M., Narayanan, J., Anseel, F., Antonakis, J., Ashford, S. P., Bakker, A. B., Bamberger, P., Bapuji, H., Bhave, D. P., Choi, V. K., Creary, S. J., Demerouti, E., Flynn, F. J., Gelfand, M. J., Greer, L. L., Johns, G., Kesebir, S., Klein, P. G., Lee, S. Y., . . . Vugt, M. V. (2021). COVID-19 and the workplace: Implications, issues, and insights for future research and action. *American Psychologist, 76*(1), 63.

Kumar, V., Smith-Renner, A., Findlater, L., Seppi, K., & Boyd-Graber, J. (2019). Why didn't you listen to me? comparing user control of human-in-the-loop topic models. *arXiv preprint arXiv:1905.09864*. https://arxiv.org/abs/1905.09864

Lynch, C. (2015). Stephen Hawking on the future of capitalism and inequality. *Counter Punch*. http://www.counterpunch.org/2015/10/15/stephen-hawkings-on-the-future-of-capitalism-and-inequality/

Ma, X., Mao, C., & Liu, G. (2022). Can robots replace human beings? Assessment on the developmental potential of construction robot. *Journal of Building Engineering, 56*, 104727.

Maimina, E., Puzynya, T., Grishina, T., Psareva, N., & Stytsyuk, R. (2019). New professions emerging out of the development of robotics. *Revista Espacios, 40*(10), 16. https://doi.org/10.18103/revistas.v40i10.1940

Manyika, J., & Sneader, K. (2018). *AI, automation, and the future of work: Ten things to solve for*. McKinsey & Company.

Mpofu, R. T., & Nicolaides, A. (2019). Frankenstein and the Fourth Industrial Revolution (4IR): Ethics and human rights considerations. *African Journal of Hospitality, Tourism and Leisure, 8*(5), 1–25.

Museum of Science, Boston. (2016, July 14). *Grave matters: The role of death in life – Sheldon Solomon, PhD* [Video]. YouTube. https://youtu.be/j7GZrgWKj9o?si=wcLUsK6KjJeTm3gV

Nakkula, M., & Ravich, S. (1998). *Matters of interpretation*. Jossey-Bass Inc., Publishers.

Ning, H., Wang, H., Lin, Y., Wang, W., Dhelim, S., Farha, F., Ding, J., & Daneshmand, M. (2023). A survey on the metaverse: The state-of-the-art, technologies, applications, and challenges. *IEEE Internet of Things Journal, 10*(16).

Oosthuizen, R. M. (2022). The fourth industrial revolution – smart technology, artificial intelligence, robotics and algorithms: Industrial psychologists in future workplaces. *Frontiers in Artificial Intelligence, 5*, 913168. https://doi.org/10.3389/frai.2022.913168

O'Sullivan, S., Nevejans, N., Allen, C., Blyth, A., Leonard, S., Pagallo, U., Holzinger, K., Holziner, A., Sajid, M., & Ashrafian, H. (2018). Legal, regulatory, and ethical frameworks for development of standards in artificial intelligence (AI) and autonomous robotic surgery. *The International Journal of Medical Robotics and Computer Assisted Surgery, 15*, Article e1968. https://doi.org/10.1002/rcs.1968.

Pfeiffer, S. (2017). The vision of 'Industrie 4.0' in the making – a case of future told, tamed, and traded. *Nanoethics, 11*, 107–121. https://doi.org/10.1007/s11569-016-0280-3
Piątkowski, M. J. (2020). Expectations and challenges in the labour market in the context of Industrial Revolution 4.0. The agglomeration method-based analysis for Poland and other EU member states. *Sustainability, 12*(13), 5437. https://doi.org/10.3390/su12135437
Reichental, J. (2023). Foundations of the fourth industrial revolution (Industry 4.0). *LinkedIn Learning*. https://www.linkedin.com/learning/foundations-of-the-fourth-industrial-revolution-industry-4-0-22810607/how-the-fourth-industrial-revolution-is-changing-the-world?u=2206009
Ross, P., & Maynard, K. (2021). Towards a 4th industrial revolution. *Intelligent Buildings International, 13*(3), 159–161. https://doi.org/10.1080/17508975.2021.1873625
Schulze, E. (2019, January 17). Everything you need to know about the fourth industrial revolution. *CNBC*. https://www.cnbc.com/2019/01/16/fourth-industrial-revolution-explained-davos-2019.html
Schwab, K. (2016). *The fourth industrial revolution*. World Economic Forum.
Sigelman, M., Taska, B., O'Kane, L., Nitschke, J., Strack, R., Baier, J., Breitling, F., & Kotsis, Á. (2022). *Shifting skills, moving targets, and remaking the workforce*. Boston Consulting Group and the Burning Glass Institute.
Silvestrini Vieira Alves, A. P. (2020). Achieving the right to work in the face of technological advances: Reflections on the occasion of the ILO's centenary. *University of Bologna Law Review, 5*(1), 226–233. https://doi.org/10.6092/issn.2531-6133/11393
Starr-Glass, D. (2019). Doing and being: Future graduates, careers and Industry 4.0. *On the Horizon, 27*(3/4), 145–152. https://doi.org/10.1108/OTH-08-2019-0048
Thibodeau, P. (2014). *One in three jobs will be taken by software or robots by 2025*. http://www.computerworld.com/article/2691607/one-in-three-jobs-will-be-taken-by-software-or-robots-by-2025.html
US Surgeon General. (2023). *Our epidemic of loneliness and isolation: The U.S. Surgeon General's advisory on healing effects of connection and community*. https://www.hhs.gov/sites/default/files/surgeon-general-social-connection-advisory.pdf
Vahratian, A., Blumberg, S. J., Terlizzi, E. P., & Schiller, J. S. (2021). Symptoms of anxiety or depressive disorder and use of mental health care among adults during the COVID-19 pandemic – United States, August 2020–February 2021. *Morbidity and Mortality Weekly Report, 70*(13), 490.
Veal, A. J. (2023). The 4-day work-week: The new leisure society? *Leisure Studies, 42*(2), 172–187.
Vyas, L. (2022). "New normal" at work in a post-COVID world: Work-life balance and labor markets. *Policy and Society, 41*(1), 155–167.
Wu, X., Xiao, L., Sun, Y., Zhang, J., Ma, T., & He, L. (2022). A survey of human-in-the-loop for machine learning. *Future Generation Computer Systems, 135*, 364–381.

Section 2

Machine Learning, AI, and Predictive Models in Behavior Science

4 Machine Learning to Support Decision-Making in Behavior Science

Current Research and Future Directions

Marc J. Lanovaz[1,2] *and Philippe Leroux*[1,2]

[1] *École de psychoéducation, Université de Montréal*

[2] *Centre de recherche de l'Institut universitaire en santé mentale de Montréal*

Correspondence

Marc J. Lanovaz, École de psychoéducation, Université de Montréal, C.P. 6128, succursale Centre-Ville, Montreal, QC, Canada, H3C 3J7. Email: marc.lanovaz@umontreal.ca, Phone: 1 514-343-6111 #81774

Regardless of its consequences on human behavior, technology has become a ubiquitous part of our daily lives. Among other things, people use technology to access news, to make online purchases, to watch movies, to stay in touch with others, and to travel to new locations. What makes technology so powerful today is not that it gives us access to information (e.g., news, music, posts about others, routes to take) but that it can learn from our behavior and make recommendations. For example, CNN will not only give you access to news but will also recommend the articles or videos that you are most likely to read or watch. Amazon and Netflix rely on your prior history to propose purchases and movies. Facebook uses your personal information to order the posts that you see on your feed first, and Google Maps learns over time what is the most efficient route to get from point A to point B in your local community. In the prior examples, each company is applying machine learning to drive sales, advertisement revenue, or both.

Beyond enabling corporations to earn more profit, machine learning may also contribute to the improvement of socially significant behavior. Fields such as medicine and education have adopted machine learning to support practitioners in making better decisions, to improve interventions and teaching procedures, and to facilitate the delivery of services (Khanal et al., 2020; Waring et al., 2020). In the same vein, integrating machine learning in behavior research may lead to the development of more accessible services and better outcomes for vulnerable populations. The problem is that behavior scientists have been slow to integrate this technology in their work when compared to other fields. To address this issue, this chapter aims to serve as a primer for the use of machine learning in behavior science by introducing the reader to machine learning methodology and algorithms, presenting published applications of machine learning with human behavior, and suggesting some future directions for research.

What Is Machine Learning?

As machine learning is a subfield of artificial intelligence, a first step is to define the latter. Artificial intelligence refers to "the study of how to make computers do things at which, at the moment, people do better" (Rich & Knight, 1991, p. 3). Thus, what artificial intelligence is and is not varies as technology improves over time. Machine learning is a subfield of

DOI: 10.4324/9781003380603-6

artificial intelligence that involves the use of algorithms to identify and utilize patterns in data (Goodfellow et al., 2016). Computer scientists typically divide machine learning procedures into three broad categories: unsupervised machine learning, supervised machine learning, and reinforcement learning. Unsupervised machine learning is designed to identify groupings or clusters of data with similar characteristics. Researchers only need to provide input data and the algorithm develops a model that creates groupings. In contrast, supervised machine learning involves providing input data with their expected responses (output). Then, the algorithm develops a model to best predict the responses using the input data. In reinforcement learning, the algorithm must take actions in an environment that contains rewards. The purpose of the algorithm is to develop a model that will optimize the quantity of rewards it contacts in the environment. This chapter focuses on supervised machine learning as it tends to produce more robust and reliable models for decision-making.

Supervised Machine Learning

When conducting supervised machine learning, the first thing that researchers need is a dataset. A dataset contains samples: Each sample is composed of features and the corresponding labels. The features are the input data that the machine learning uses to make a prediction.[1] Machine learning may use many different types of features, such as behavioral measurements, audio recordings, physiological data, images, and even videos. In contrast, the labels involve the output that the researcher is trying to predict. The values of the labels may be a category (classification) or a continuous value (regressor). In more behavioral terms, the features resemble discriminative stimuli, the labels the correct responses to these stimuli, and the samples the exemplars.

Once researchers have organized their data into features and labels, the next step involves setting aside part of their samples to test their future models for generalization. Researchers may use three different approaches, or cross-validation methods, to address this issue: hold-out, *k*-fold, and leave-one-out. Hold-out cross-validation involves splitting the dataset into two subsets: one test set and one training set. Researchers then use the training set to train their models and the test set to assess generalization. The *k*-fold cross-validation method divides the dataset into *k* groups (or folds). Each group is in the test set once while the model is trained with the other groups. This process is repeated *k* times until all groups have been part of the test set once. Finally, the leave-one-out cross-validation is similar to *k*-fold, except that each test group is composed of a single sample. Hence, each sample is in the test set once and in the training set for all the other iterations. The number of iterations is equal to the number of samples.

Following the selection of a cross-validation methodology, researchers should choose an algorithm. In supervised machine learning, an algorithm is a series of computer instructions designed to uncover patterns in the features to predict the labels (see the "Common Algorithms" section, following, for more details). This algorithm is then used to train a model to identify patterns in behavior. At this point, we should define what computer scientists mean by "training," as it differs from its traditional meaning in human and animal learning. When training a model, researchers provide the features and labels of the *training* set to the algorithm, which will then develop a model with parameters optimized to categorize the samples correctly. That is, training involves the algorithm using the features to best predict the labels that researchers provide. More specifically, each algorithm uses a different strategy to adjust the parameters of a model (e.g., weights, function variables of the algorithm) in order to optimize the number of labels that are identified correctly. The result of training is a model with parameter values that can then be used to identify label values on novel data. Following training, the final step involves applying the model to the *test* set and then comparing the results to the true values. The objective of this process is to develop models that produce labels that match the true label values.

This brief introduction to machine learning leaves out some more advanced topics, which are beyond the scope of the chapter (e.g., hyperparameter tuning, feature selection, data augmentation, outcome measures). The reader can find step-by-step tutorials discussing these more advanced topics elsewhere (see Lanovaz & Bailey, 2024; Turgeon & Lanovaz, 2020). What is important to remember is the general logic underlying supervised machine learning wherein (a) a researcher provides features and labels to an algorithm, (b) this algorithm produces a model by learning patterns on a training set, and (c) the model is then applied to a test set, which was not used during training, to assess for generalization.

Common Algorithms

This section introduces some algorithms commonly used in machine learning. It should be noted that it is the methodological approach, rather than the algorithm itself, that determines whether a researcher is conducting machine learning. For example, the application of logistic regression to test hypotheses using *p*-values would not be considered as machine learning. In comparison, researchers using a cross-validation design to examine the predictive accuracy of models developed using logistic regression would be doing machine learning. The manner in which researchers apply algorithms determines whether the study involves machine learning or not.

Logistic Regression

Logistic regression is designed to handle classification tasks involving categorical target variables (Bisong, 2019). In such problems, the algorithm aims to establish a relationship between the features and the label, enabling the prediction of the probability that a new instance belongs to a specific target class. To achieve its purpose, the regression model incorporates the sigmoid function, resembling an S curve that starts at zero, rises, and levels off at one. This function ensures that the output produces probabilities within the range of zero to one.

K-Nearest Neighbor

The *k*-nearest neighbors algorithm is used for both classification and regression tasks (Cunningham & Delany, 2022). In the training phase, the algorithm memorizes the entire training dataset, storing the feature vectors and their corresponding class labels (for classification) or target values (for regression) in memory. When making predictions for a new data point, the algorithm finds the *k* nearest data points from the training dataset based on a similarity measure. These *k* data points are the neighbors of the new data point. The algorithm assigns the class label to the new data point based on a majority voting among its *k* nearest neighbors.

Random Forest

The random forest is an ensemble learning technique in the family of decision tree-based algorithms used for classification and regression tasks (Biau & Scornet, 2016). To create each tree, random forests randomly select subsets of the training data. This manipulation produces diverse datasets for each tree. During tree construction, a random subset of features is considered at each potential split based on a specific feature and its corresponding threshold or condition. The trees are grown through repeatedly splitting the data based on the selected features until reaching stopping criteria. Its main objective is to enhance prediction accuracy and robustness by aggregating the outputs of multiple individual decision trees.

Support Vector Machine

Support vector machines aim to find the optimal decision boundary (hyperplane) that maximizes the margin between two classes projected in a higher dimension (feature space) for classification and regression tasks (Campbell & Ying, 2022). The margin represents the distance between the boundary and the closest data points of each class on each side. These data points, known as support vectors, determine the margin and the decision boundary, influencing the hyperplane position. Ultimately, it seeks the hyperplane that provides the best prediction on untrained data.

Neural Networks

Neural networks serve multiple purposes beyond regression and classification tasks, making them versatile algorithms for machine learning (Wu & Feng, 2018). The fundamental units of neural networks are neurons, which are arranged in three types of layers: an input layer, one or more hidden layers, and an output layer. The input layer receives the raw data, the hidden layers perform intermediate computations, and the output layer provides the final predictions or classifications. The primary objective in training a neural network is to minimize the loss (error) function, which is the output of the neural network compared to the true target values. The algorithm achieves this objective by using an optimization technique known as backpropagation. Backpropagation calculates the gradients of the loss function with respect to the model weights and biases, enabling the model to fine-tune these parameters and reduce errors. Therefore, the training process involves feeding data through the neural network, computing the loss, and iteratively updating the weights and biases using backpropagation. These iterations, or epochs, continue until the loss is minimized, resulting in an optimized model.

A Behavioral Exemplar

The prior descriptions may seem abstract for behavior scientists unfamiliar with computer science. We thus walk the reader through a recently published example from the research literature: training models to identify whether AB graphs show a behavior change (see Figure 4.1 for exemplars). Although researchers and practitioners often rely on visual inspection of AB graphs to determine whether to continue, interrupt, or modify their interventions, several researchers have shown that visual inspection can be unreliable (see Ninci et al., 2015). To address this issue, Lanovaz and Hranchuk (2021) conducted a study to examine

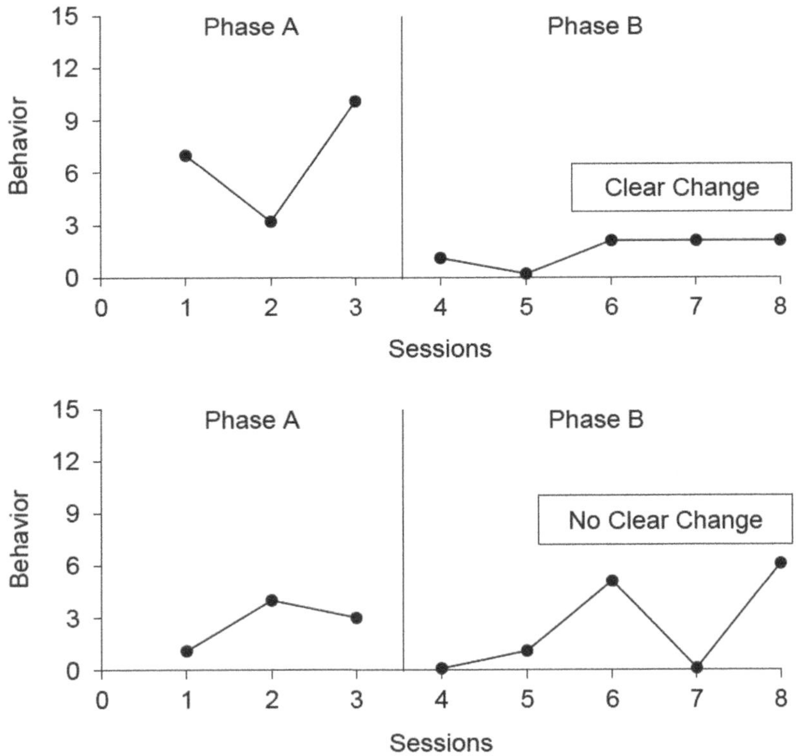

Figure 4.1 Exemplars of single-case AB graphs

whether models derived from machine learning could produce more accurate results than expert visual raters.

To conduct their study, Lanovaz and Hranchuk (2021) used a hold-out cross-validation design that included two sets of data: a training set containing 96,000 samples and a test set containing 1,024 samples. Note that researchers may apply machine learning to datasets with as few as 50 samples (e.g., Bailey et al., 2021), but the more samples the better. Each sample involved a graph simulated using the Monte Carlo method.[2] For each graph, the researchers extracted eight features: the means of Phases A and B, the standard deviations of Phases A and B, and the slopes and intercepts of Phases A and B. The label was a binary class: A value of one represented a graph with a behavior change (an effect term was added to simulate a behavior change), and a value of zero represented a graph with no behavior change (no effect term was added). As prior research had shown promising results, Lanovaz and Hranchuk focused on using logistic regression and support vector machines. These two algorithms trained models on the 96,000 samples of the training set.

Following training, Lanovaz and Hranchuk (2021) applied their newly trained models to 1,204 graphs (never used during training) that had also been rated by expert visual raters. Their analyses then compared the accuracy of their models with those produced by the visual raters. Both their models had higher accuracy than all the expert human raters. Put differently, the model identified the true value of the label more frequently than each human rater. This exemplar illustrates how behavior scientists may apply machine learning to improve clinical decision-making.

Current Research and Future Directions

As indicated in the introduction to this chapter, applications of machine learning to human behavior remain limited in behavior science. Nonetheless, a growing number of studies have reported encouraging results when using machine learning. As the focus of the current chapter is decision-making, the current section focuses on emerging areas that have the potential to facilitate and improve processes used to assess and change human behavior (i.e., applied behavioral research). The reader should note that our study is not meant to provide a comprehensive review of all applications of machine learning but rather to highlight areas of research that could improve decision-making when implementing behavioral interventions. Examples of areas of research relevant to behavior scientists not reviewed in the current chapter include the application of machine learning to monitor animal behavior (e.g., Hsu & Yttri, 2021; Mathis et al., 2018; Plessas et al., 2022) and to improve diagnostic procedures in mental health (e.g., Alqaysi et al., 2022; Verma et al., 2023).

Single-Case Methodology

In the previous section, we presented a study that used machine learning to support decision-making on quasi-experimental AB graphs (Lanovaz & Hranchuk, 2021). This study was part of a series examining the use of machine learning to analyze single-case designs (e.g., Lanovaz & Bailey, 2024; Lanovaz et al., 2020; Taylor & Lanovaz, 2022). In general, the results of these studies showed that machine learning holds promise in supporting behavior scientists in reducing the number of graph interpretation errors. For example, Lanovaz and Hranchuk (2021) reported that even when large behavior changes are present, the average false negative rate was approximately 20% for expert human raters whereas it was near 0% for the machine learning models. If these were actual clinical data, behavior scientists would be interrupting effective treatment in a significant number of cases, increasing the time and resources associated with service delivery.

To date, all published studies on the topic have been conducted by Lanovaz and colleagues. Research from independent laboratories must replicate their work to examine the robustness of their findings. Moreover, Lanovaz and colleagues have been aggregating within-phase data (i.e., mean, standard deviation, slope, intercept) to function as features during training and testing. To our knowledge, there is no empirical evidence for using these features over others. Trying other sets of features may possibly produce better outcomes. Another limitation is that the methodology has been mainly applied to quasi-experimental designs. The only model trained specifically for experimental designs was for the multiple baseline design (see Lanovaz & Bailey, 2024). Extending the work to other types of design appears paramount for a broader adoption within the research community. Finally, future research should also examine how machine learning may guide behavior scientists in selecting the optimal number of baseline and treatment sessions to conduct based on observed responding.

Behavioral Observation and Measurement

One important task in research and practice involves behavioral observation and measurement. In conjunction with single-case designs, behavioral measurement allows researchers and practitioners to determine whether an intervention is effective with a given client. Data collection presents two challenges: Data collection by nonexpert observers can produce unreliable measurements, and expert observers can be costly (Dufour et al., 2020). To automate the process and reduce costs, several researchers have developed machine learning models to detect behavior (e.g., Dufour et al., 2020; Goodwin et al., 2011; Jazouli et al., 2019; Maharaj et al., 2020; Rad & Furlanello, 2016). One of the limitations of this line of research is that most models have only been tested in contrived environments, which limits their applicability in natural settings. Furthermore, all the previously studies have focused on measuring repetitive vocal and motor behavior, mainly in autistic children. The next step would involve broadening the behavioral topographies, populations, and settings targeted to develop more generalizable measurement systems.

As such, behavioral measurement may be a potentially fertile area for the use of videos, images, and audio recordings as features in behavior science. As indicated earlier, researchers have already developed models to monitor and identify animal behavior by relying on video recordings (e.g., Mathis et al., 2018). Applying similar approaches to videos for measuring human behavior of social significance may facilitate data collection in both research and practice. Machine learning may also use audio recordings, or text transcriptions, as input data. Researchers could develop models that rely on audio recordings to identify verbal behavior when conducting basic or applied research. This area of research could build upon prior research that has used audio recordings and textual transcriptions to conduct sentiment analysis (Ezzat et al., 2012; Wankhade et al., 2022). The analysis of images may also contribute to the development of our science. Notably, behavior researchers could use images with machine learning to measure permanent products such as the amount of food consumed during feeding interventions (Taylor & Taylor, 2023) or photographic changes in hair density in the treatment of trichotillomania (Houghton et al., 2016).

Machine learning may also support behavior scientists when deciding what system of measurement to use with a given client. Researchers have already proposed empirically derived rules for selecting methods of measurement (Leblanc et al., 2016). To enhance these recommendations, researchers may train novel machine learning models to predict which method is most likely to produce the smallest error while requiring the least effort. The new models may then assist behavior scientists in selecting the method best suited to a participant's behavior. Another area where machine learning may prove fruitful involves the observation of precursor behavior to prevent the occurrence of challenging behavior. Researchers have conducted a handful of studies training models with physiological data, collected via smartwatches, to predict challenging behavior (Alban et al., 2023; Goodwin et al., 2019; Imbiriba et al., 2020; Zheng et al., 2021). For example, Goodwin et al. (2019) were able to predict with a warning period of one to two minutes that a child with autism was going to engage in aggression. If a practitioner had access to this technology to support their observations, they could implement a preventative intervention before the behavior even occurs. Machine learning may allow behavior scientists to observe and identify subtle physiological patterns associated with challenging behavior. That said, this line of research suffers from similar limitations as the one on measuring repetitive behavior: Most of the studies have focused on children with autism, and none of the models are ready for use in practical settings. Collecting more diverse datasets to train novel models appears essential for a broader adoption of the technology.

Functional Assessment

Machine learning may assist behavior scientists in conducting functional assessment more efficiently. The gold standard when identifying the function of challenging behavior remains functional analysis (Iwata & Dozier, 2008). Several researchers have documented the limitations of conducting functional analyses, which include ethical issues related to evoking challenging behavior as well as the expertise, time, and resources required to conduct a thorough analysis (Hanley, 2012). One potential solution involves using indirect assessments, such as the Questions About Behavioral Function (QABF; Matson & Vollmer, 1995), but it struggles in identifying the functions of multiply-controlled behavior (e.g., Romani et al., 2023; Watkins & Rapp, 2013). To address this issue, Bailey et al. (2021) examined whether using machine learning would improve the accuracy of the QABF. Their findings showed that using the traditional rules of the QABF led to the correct identification of all functions less than 50% of the time whereas machine learning–derived models identified all the functions correctly in nearly 90% of cases. Given that the QABF only takes 10 minutes to complete, these results may have significant applications by reducing the cost and time of identifying behavioral function.

To our knowledge, Bailey et al. (2021) conducted the only study on using machine learning for the QABF. Their results will need to be replicated prior to adoption in practical settings. Another potential application of functional assessment involves the analysis of the Open-Ended Functional Assessment Interview developed by Hanley (2012). This interview has been the topic of numerous studies as part of the interview-informed synthesized contingency analysis (Coffey et al., 2020). Currently, behavior scientists must rely on their qualitative analysis of the data to hypothesize a function. Using supervised machine learning with natural language processing may lead to models that produce more consistent interpretations. Similarly, researchers could apply the same tools to analyzing ABC (antecedent-behavior-consequence) narrative recordings or even descriptive data, which are highly used but have little support in the research literature. Recently, Plessas et al. (2022) have developed and tested models to identify reinforcement schedules in rats using descriptive data. Eventually, researchers may develop similar models to identify schedules operating on a children's behavior in school or childcare settings.

Treatment Selection and Prognosis

Even though the science of behavior has led to the development of numerous evidence-based practices, researchers and practitioners still typically rely on their clinical judgment when selecting an intervention to improve the well-being of a client. For example, a behavior scientist who wants to reduce vocal stereotypy in a child with autism has a number of treatment options to choose from but little guidance as to which one would work best for a specific client (Wang et al., 2020). To address this concern, some researchers have developed and tested criteria to improve treatment selection in behavior science (e.g., Hagopian et al., 2015); however, we could not find any example using machine learning. By using variables such as age, diagnosis, baseline rates of behavior, and function as features and the intervention outcome as labels (i.e., effective or not effective), researchers may develop models to guide behavior scientists in their treatment choices.

In the same vein, predicting the performance of individuals over time may also improve the individualization of interventions. For example, some researchers have examined whether machine learning could predict the outcome of early behavioral intervention in autism (Linstead et al., 2015; Préfontaine et al., 2022). If more robust models were developed, behavior scientists may take into consideration these results to adapt their interventions. Similarly, professors of behavior science could develop models to predict student performance over time (Yan & Au, 2019). By identifying students more likely to struggle, educators may provide preventative individualized supports. By developing models to predict with whom a behavioral or educational intervention is likely to fail, students and clients may have access to services better tailored to their needs.

Conclusion

The application of machine learning in behavior science is still in its infancy. The current chapter reviews some of the literature on using machine learning to improve decision-making in behavior science and makes some general recommendations on where research may go next. No one can foresee where the application of machine learning will lead our science in the future, but one can conservatively predict that its influence will only grow in the years to come. Hence, behavior scientists should reflect on how machine learning is already impacting their research and the behavior of their knowledge users and how integrating machine learning could lead to improvements in procedures used in research and practice.

Notes

1 In machine learning, the words "prediction" and "predict" are not used in their traditional sense (i.e., future forecasting). A prediction is the label value generated by a model that was trained by an algorithm. Therefore, a model predicts label values. These label values can represent current or future stimulus events.

2 The Monte Carlo method involved using pseudorandom number generators to produce a large number of graphs with known properties.

References

Alban, A. Q., Alhaddad, A. Y., Al-Ali, A., So, W.-C., Connor, O., Ayesh, M., Ahmed Qidwai, U., & Cabibihan, J.-J. (2023). Heart rate as a predictor of challenging behaviours among children with autism from wearable sensors in social robot interactions. *Robotics, 12*(2), 55. https://doi.org/10.3390/robotics12020055

Alqaysi, M. E., Albahri, A. S., & Hamid, R. A. (2022). Diagnosis-based hybridization of multimedical tests and sociodemographic characteristics of autism spectrum disorder using artificial intelligence and machine learning techniques: A systematic review. *International Journal of Telemedicine and Applications, 2022*, 3551528.

Bailey, J. D., Baker, J. C., Rzeszutek, M. J., & Lanovaz, M. J. (2021). Machine learning for supplementing behavioral assessment. *Perspectives on Behavior Science, 44*(4), 605–619. https://doi.org/10.1007/s40614-020-00273-9

Biau, G., & Scornet, E. (2016). A random forest guided tour. *Test, 25*(2), 197–227. https://doi.org/10.1007/s11749-016-0481-7

Bisong, E. (2019). Logistic regression. In E. Bisong (Ed.), *Building machine learning and deep learning models on Google Cloud platform: A comprehensive guide for beginners* (pp. 243–250). Apress. https://doi.org/10.1007/978-1-4842-4470-8_20

Campbell, C., & Ying, Y. (2022). *Learning with support vector machines*. Springer Nature.

Coffey, A. L., Shawler, L. A., Jessel, J., Nye, M. L., Bain, T. A., & Dorsey, M. F. (2020). Interview-informed synthesized contingency analysis (IISCA): Novel interpretations and future directions. *Behavior Analysis in Practice, 13*, 217–225.

Cunningham, P., & Delany, S. J. (2022). k-nearest neighbour classifiers: 2nd edition (with Python examples). *ACM Computing Surveys, 54*(6), 1–25. https://doi.org/10.1145/3459665

Dufour, M.-M., Lanovaz, M. J., & Cardinal, P. (2020). Artificial intelligence for the measurement of vocal stereotypy. *Journal of the Experimental Analysis of Behavior, 114*(3), 368–380. https://doi.org/10.1002/jeab.636

Ezzat, S., El Gayar, N., & Ghanem, M. M. (2012). Sentiment analysis of call centre audio conversations using text classification. *International Journal of Computer Information Systems and Industrial Management Applications, 4*(1), 619–627.

Goodfellow, I., Bengio, Y., & Courville, A. (2016). Deep learning. MIT Press.

Goodwin, M. S., Intille, S. S., Albinali, F., & Velicer, W. F. (2011). Automated detection of stereotypical motor movements. *Journal of Autism and Developmental Disorders, 41*(6), 770–782. https://doi.org/10.1007/s10803-010-1102-z

Goodwin, M. S., Mazefsky, C. A., Ioannidis, S., Erdogmus, D., & Siegel, M. (2019). Predicting aggression to others in youth with autism using a wearable biosensor. *Autism Research: Official Journal of the International Society for Autism Research, 12*(8), 1286–1296. https://doi.org/10.1002/aur.2151

Hagopian, L. P., Rooker, G. W., & Zarcone, J. R. (2015). Delineating subtypes of self-injurious behavior maintained by automatic reinforcement. *Journal of Applied Behavior Analysis, 48*(3), 523–543. https://doi.org/10.1002/jaba.236

Hanley, G. P. (2012). Functional assessment of problem behavior: Dispelling myths, overcoming implementation obstacles, and developing new lore. *Behavior Analysis in Practice, 5*, 54–72. https://doi.org/10.1007/BF03391818

Houghton, D. C., Franklin, M. R., Twohig, M. P., Franklin, M. E., Compton, S. N., Neal-Barnett, A. M., Saunders, S. M., & Woods, D. W. (2016). Photographic assessment of change in trichotillomania: Psychometric properties and variables influencing interpretation. *Journal of Psychopathology and Behavioral Assessment, 38*, 505–513. https://doi.org/10.1007/s10862-016-9536-z

Hsu, A. I., & Yttri, E. A. (2021). B-SOiD, an open-source unsupervised algorithm for identification and fast prediction of behaviors. *Nature Communications, 12*(1), 5188.

Imbiriba, T., Cumpanasoiu, D. C., Heathers, J., Ioannidis, S., Erdoğmuş, D., & Goodwin, M. S. (2020). Biosensor prediction of aggression in youth with autism using kernel-based methods. *Association for Computing Machinery, 13*, 1–6. https://doi.org/10.1145/3389189.3389199

Iwata, B. A., & Dozier, C. L. (2008). Clinical application of functional analysis methodology. *Behavior Analysis in Practice, 1*, 3–9. https://doi.org/10.1007/BF03391714

Jazouli, M., Majda, A., Merad, D., Aalouane, R., & Zarghili, A. (2019). Automatic detection of stereotyped movements in autistic children using the Kinect sensor. *International Journal of Biomedical Engineering and Technology, 29*(3), 201–220. https://doi.org/10.1504/IJBET.2019.097621

Khanal, S. S., Prasad, P. W. C., Alsadoon, A., & Maag, A. (2020). A systematic review: Machine learning based recommendation systems for e-learning. Education and Information Technologies, 25, 2635–2664. https://doi.org/10.1007/s10639-019-10063-9

Lanovaz, M. J., & Bailey, J. D. (2024). Tutorial: Artificial neural networks to analyze single-case experimental designs. *Psychological Methods, 29*(1), 202–218. https://doi.org/10.1037/met0000487

Lanovaz, M. J., Giannakakos, A. R., & Destras, O. (2020). Machine learning to analyze single-case data: A proof of concept. *Perspectives on Behavior Science, 43*(1), 21–38. https://doi.org/10.1007/s40614-020-00244-0

Lanovaz, M. J., & Hranchuk, K. (2021). Machine learning to analyze single-case to analyze single-case graphs: A comparison to visual analysis. *Journal of Applied Behavior Analysis, 54*(4), 1541–1552. https://doi.org/10.1002/jaba.863

LeBlanc, L. A., Raetz, P. B., Sellers, T. P., & Carr, J. E. (2016). A proposed model for selecting measurement procedures for the assessment and treatment of problem behavior. *Behavior Analysis in Practice, 9*(1), 77–83. https://doi.org/10.1007/s40617-015-0063-2

Linstead, E., German, R., Dixon, D., Granpeesheh, D., Novack, M., & Powell, A. (2015, December). An application of neural networks to predicting mastery of learning outcomes in the treatment of autism spectrum disorder. In *2015 IEEE 14th international conference on machine learning and applications (ICMLA)* (pp. 414–418). IEEE. https://doi.org/10.1109/ICMLA.2015.214

Maharaj, A. V., Gutierrez, A., Cueto, C., & Cadavid, S. (2020). Automated measurement of repetitve behavior using the Microsoft Kinect: A proof of concept. *Behavioral Interventions, 35*(4), 488–497. https://doi.org/10.1002/bin.1746

Mathis, A., Mamidanna, P., Cury, K. M., Abe, T., Murthy, V. N., Mathis, M. W., & Bethge, M. (2018). DeepLabCut: Markerless pose estimation of user-defined body parts with deep learning. *Nature Neuroscience, 21*(9), 1281–1289. https://doi.org/10.1038/s41593-018-0209-y

Matson, J. L., & Vollmer, T. R. (1995). *User's guide – questions about behavioral function (QABF)*. Scientific Publishers.

Ninci, J., Vannest, K. J., Willson, V., & Zhang, N. (2015). Interrater agreement between visual analysts of single-case data: A meta-analysis. Behavior Modification, 39(4), 510–541. https://doi.org/10.1177/0145445515581327

Plessas, A., Espinosa-Ramos, J. I., Parry, D., Cowie, S., & Landon, J. (2022). Machine learning with a snapshot of data: Spiking neural network 'predicts' reinforcement histories of pigeons' choice behavior. *Journal of the Experimental Analysis of Behavior, 117*(3), 301–319. https://doi.org/10.1002/jeab.759

Préfontaine, I., Lanovaz, M. J., & Rivard, M. (2022). Brief report: Machine learning for estimating prognosis of children with autism receiving early behavioral intervention – a proof of concept. *Journal of Autism and Developmental Disorders*. https://doi.org/10.1007/s10803-022-05641-9

Rad, N. M., & Furlanello, C. (2016). Applying deep learning to stereotypical motor movement detection in autism spectrum disorders. In *2016 IEEE 16th international conference on data mining workshops (ICDMW)* (pp. 1235–1242). https://doi.org/10.1109/ICDMW.2016.0178

Rich, E., & Knight, K. (1991). *Artificial intelligence*. McGraw-Hill Education.

Romani, P. W., Luehring, M. C., Hays, T. M., & Boorse, A. L. (2023). Comparisons of functional behavior assessment procedures to the functional analysis of problem behavior. *Behavior Analysis: Research and Practice, 23*(1), 36–48. https://doi.org/10.1037/bar0000258

Taylor, T., & Lanovaz, M. J. (2022). Agreement between visual inspection and objective methods of analyses: A replication and extension. *Journal of Applied Behavior Analysis, 55*(3), 986–996. https://doi.org/10.1002/jaba.921

Taylor, T., & Taylor, S. A. (2023). Reporting treatment processes and outcomes for paediatric feeding disorders: A current view of the literature. *European Journal of Behavior Analysis*. https://doi.org/10.1080/15021149.2023.2259219

Turgeon, S., & Lanovaz, M. J. (2020). Tutorial: Applying machine learning in behavioral research. *Perspectives on Behavior Science, 43*(4), 697–723. https://doi.org/10.1007/s40614-020-00270-y

Verma, S., Goel, T., Tanveer, M., Ding, W., Sharma, R., & Murugan, R. (2023). Machine learning techniques for the Schizophrenia diagnosis: A comprehensive review and future research directions. *Journal of Ambient Intelligence and Humanized Computing, 14*(5), 4795–4807. https://doi.org/10.1007/s12652-023-04536-6

Wang, D., Mason, R. A., Lory, C., Kim, S. Y., David, M., & Guo, X. (2020). Vocal stereotypy and autism spectrum disorder: A systematic review of interventions. *Research in Autism Spectrum Disorders, 78*, 101647. https://doi.org/10.1016/j.rasd.2020.101647

Wankhade, M., Rao, A. C. S., & Kulkarni, C. (2022). A survey on sentiment analysis methods, applications, and challenges. *Artificial Intelligence Review, 55*(7), 5731–5780. https://doi.org/10.1007/s10462-022-10144-1

Waring, J., Lindvall, C., & Umeton, R. (2020). Automated machine learning: Review of the state-of-the-art and opportunities for healthcare. *Artificial Intelligence in Medicine, 104*, 101822. https://doi.org/10.1016/j.artmed.2020.101822

Watkins, N., & Rapp, J. T. (2013). The convergent validity of the questions about behavioral function scale and functional analysis for problem behavior displayed by individuals with autism spectrum disorder. *Research in Developmental Disabilities, 34*(1), 11–16. https://doi.org/10.1016/j.ridd.2012.08.003

Wu, Y., & Feng, J. (2018). Development and application of artificial neural network. *Wireless Personal Communications, 102*(2), 1645–1656. https://doi.org/10.1007/s11277-017-5224-x

Yan, N., & Au, O. T. S. (2019). Online learning behavior analysis based on machine learning. *Asian Association of Open Universities Journal, 14*(2), 97–106. https://doi.org/10.1108/AAOUJ-08-2019-0029

Zheng, Z. K., Staubitz, J. E., Weitlauf, A. S., Staubitz, J., Pollack, M., Shibley, L., Hopton, M., Martin, W., Swanson, A., Juárez, P., Warren, Z. E., & Sarkar, N. (2021). A predictive multimodal framework to alert caregivers of problem behaviors for children with ASD (PreMAC). *Sensors, 21*(2), 370. https://doi.org/10.3390/s21020370

5 Reinforcement Learning in Behavior Science and Artificial Intelligence

David J. Cox, Laura Weil, Joshua Farrow, Adrienne M. Jennings, Carlos Santos, and Jacob Sosine

Selection by consequences is a fundamental principle guiding the study and interpretation of living things or machines made by living things (Skinner, 1981). Here, selection by phylogenetic consequences might be a fundamental principle used to explain how organisms change and adapt to their environment (e.g., biologists studying fungi, fruit flies, or flamingos). Similarly, selection by ontogenetic consequences might shape the ideas, theoretical constructs, and approaches to experiments and problem-solving emitted by the scientists themselves. The work of scientists over the past 120 years has led to a rigorous experimental and naturalistic literature that demonstrates the broad utility of selection by consequences for describing, predicting, and controlling a range of phenomena (e.g., Darwin, 1859; Pavlov, 1927; Skinner, 1938; Turing, 1950).

In this chapter, we focus on two use cases of selection by consequences. Specifically, the similarities and differences of selection by consequences as used by behavior scientists studying conditioning processes in biological organisms and as used by computer scientists building artificial systems via reinforcement learning (RL). In the remainder of this chapter, we hope to accomplish three things. First, we outline the unique histories of these two disciplines so that readers better understand the context under which various terms and experimental methods were developed. Second, we highlight similarities and differences in the general goals, terms used, and primary areas of focus. Last, we identify areas whereby researchers might use learnings from each area to advance their own research agendas.

Reinforcement Learning in Behavior Science

The concept of reinforcement in behavior science can be traced back to a variety of experiments conducted by Thorndike (1898), Watson (1913), Pavlov (1927), and Skinner (1938). Behavior scientists generally focus on understanding how biological organisms behave as a function of their interaction with the environment and how they can use that information to change specific patterns of behavior. Understanding behavior is the chief concern.

Pavlov's work emphasized the study of respondent conditioning (a.k.a. classical conditioning). Respondent conditioning describes how organisms' behavior changes as a function of changes in the relation between stimuli. For example, when an unconditioned stimulus (US) is presented (e.g., food), it might elicit behavior without any training needed (e.g., salivation). Through repeated pairing of a neutral stimulus (NS; one that does not elicit any response originally) with a US, the organism may come to respond to the neutral stimulus in a way that is functionally similar to an unconditioned stimulus. From this, a behavior

DOI: 10.4324/9781003380603-7

scientist may infer that the organism learned this stimulus-stimulus relation as the previously NS would now elicit a similar behavior to the unconditioned stimulus (the NS would become a conditioned stimulus, a CS).

Thorndike also demonstrated learning but via response-consequence relations rather than stimulus-stimulus relations. For example, in one experiment, Thorndike placed a cat in a "puzzle box" with food outside of the box in view. The cat had to emit a specific response to escape (e.g., press a lever, pull a wire, push a door). Through trial and error, the cat's escape time gradually decreased, leading Thorndike to claim that animals learn by associating behavior with consequences rather than by reasoning. This led to the "law of effect": Actions that gain the animal pleasure are strengthened (Donahoe, 1999).

Skinner (1938, 1953) expanded on Thorndike's work to develop a more comprehensive explanatory system using behavior-consequence relations via reinforcement and punishment. Here, reinforcement is the process whereby a stimulus change following behavior increases the future probability of that class of behavior. Punishment is the process whereby a stimulus change following behavior decreases the future probability of that class of behavior. Some reinforcers will serve as reinforcers under the right biological conditions and without any learning due to their biological significance (i.e., primary reinforcers; e.g., food, water, sexual contact). However, many environmental consequences, especially for humans, may have little direct biological significance and their ability to reinforce responding may not be known *a priori* (e.g., Netflix, smartphones). Stimuli serving as punishers are similar in that primary punishers can likely be predicted *a priori* (e.g., physical damage, removal of food or water, excessive heat or cold) and conditioned punishers may only be determined following analysis (e.g., loss of money, reprimands).

Respondent (stimulus-stimulus) and operant (behavior-consequence) conditioning in biological organisms have significantly expanded in the number of scientists who use these frameworks as well as their application in broader societal contexts. For example, researchers have demonstrated how the strength of respondent conditioning (i.e., degree of learning) is influenced by the temporal order with which CS and US are paired (e.g., trace conditioning, delay conditioning), the length of the CS-US intertrial interval, the contingency between CS-US,[1] characteristics of the stimuli (e.g., intensity), prior experience with the stimuli, and the number of CS-US pairings (Chance, 2013). Similarly, operant conditioning has advanced significantly over the past century. Methodologically, researchers have expanded the types of schedules of reinforcement and punishment studied from simple, single schedules of reinforcement (e.g., FR, VR, FI, VI) to compound and complex schedules of reinforcement (e.g., mixed, multiple, concurrent, chained, tandem, conjunctive; Morgan, 2010). The result of this work has been significant advances in our understanding of stimulus control (e.g., Lattal, 1975; Morse & Skinner, 1958), the generalization and maintenance of behavior (e.g., Hoffman & Fleshler, 1961; Schlosberg, 1959), remembering (e.g., Palmer, 1991), time perception (e.g., Church, 1999; Reynolds, 1966), the uniqueness of verbal stimuli and behavior (e.g., Palmer, 2008; Petursdottir, 2018), judgment and decision-making (e.g., Fantino, 1998), scaled relations to neuroscience (e.g., Moore, 2002), and scaled relations to social groups (e.g., Glenn, 1988; Tourinho & Vichi, 2012).

Much early work in behavior science provided crude predictions of the direction behavior would likely change as a function of simple, complex, and compound schedules of reinforcement. Beginning in the 1970s, quantitative analyses of behavior ushered in a new level of precision in researchers' understanding of operant and respondent behavior. Here, researchers parametrically manipulate independent variables across the many values it can take. Respondent conditioning examples include the Rescorla and Wagner (1972) model for how biological organisms learn associations and the Mackintosh (1975) and Hall and Pearce (1979) models predicting to what stimuli biological organisms attend. Operant conditioning examples include choice among response options (e.g., Baum, 1974; Herrnstein, 1970); the effects of delay and uncertainty to contacting consequences (e.g., Kahneman & Tversky, 1979; Rachlin, 2006); how changing effort impacts reinforcement earned (e.g., Hursh & Silberberg, 2008); when and to what extent relapse might occur (e.g., Shahan & Craig, 2017); and how multiple models might aggregate into a single theory (e.g., Killeen & Sitomer, 2003). Today, behavior scientists have identified at least 22 different categories of models to describe and predict behavior change in biological organisms as a function of changes in the environment that surrounds them (Cox, 2023).

Reinforcement Learning in Artificial Intelligence

RL in computer science conceptually sits at the intersection of many different scientific fields (Figure 5.1). Whereas behavior scientists study learning primarily in human and nonhuman animals, computer scientists study learning primarily in machines. In so doing, researchers leverage concepts from conceptually related fields such as engineering (optimal control)

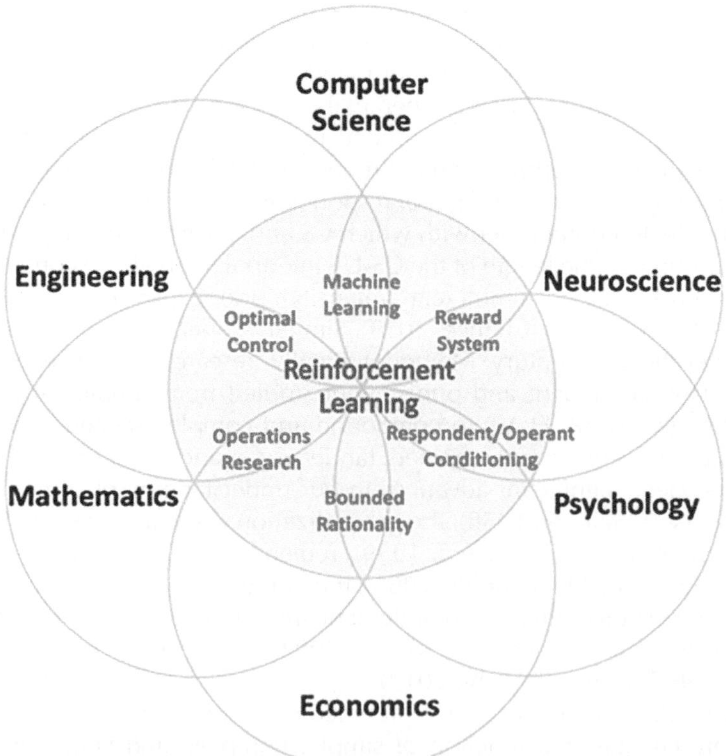

Figure 5.1 Overview of the many scientific fields that contribute ideas and methods to modern RL.

Note: This image is adapted from David Silver's *Introduction to Reinforcement Learning* course published by Google DeepMind in 2015. Readers interested in this area are strongly encouraged to check out this resource.

and neuroscience (neural networks). Scientists working from the artificial intelligence (AI) lens generally focus on how artificial agents ought to behave in specific environments to maximize cumulative reward or minimize cumulative punishment. Here, behavior is the means to achieving a specific goal set forth by the programmer.

The first article that discussed the possibility of mechanized, human-style intelligence was published by Alan Turing in 1950. In addition to describing the famous "Turing test," Turing also described a strategy to produce programs with human-level intelligence by teaching machines as one might teach a child, rather than developing a program that simulates the adult mind. Several meetings in the 1950s and 1960s formalized the field of AI, with the most notable occurring at Dartmouth College in 1956. Here, Allen Newell and colleagues presented, arguably, the first AI program in the logic theorist that mimicked human problem-solving (Newell & Simon, 1956). Though the conference reportedly fell short of expectations, it suggested AI was feasible under the assumption that every aspect of learning and intelligence can be described so precisely that a machine can simulate it (Moor, 2006).[2]

People can build machines that learn and emit intelligent behavior in many different ways (for an overview, see Russell & Norvig, 2010). This chapter is about one area in AI termed machine learning (ML) in which machines learn to behave from examples. ML is largely separated into supervised, unsupervised, and RL. Supervised learning refers to situations where the output of the task is known and the machine is taught to learn a precise or accurate mapping between the system's inputs and the known output. Unsupervised learning refers to situations where there are no known system outputs and the machine's goal is to learn patterns or groupings in the dataset. RL refers to situations where programmers want a system to automatically engage in goal-directed learning and decision-making by learning optimal actions through reward and punishment (Sutton & Barto, 2018). RL in AI is considered a class of problems as opposed to a set of techniques, preparations, or processes (Kaelbling et al., 1996). As a result, several different RL approaches exist such as trial-and-error, model-based, imitation, informed exploration, and hybrid approaches.

Trial-and-error learning has been described in the biological learning literature since the 1850s (Woodworth & Schlosberg, 1938) and was a suggested mechanism to develop AI from the outset (Turing, 1948/2004). One of the first demonstrations of an artificial agent using trial-and-error learning via feedback through rewards was Theseus, a maze-running mouse (Klein, 2018; Shannon, 1952). Interestingly, and familiar to behavior scientists, the mouse was directed via magnets and relays under its floor such that it was the environment itself – the maze – that learned how to successfully guide the mouse rather than anything inside the mouse (Sutton & Barto, 2018). Other early fundamental RL work included stochastic learning components (Minsky, 1954), simulating self-organizing systems in digital computers (Farley & Clark, 1954), the first uses of the term "RL" in the literature (e.g., Mendel, 1966; Waltz & Fu, 1965), and the introduction of the credit assignment problem (Minsky, 1961).[3]

An early system combining these prior elements was MENACE: Machine Educable Noughts and Crosses Engine (a.k.a. tic-tac-toe; Michie, 1961). Built from matchboxes, every possible game state was drawn on a unique matchbox. Inside each matchbox were differently colored beads, with each corresponding to a move MENACE could make in that game state. To make a move, the matchbox associated with the game state was found, the box was shaken and then opened to reveal a single bead, and the corresponding move was played. MENACE's opponent then played, and the process was repeated until the game was over. If MENACE lost, the beads chosen were removed, making it less likely that response was emitted in the future in that game state. If MENACE won, three beads of the response emitted were added to the box, making it more likely that response was emitted in the future in that game state. If MENACE tied, one bead of the response emitted was added to the box such that no change in the probability of emitting that response occurred. Note, here, the equal distribution of reinforcement or punishment across all responses within the chain that led to the terminal reinforcer (winning) or punisher (losing).

MENACE had complete knowledge of all environments and possible actions. In many situations, biological organisms do not have complete knowledge of the environment. BOXES sought to solve this challenge via a pole-balancing task where the agent must learn how to balance a pole upright on a cart with two wheels that can only move left and right (Michie & Chambers, 1968). Here, the complexity of the environment made the learning mechanism from MENACE difficult to use. Michie and Chambers (1968) showed that situations with incomplete environmental information could be solved by decomposing the large task (balancing the pole upright) into many independent, smaller tasks where optimal responding could be learned for each (for an overview of the algorithm, see Sammut, 2023).

Another challenge when designing artificial agents is to program how they will learn about and allocate responding among all responses. Here, the agent must balance *exploration* and *exploitation* – that is, balancing acquiring new knowledge by *exploring* what happens when they emit different responses and maximizing total return by *exploiting* what they have already learned about each response. One solution still in use today is formalized as *n*-armed bandit problems and solved via Monte Carlo methods.[4] Monte Carlo methods use repeated random sampling of available responses to statistically estimate reward values for each response. Using this approach, the agent eventually converges toward an exact estimate of response values as the number of samples increases. Early important work here includes Bellman's (1952, 1958) mathematical optimization approach (dynamic programming), which informs many RL algorithms; Howard's (1960) introduction of policy iteration for Markov decision processes;[5] Tsetlin's (1973) work on learning automata that learned via a nonassociative, purely selectionistic approach using outcome probability distributions; and Holland's (1975) general theory of adaptive systems based on trial-and-error learning of associations, value functions, and the use of evolutionary methods in *n*-armed bandit problems.

Another critical advance in modern RL came from attempts to solve the limitations of Monte Carlo methods and dynamic programming methods. Specifically, Monte Carlo methods require complete episodes to compute value estimates, which can be challenging with continuous tasks or very long episodes. Monte Carlo methods also can be slow to converge when rewards are stochastic and have high variance in estimates. Dynamic programming methods (e.g., value iteration, policy iteration) require a complete model of the environment including transition probabilities and reward functions, which are often not available in nonlaboratory, real-world problems. Dynamic programming methods can also be computationally expensive, which increases as the size of the state space increases.

Temporal difference methods (Barto et al., 1983; Sutton, 1988) address these limitations by updating current value estimates using other current estimates. This allows an agent to update values in each time step as opposed to at the end of each complete episode (Figure 5.2). As outlined in detail by Sutton and Barto (2018), temporal difference methods are related to the idea of secondary (conditioned) reinforcers (Minsky, 1954; Samuel, 1959). The idea is to have the agent learn the association between two states: (1) the current state change as a function of a response and (2) the eventual reinforcer.[6] Mathematically, this allows for modeling response chains where many actions lead to a terminal primary reinforcer and where states along the way serve as secondary reinforcers. More recently, RL

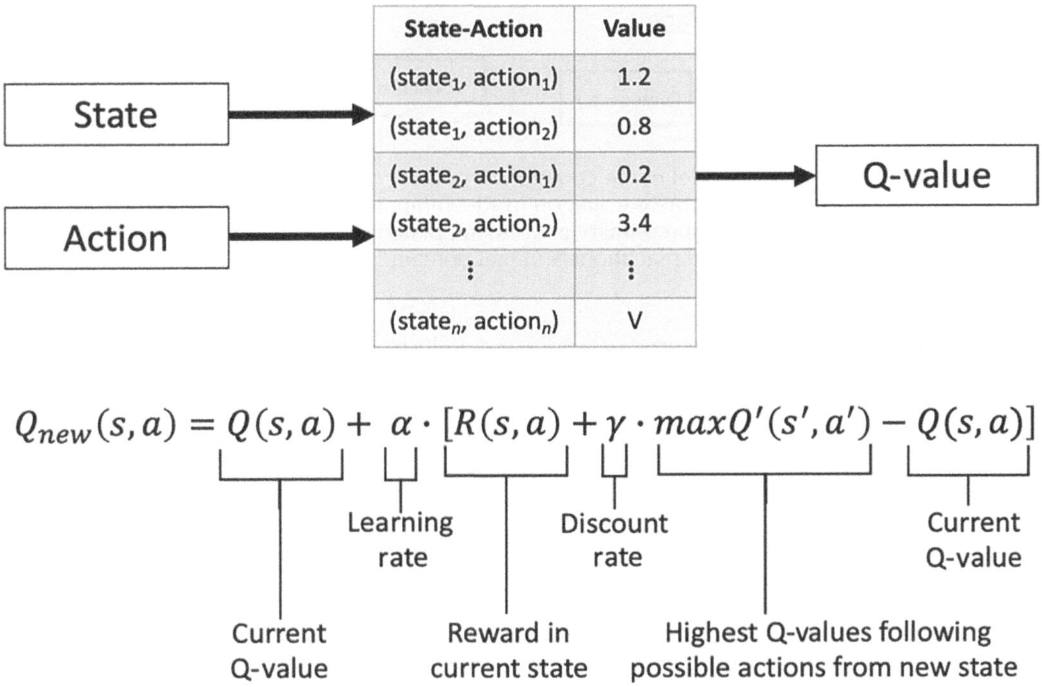

Figure 5.2 Overview of Q-learning and how Q values update. Note how the current state, Q(s, a), is related to the most informative state that immediately follows it, maxQ′(s′, a′), similar to molecular arguments for response chains in behavior science.

algorithms have extended temporal difference learning to Q-learning (Watkins & Dayan, 1992) and SARSA (Sutton & Barto, 2018); where a Q-table is maintained that represents the value of taking specific actions in specific states (Q-learning; SARSA) as opposed to representing only the value of states (temporal difference).

Much of the aforementioned RL work stems from trial-and-error approaches. However, alternative approaches have been developed. These include model-based RL, imitation learning, informed exploration, and hybrid approaches. Model-based RL (e.g., Moerland et al., 2023) uses a model of an environment's dynamics, allowing the agent to find optimal actions without trying them all. Imitation learning involves an agent observing an expert's behavior so that they need not try all actions in all states (e.g., Osa et al., 2018). Informed exploration involves the agent's exploration being guided by probability distributions of possible environmental models (e.g., Sankaranarayanan et al., 2018). Last, hybrid approaches combine different approaches depending on the specific problem, the available data, and the desired behavior of the system.

Finally, as with behavior science, RL has significantly advanced and become more complex over time and has broad utility across many industries (e.g., Winder, 2021). As with many areas of AI, efficiency gains in data collection and computational processing now allow deep learning techniques and ensemble methods to be combined with classic RL techniques (e.g., Alavizadeh et al., 2022; Hua et al., 2021; Yin et al., 2018). RL is currently used in many societally relevant applications such as self-driving cars (e.g., Aradi, 2022), robotics (e.g., Singh et al., 2022), managing building life cycles (e.g., Hong et al.,

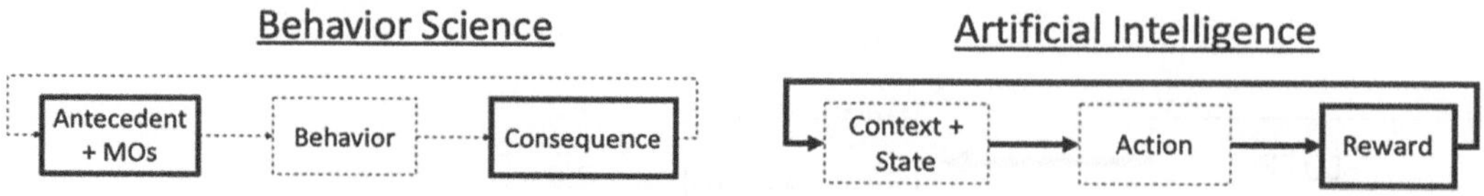

Figure 5.3 Graphical-textual model of the common three-term contingency used in behavior science (left panel) and its counterpart jargon in RL within AI (right panel). The thick lines (boxes and arrows) highlight the primary areas manipulated to change behavior toward a desired end by researchers and practitioners in that domain.

2020), controlling energy systems (e.g., Perera & Kamalaruban, 2021), helicopter control (e.g., Abbeel et al., 2006), routing in wireless networks (e.g., Al-Rawi et al., 2015), production scheduling (e.g., Wang & Usher, 2005), systems security (e.g., Alavizadeh et al., 2022), and beating humans in games such as Checkers and Go (e.g., BBC, 2016; Harding & Barden, 2011).

Comparing and Contrasting Reinforcement Learning Across Disciplines

Figures 5.3 and 5.4 highlight differences and similarities between the two fields via diagrams commonly used in each field. Similarities exist in the information being analyzed to describe, predict, and control the behavior of an organism situated in a larger environment through reinforcement and punishment. Differences exist in the purpose of the analysis, the techniques used, areas of emphasis, mechanisms, and the overall complexity of the system. Here we expand on these similarities and differences, though there is more of a gradient than a hard boundary delineating work in each area.

Similarities

In behavior science and RL in AI, humans attempt to describe, predict, and control the behavior of a system, biological in the case of the behavior scientist, artificial in the case of the computer scientist. That system exists in a larger environment. At each time step, the organism exists in a specific physical state (biological or artificial). That physical state interacts with the current context and past feedback from the environment (i.e., their learning history) to inform the organism what actions are possible and likely to contact reinforcement or avoid punishment. The organism emits a response, which changes the environment and their physical state. This change often includes feedback in the form of reinforcement or punishment. And, this loop of . . .→ environment/context → physical state → behavior → environment/context → . . . continues forward in time. Throughout, the organism learns associations among the environment, their state, and contact with reward or punishment as a result of their behavior. Stated differently, the mechanism of learning in both is the selection of behavior by consequences.

Differences

In behavior science, the purpose of analysis is to identify the function of a behavior (or response class) to change the rate at which that, or other functionally related, behavior occurs. Questions include: What schedules of reinforcement maintain a response? What contextual stimuli signal the availability of reinforcement/punishment? How does an

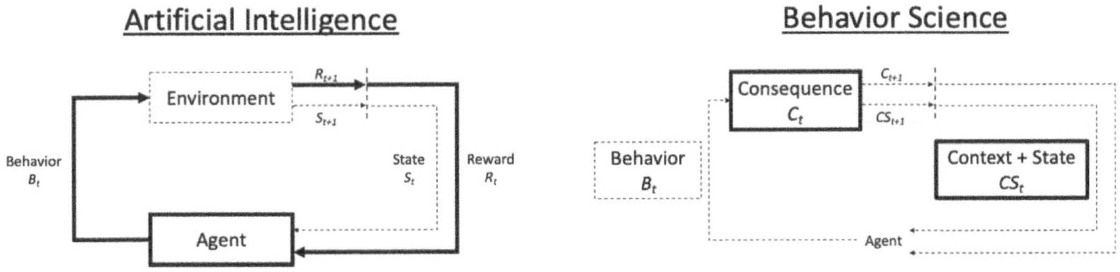

Figure 5.4 Graphical-textual model of the common feedback loop to denote agent learning in artificial intelligence (left panel) and its counterpart jargon in behavior science (right panel). The text in boxes and larger font highlight primary areas of emphasis. The thick lines (boxes and arrows) highlight the primary areas manipulated to change behavior toward a desired end by researchers and practitioners in that domain.

Note: Some of the terms had to be rearranged for behavior science to fit it into the commonly espoused three-term contingency. Thus, though the same parts are present in both, the location is not a perfect 1:1 mapping.

organism's current biobehavioral state (i.e., motivating operations)[7] influence the behavior emitted? How do schedules of reinforcement/punishment interact to influence behavior? How does one's learning history impact the control of behavior via contextual information and reinforcement/punishment schedules? And, how can the researcher/practitioner use this information to change behavior in a desired direction? As highlighted in Figures 5.3 and 5.4, emphasis is placed on observing, measuring, and manipulating the context + state (stimulus control; motivating operations [MOs]) and the consequences that follow behavior. The end goal is directional control over a specific response (or response class). Though the organism obviously exists, direct analysis of the totality of the organism is typically impractical (more following) and, thus, deemphasized.

In the domain of computer science, the purpose of analysis is to precisely specify algorithm(s) that interact with a precisely defined model of the environment to optimize the agent's performance on a specific task. Here, questions include: How mathematically precise can the environment be modeled? How thoroughly can we define actions that can occur in a specific state? What algorithm will lead to (as close to) optimal performance via mapping actions to environmental states? How can reward and punishment be manipulated to improve the agent's learning rate? And, how can the researcher/engineer use this information to control the agent toward a specifically defined environmental goal state as precisely as possible? As highlighted in Figures 5.3 and 5.4, emphasis is placed on accurately modeling the environment (not manipulating it), the algorithm that maps actions to the environment, and modifying reward/punishment amounts to improve performance over time. Though the states and actions obviously exist, they are explicitly known and described, and they transfer information between the agent and the environment.

The techniques and mechanisms also differ between the two sciences. In behavior science, the researcher/practitioner primarily manipulates (a) prior access to stimuli to contrive MOs, (b) stimuli in the environment signaling the availability of reinforcement/punishment for specific responses, (c) the addition of prompts or cues to reduce the need for trial-and-error learning and increase the learning rate, and (d) the consequences that follow responding – typically only reinforcement or extinction. Here, the researcher/practitioner may use many types of reinforcement schedules, prompting hierarchies, and stimulus fading procedures to increase the probability that responses change in a desired direction (e.g., rate, duration, intensity, latency). The mechanism or process of change is broadly reinforcement or extinction with the details being specific techniques for presenting stimuli, prompting, and delivering consequences following desired or undesired responses. In total, the environment is manipulated around the organism to change specific behaviors in a desired direction (thick solid lines in Figures 5.3 and 5.4).

The techniques and mechanisms of change are a bit different for artificial agents. Here, the researcher/engineer primarily operates by (a) improving the agent's ability to sense and subsequently model the environmental context, (b) improving their ability to model the agent's current state, (c) balancing exploration-exploitation to efficiently model how actions lead to specific goals, (d) modifying reward signals to provide the agent feedback on performance (typically reward and punishment), and (e) modifying the algorithm(s) that map context, states, actions, and rewards to each other. Emphasis is placed on explicit and precise mathematical definitions of the environment, the agent state and actions, the reward amounts, and how the agent transitions from one state to the next (see the thick, solid lines in Figures 5.3 and 5.4). In total, the agent is manipulated mathematically so it learns how the world works, adjusts its behavior accordingly, and achieves a specific environmental state.

A final difference is the differential complexity of the systems analyzed. Biological organisms necessarily consist of physiological systems and processes adapted over the course of their species' evolutionary history. Their current behavioral repertoires have been shaped through a lifetime of contact with respondent and operant contingencies, leading to a largely unmeasured and imprecisely known learning history. Though assumed to be largely deterministic, entire scientific fields within biology continuously fill in gaps in our understanding of the molecular-to-systemic workings of the 8.7 million species estimated to exist (National Geographic, 2023). Thus, a very low probability exists that the exact physical state, perceptive capabilities, mechanisms for transitioning among dynamically changing states, and mathematical relations among environment-states-actions can be defined with the same level of precision as artificial agents. Relatedly, biological organisms constantly respond to dozens to hundreds of determiners around bio-socio-behavioral homeostasis as opposed to optimizing toward a single goal.[8]

Artificial agents, in contrast, are currently systemically much less complex though mathematically described with greater complexity than biological systems. Built by humans, artificial agents have a well-defined number and variety of working parts, and the interaction among the different components is precisely defined. In turn, the current behavioral repertoires and learning histories of artificial agents is likely to be completely, or nearly completely, known. Further, as noted prior, many RL algorithms make heavy use of stochastic processes, which differs from the assumed deterministic processes of most bio-socio-behavioral processes. Finally, artificial agents built via RL often have one, or perhaps a few, specific goals or end states they optimize toward.

Bridging the Gap: Combining Evidence and Methodologies from Both Fields

Computer science and behavior science, while distinct, each have many strengths based on the historical context within which they developed and the problems researchers in each area seek to address. Researchers working in each area may develop a richer understanding of their own work by incorporating insights from the other. Though many possibilities exist, definitive benefits likely emerge around the differences noted previously.

To begin, the areas of emphasis within Figures 5.3 and 5.4 led each area to develop sophisticated methods to meet the purpose of their analysis that the other might borrow. For example, behavior scientists largely focus on few environmental stimuli and the function of one response (or response class). However, by including a broader set of states and actions, precisely defining those states and actions, and precisely defining an organism's perception of their physical and environmental states, behavior scientists can use algorithms and techniques to quantitatively map more complex environmental contexts to multiple response classes as a function of many differential consequences for behavior. Such an approach may allow behavior scientists to directly model the complex multiple control of behavior dynamically as it changes across an organism's day, month, year, and lifetime.

Computer scientists may benefit from the sophisticated control of specific responses that behavior scientists have developed via environmental manipulations antecedent and consequential to responding. For example, behavior scientists have a robust literature around how changing the amount, type, delay, and schedule of reinforcement delivery will influence the rate, intensity, duration, and latency of specific responses and the relation of different responses to each other. All of this occurs in biological systems that constantly change irrespective of the specific contingencies in effect. As artificial agents advance to integrate many different response classes and need to balance many competing goals and states while adapting to a changing environment, the rich literature from behavior science may allow computer scientists to predict and control the agents more easily. Natural selection has led complex biological organisms to behave in predictable ways based on such environmental manipulations. Artificial agents likely will benefit from behavior scientists' analyses of that history.

Both areas also must handle the thorny problem of behavior in time. This includes things like exactly how an organism's past experiences influence behavior in their current state and how choice should change based on the probability that future events will occur at some delay. Both sciences have tackled these challenges in their own unique way though largely converging on similar ideas around temporally weighting past events and discounting future events. Here, behavior scientists may benefit from the mathematical precision with which an organism's learning history is described, and discounting is embedded in algorithms to predict current behavior and optimal responding. Computer scientists may benefit from the robust literature on how learning history can positively or negatively impact future learning as well as how patterns of probability and delay discounting can lead to suboptimal response patterns that artificial agents often want to avoid.

Last, the working environments of both fields offer many opportunities to expand each science in new ways. For example, the *modus operandi* of RL in AI is to develop an agent that acts in a specific environment and learns to optimally respond to produce a specific goal state. Behavior scientists work daily in specific environments and attempt to behave optimally to produce some outcome (e.g., maximize patient progress, understand the interaction among basic processes). The simulation approach offered by RL may provide a method for building artificial agents that teach behavior scientists how to make better decisions for the outcomes they seek in their work (e.g., McDowell, 2019). Similarly, behavior scientists have worked for decades to meticulously collect data on the environment, the behavior, the consequences that follow, and how this feedback loop allows complex biological organisms to adapt and survive over a lifetime. These rich datasets and fundamental descriptions of selective processes in biological organisms may provide insight for how computer scientists can best scale artificial agents to behave effectively in higher dimensional and more complex tasks that involve longer-term adaptive survival mechanisms.

Moving Forward

Integrating behavior and computer science will require several advances. First, RL often works well with datasets that precisely define environments, states, and reward/punishment amounts. Such datasets are currently limited in behavior science, but two options may exist. First, behavior scientists could use technologies and apps designed to monitor behaviors, biomarkers, and the larger environment (i.e., ambient hovering, Augusto et al., 2010; Internet of Things, Salih et al., 2022). Second, behavior scientists could use platforms specifically designed to collect data on more variables (e.g., Arce et al., 2023). Once collected, more precise and personalized behavior change interventions can be developed that may uncover patterns of behavior-environment relations previously difficult for humans to identify (Mnih et al., 2015; Neely et al., 2022; Wong et al., 2021).

To handle larger and more complex datasets for real-time predictions requires increasingly complex algorithms and processing speed. For example, much current and near-future state-of-the-art work here will likely use deep RL (Graesser & Keng, 2019) and quantum computing with non-Markov decision processes (e.g., White et al., 2020). As technologies embedded with RL agents become more prevalent in households and workplaces, the challenges of computationally handling and processing such datasets may outpace our advances in technology. Here, past work with biological organisms may help to identify which environmental stimuli are worth attending to as well as more sophisticated use of RL with human feedback to individually tailor reward functions (Christiano et al., 2017).

Regardless of the path any of this follows, interdisciplinary research will be critical. Behavior and computer scientists will need to collaborate to ensure the fairness, safety, security, and transparency of these applications. Each science has a tremendous amount to offer the other in terms of methodologies, tools, approaches, and conceptual frameworks that have been rigorously developed by unique historical contexts and objectives. The brave new world we are entering will require a thorough understanding of each discipline's unique perspective and creative integration and collaboration historically not seen.

Notes

1 The contingency is the mathematical covariance.
2 Note the parallel to what researchers who work in the quantitative analyses of behavior are after.
3 In RL, the credit assignment problem refers to the challenge of distributing credit for a success (the reward) among the many decisions and behaviors that might have been involved in producing it. In behavior science, this challenge exists in how an organism "knows" which response (of the many emitted) led to a reinforcer such that reinforcement increases that response and not others (e.g., Hutchison, 2012; Staddon, 2001; Staddon & Zhang, 2017; Touretzky & Saksida, 1997).
4 A one-armed bandit is likened to a single slot machine. A multiarmed bandit is likened to an agent having multiple slot machines to choose from. A n-armed bandit problem, thus, is where n slot machines exist to choose from. Note the centrality of randomness in choice and payouts.
5 Markov decision processes (MDPs) are formal representations of decision-making problems that define the environment for RL via the tuple (S, A, P, R, γ). Here, S is the set of states; A is the set of actions; P is the state transition probability matrix; R is the reward function; and γ is the discount factor.
6 Note the similarity to respondent conditioning where stimulus-stimulus relations are learned. Coincidentally, several researchers used temporal difference learning to create models of classical conditioning for biological organisms (Klopf, 1988; Sutton & Barto, 1987, 1990).
7 For an easy conceptual link between these two areas, see Clark and Mangel (2000).
8 The reader should not infer anything spooky here. Rather, we are using this language to draw parallels between multiple concurrent and compound schedules in behavior science and the explicitly specified goals with artificial agents.

References

Abbeel, O., Coates, A., Quigley, M., & Ng, A. Y. (2006). An application of reinforcement learning to aerobatic helicopter flight. *Proceedings of the 19th International Conference on Neural Information Processing Systems*, 1–8. https://proceedings.neurips.cc/paper_files/paper/2006/file/98c39996bf1543e974747a2549b3107c-Paper.pdf

Alavizadeh, H., Alavizadeh, H., & Jang-Jaccard, J. (2022). Deep Q-learning based reinforcement learning approach for network intrusion detection. *Computers, 11*(3), 41. https://doi.org/10.3390/computers11030041

Al-Rawi, H. A. A., Ng, M. N., & Yau, K. L. A. (2015). Application of reinforcement learning to routing in distributed wireless networks: A review. *Artificial Intelligence Review, 43*, 381–416. https://doi.org/10.1007/s10462-012-9383-6

Aradi, S. (2022). Survey of deep reinforcement learning for motion planning of autonomous vehicles. *IEEE Transactions on Intelligent Transportation Systems, 32*(2), 740–759. https://doi.org/10.1109/TITS.2020.3024655

Arce, W. S., Walker, S. G., Hurtz, M. L., & Gehringer, J. E. (2023). Cometrics: A new software tool for behavior-analytic clinicians and machine learning researchers. *Behavior Analysis in Practice*. https://doi.org/10.1007/s40617-023-00817-w

Augusto, J. C., Nakashima, H., & Aghajan, H. (2010). Ambient intelligence and smart environments: A state of the art. In H. Nakashima, H. Aghajan, & J. C. Augusto (Eds.), *Handbook of ambient intelligence and smart environments* (pp. 3–31). Springer. https://doi.org/10.1007/978-0-387-93808-0_1

Barto, A. G., Sutton, R. S., & Anderson, C. W. (1983). Neuronlike adaptive elements that can solve difficult learning control problems. *IEEE Transactions on Systems, Man, and Cybernetics, 13*(5), 834–846. https://doi.org/10.1109/TSMC.1983.6313077

Baum, W. M. (1974). On two types of deviation from the matching law: Bias and undermatching. *Journal of the Experimental Analysis of Behavior, 22*(1), 231–242.

BBC. (2016, March). Artificial intelligence: Google's AlphaGo beats Go master Lee Se-dol. *BBC*. https://www.bbc.com/news/technology-35785875

Bellman, R. (1952). On the theory of dynamic programming. *Proceedings of the National Academy of Sciences of the United States of America, 38*(8), 716–719. https://doi.org/10.1073/pnas.38.8.716

Bellman, R. (1958). Dynamic programming and stochastic control processes. *Information and Control, 1*(3), 228–239. https://doi.org/10.1016/S0019-9958(58)80003-0

Chance, P. (2013). *Learning and behavior*. Cengage Learning.

Christiano, P. F., Leike, J., Brown, T. B., Martic, M., Legg, S., & Amodei, D. (2017). Deep reinforcement learning from human preferences. *Stat, 1050*, 13.

Church, R. M. (1999). Evaluation of quantitative theories of timing. *Journal of the Experimental Analysis of Behavior, 71*(2), 253–291.

Clark, C. W., & Mangel, M. (2000). *Dynamic state variable models in ecology: Methods and applications*. Oxford University Press.

Cox, D. J. (2023, May). *Mapping the landscape of quantitative models of behavior-environment relations*. 45th Meeting of the Society for the Quantitative Analyses of Behavior, Denver, CO.

Darwin, C. (1859). *On the origin of species by means of natural selection, or the preservation of favoured races in the struggle for life*. John Murray. http://darwin-online.org.uk/content/frameset?itemID=F373&viewtype=text&pageseq=1

Donahoe, J. W. (1999). Edward L. Thorndike: The selectionist connectionist. *Journal of the Experimental Analysis of Behavior, 72*(3), 451–454.

Fantino, E. (1998). Judgment and decision making: Behavioral approaches. *The Behavior Analyst, 21*(2), 203–218.

Farley, B. G., & Clark, W. A. (1954). Simulation of self-organizing systems by digital computer. *IRE Transactions on Information Theory, 4*, 76–84.

Glenn, S. S. (1988). Contingences and metacontingencies: Toward a synthesis of behavior analysis and cultural materialism. *The Behavior Analyst, 11*(2), 161–179.

Graesser, L., & Keng, W. L. (2019). *Foundations of deep reinforcement learning: Theory and practice in Python*. Addison-Wesley Professional. ISBN: 0135172381

Hall, G., & Pearce, J. M. (1979). Latent inhibition of a CS during CS-US pairings. *Journal of Experimental Psychology: Animal Behaviour Processes, 5*(1), 31–42. https://doi.org/10.1037/0097-7403.5.1.31

Harding, L., & Barden, L. (2011, May). From the archive, May 12, 1997: Deep blue win a giant step for computerkind. *The Guardian*. https://www.theguardian.com/theguardian/2011/may/12/deep-blue-beats-kasparov-1997

Herrnstein, R. J. (1970). On the law of effect. *Journal of The Experimental Analysis of Behavior, 13*(2), 243–266. https://doi.org/10.1901/jeab.1970.13-243
Hoffman, H. S., & Fleshler, M. (1961). Stimulus factors in aversive controls: The generalization of conditioned suppression. *Journal of the Experimental Analysis of Behavior, 4*(4), 371–378. https://doi.org/10.1901/jeab.1961.4-371
Holland, J. H. (1975). *Adaptation in natural and artificial systems*. University of Michigan Press.
Hong, T., Wang, Z., Luo, X., & Zhang, W. (2020). State-of-the-art on research and applications of machine learning in the building life cycle. *Energy and Buildings, 212*, 109831. https://doi.org/10.1016/j.enbuild.2020.109831
Howard, R. A. (1960). *Dynamic programming and Markov processes*. The MIT Press. ISBN: 0262080095
Hua, J., Zeng, L., Li, G., & Ju, Z. (2021). Learning for a robot: Deep reinforcement learning, imitation learning, and transfer learning. *Sensors, 21*(4), 1278. https://doi.org/10.3390/s21041278
Hursh, S. R., & Silberberg, A. (2008). Economic demand and essential value. *Psychological Review, 115*(1), 186–198. https://doi.org/10.1037/0033-295X.115.1.186
Hutchison, W. R. (2012). The central role for behavior analysis in modern robotics, and vice versa. *The Behavior Analyst, 35*(1), 29–35. https://doi.org/10.1007%2FBF03392262
Kaelbling, L. P., Littman, M. L., & Moore, A. W. (1996). Reinforcement learning: A survey. *Journal of Artificial Intelligence, 4*, 237–285. https://jair.org/index.php/jair/article/view/10166/24110
Kahneman, D., & Tversky, A. (1979). Prospect theory: An analysis of decisions under risk. *Econometrica, 47*, 263–291.
Killeen, P. R., & Sitomer, M. T. (2003). MPR. *Behavioural Processes, 62*, 49–64. https://doi.org/10.1016/S0376-6357(03)00017-2
Klein, D. (2018, December). Mighty mouse. *MIT Technology Review*. https://www.technologyreview.com/2018/12/19/138508/mighty-mouse/
Klopf, A. H. (1988). A neuronal model of classical conditioning. *Psychobiology, 16*, 85–125.
Lattal, K. A. (1975). Reinforcement contingencies as discriminative stimuli. *Journal of the Experimental Analysis of Behavior, 23*(2), 241–246.
Mackintosh, N. J. (1975). A theory of attention: Variations in the associability of stimuli with reinforcement. *Psychological Review, 82*(4), 276–298. https://doi.org/10.1037/h0076778
McDowell, J. J. (2019). On the current status of the evolutionary theory of behavior dynamics. *Journal of the Experimental Analysis of Behavior, 111*(1), 130–245. https://doi.org/10.1002/jeab.495
Mendel, J. M. (1966). A survey of learning control systems. *ISA Transactions, 5*, 297–303.
Michie, D. (1961). Trial and error. *Science Survey*, 129–145. https://people.csail.mit.edu/brooks/idocs/matchbox.pdf
Michie, D., & Chambers, R. A. (1968). BOXES: An experiment in adaptive control. In E. Dale & D. Michie (Eds.), *Machine intelligence 2* (pp. 137–152). Oliver and Boyd.
Minsky, M. L. (1954). *Theory of neural-analog reinforcement systems and its application to the brain-model problem* [Ph.D. thesis, Princeton University]. https://www.proquest.com/docview/301998727
Minsky, M. L. (1961). Steps toward artificial intelligence. *Proceedings of the Institute of Radio Engineers, 49*, 8–30. https://courses.csail.mit.edu/6.803/pdf/steps.pdf
Mnih, V., Kavukcuoglu, K., Silver, D., Rusu, A. A., Veness, J., Bellemare, M. G., Graves, A., Riedmiller, M., Fidjeland, A. K., Ostrovski, G., Petersen, S., Beattie, C., Sadik, A., Antonoglou, I., King, H., Kumaran, D., Wierstra, D., Legg, S., & Hassabis, D. (2015). Human-level control through deep reinforcement learning. *Nature, 518*(7540), 529–533. https://doi.org/10.1038/nature14236
Moerland, T. M., Broekens, J., Plaat, A., & Jonker, C. M. (2023). Model-based reinforcement learning: A survey. *Machine Learning, 16*(1), 1–118. http://dx.doi.org/10.1561/2200000086
Moor, J. (2006). The Dartmouth College artificial intelligence conference: The next fifty years. *AI Magazine, 27*(4), 87–91. https://aaai.org/ojs/index.php/aimagazine/article/view/1911/1809
Moore, J. (2002). Some thoughts on the relation between behavior analysis and behavioral neuroscience. *The Psychological Record, 52*, 261–279.
Morgan, D. L. (2010). Schedules of reinforcement at 50: A retrospective appreciation. *Psychological Record, 60*, 151–172. https://doi.org/10.1007/BF03395699
Morse, W. H., & Skinner, B. F. (1958). Some factors involved in the stimulus control of operant behavior. *Journal of the Experimental Analysis of Behavior, 1*(1), 103–107. https://doi.org/10.1901/jeab.1958.1-103
National Geographic. (2023). *Biodiversity*. https://education.nationalgeographic.org/resource/biodiversity/

Neely, L., Carnett, A., Quarles, J., MacNaul, H., Park, S.-W., Oyama, S., Chen, G., Desai, K., & Najafirad, P. (2022). The case for integrated advanced technology in applied behavior analysis. *Advances in Neurodevelopmental Disorders*. https://doi.org/10.1007/s41252-022-00309-y

Newell, A., & Simon, H. (1956). The logic theory machine: A complex information processing system. *RE Transactions on Information Theory, 2*(3), 61–79. https://doi.org/10.1109/TIT.1956.1056797

Osa, T., Pajarinen, J., Neumann, G., Bagnell, J. A., Abbeel, P., & Peters, J. (2018). An algorithmic perspective on imitation learning. *Foundations and Trends in Robotics, 7*(1–2), 1–179. http://dx.doi.org/10.1561/2300000053

Palmer, D. C. (1991). A behavioral interpretation of memory. In L. J. Hayes & P. N. Chase (Eds.), *Dialogues on verbal behavior* (pp. 261–279). Context Press.

Palmer, D. C. (2008). On Skinner's definition of verbal behavior. *International Journal of Psychology and Psychological Therapy, 8*(3), 295–307.

Pavlov, I. P. (1927). *Conditioned reflexes; an investigation of the physiological activity of the cerebral cortex*. Oxford University Press. https://psycnet.apa.org/record/1927-02531-000

Perera, A. T. D., & Kamalaruban, P. (2021). Applications of reinforcement learning in energy systems. *Energy Reviews, 137*, 110618. https://doi.org/10.1016/j.rser.2020.110618

Petursdottir, A. I. (2018). The current status of the experimental analysis of verbal behavior. *Behavior Analysis: Research and Practice, 18*(2), 151–168. http://dx.doi.org/10.1037/bar0000109

Rachlin, H. (2006). Notes on discounting. *Journal of the Experimental Analysis of Behavior, 85*(3), 425–435. https://doi.org/10.1901/jeab.2006.85-05

Rescorla, R. A., & Wagner, A. R. (1972). A theory of Pavlovian conditioning: Variations in the effectiveness of reinforcement and nonreinforcement. In A. H. Black & W. F. Prokasy (Eds.), *Classical conditioning II: Current research and theory* (pp. 64–99). Appleton-Century-Crofts.

Reynolds, G. S. (1966). Discrimination and emission of temporal intervals by pigeons. *Journal of the Experimental Analysis of Behavior, 9*(1), 65–68.

Russell, S., & Norvig, P. (2010). *Artificial intelligence: A modern approach* (3rd ed.). Prentice Hall. ISBN: 0-13-604259-7

Salih, K. O. M., Rashid, T. A., Radovanovic, D., & Bacanin, N. (2022). A comprehensive survey on the Internet of Things with the industrial marketplace. *Sensors, 22*(3), 730. https://doi.org/10.3390/s22030730

Sammut, C. (2023). *BOXES learning to control a pole and cart*. http://www.cse.unsw.edu.au/~claude/research/machine_learning/reinforcement_learning/boxes.html

Samuel, A. L. (1959). Some studies in machine learning using the game of checkers. *IBM Journal, 3*(3), 535–554. http://people.csail.mit.edu/brooks/idocs/Samuel.pdf

Sankaranarayanan, S., Annasamy, R. M., Sycara, K., & Penstein Rose, C. (2018). Combining mode-free Q-ensembles and model-based approaches for informed exploration. *arXiv*. https://arxiv.org/pdf/1806.04552.pdf

Schlosberg, H. (1959). A flexible model for generalization gradients. *Journal of the Experimental Analysis of Behavior, 2*(4), 319–321. https://doi.org/10.1901%2Fjeab.1959.2–319

Shahan, T. A., & Craig, A. R. (2017). Resurgence as choice. *Behavioural Processes, 141*, 100–127. http://dx.doi.org/10.1016/j.beproc.2016.10.006

Shannon, C. E. (1952). *Theseus*. https://webmuseum.mit.edu/detail.php?module=objects&type=related&kv=76066

Singh, B., Kumar, R., & Singh, V. P. (2022). Reinforcement learning in robotic applications: A comprehensive survey. *Artificial Intelligence Review, 55*, 945–990. https://doi.org/10.1007/s10462-021-09997-9

Skinner, B. F. (1938). *The behavior of organisms: An experimental analysis*. Appleton-Century. ISBN: 1-58390-007-1

Skinner, B. F. (1953). *Science and human behavior*. Macmillan.

Skinner, B. F. (1981). Selection by consequences. *Science, 231*(4507), 501–504. https://doi.org/10.1126/science.7244649

Staddon, J. E. R. (2001). *Adaptive dynamics: The theoretical analysis of behavior*. Bradford Books. ISBN: 0262194538

Staddon, J. E. R., & Zhang, Y. (2017). On the assignment-of-credit problem in operant learning. In M. L. Commons, S. Grossberg, & J. Staddon (Eds.), *Neural network models of conditioning and action* (pp. 279–293). Routledge. ISBN: 9781138192126

Sutton, R. S. (1988). Learning to predict by the methods of temporal difference. *Machine Learning, 3*, 9–44.

Sutton, R. S., & Barto, A. G. (1987). A temporal-difference model of classical conditioning. In *Proceedings of the ninth annual conference of the cognitive science society* (pp. 355–378). Erlbaum.
Sutton, R. S., & Barto, A. G. (1990). Time-derivative models of Pavlovian reinforcement. In M. Gabriel & J. Moore (Eds.), *Learning and computational neuroscience: Foundations of adaptive networks* (pp. 497–537). MIT Press.
Sutton, R. S., & Barto, A. G. (2018). *Reinforcement learning: An introduction* (2nd ed.). Bradford Books.
Thorndike, E. L. (1898). Animal intelligence: An experimental study of the associative processes in animals. *The Psychological Review: Monograph Supplements, 2*(4), i.
Touretzky, D. S., & Saksida, L. M. (1997). Operant conditioning in Skinnerbots. *Adaptive Behavior, 5*(3–4), 219–247. https://doi.org/10.1177/105971239700500302
Tourinho, E. Z., & Vichi, C. (2012). Behavioral-analytic research of cultural selection and the complexity of cultural phenomena. *Revista Latinoamericana de Psicologia, 44*(1), 169–179.
Tsetlin, M. L. (1973). *Automaton theory and modeling of biological systems*. Academic Press.
Turing, A. M. (1950). Computing machinery and intelligence. *Mind, 56*(236), 433–460. http://www.jstor.org/stable/2251299
Turing, A. M. (2004). Intelligent machinery, a heretical theory. In S. Shieber (Ed.), *The Turing test: Verbal behavior as the hallmark of intelligence* (pp. 105–110). The MIT Press. (Original work published 1948)
Waltz, M. D., & Fu, K. S. (1965). A heuristic approach to reinforcement learning control systems. *IEEE Transactions on Automatic Control, 10*, 390–398. https://doi.org/10.1109/TAC.1965.1098193
Wang, Y. C., & Usher, J. M. (2005). Application of reinforcement learning for agent-based production scheduling. *Engineering Applications of Artificial Intelligence, 18*(1), 73–82. https://doi.org/10.1016/j.engappai.2004.08.018
Watkins, C. J. C. H., & Dayan, P. (1992). *Q*-learning. *Machine Learning, 8*, 279–292. https://doi.org/10.1007/BF00992698
Watson, J. B. (1913). Psychology as the behaviorist views it. *Psychological Review, 20*, 158–177.
White, G. A. L., Hill, C. D., Pollock, F. A., Hollenberg, L. C. L., & Modi, K. (2020). Demonstration of non-Markovian process characterisation and control on a quantum processor. *Nature Communications, 11*(1), 6301. https://doi.org/10.1038/s41467-020-20113-3
Winder, P. (2021). *Reinforcement learning: Industrial applications of intelligent agents*. O'Reilly Media. ISBN: 978-1-098-11483-1
Wong, C. M. V., Chan, R. Y.-Y., Yum, Y. N., & Wang, K. (2021). Internet of Things (IoT)-enhanced applied behavior analysis (ABA) for special education needs. *Sensors (Basel, Switzerland), 21*(19), 6693. https://doi.org/10.3390/s21196693
Woodworth, R. S., & Schlosberg, H. (1938). *Experimental psychology*. Henry Holt and Company.
Yin, H., Chen, J., & Pan, S. J. (2018). Hashing over predicted future frames for informed exploration of deep reinforcement learning. *arXiv*. https://arxiv.org/pdf/1707.00524.pdf

6 Extending Neural Network Predictions of Human Behaviors

Chris Ninness, Christine Bergan, Lee Mason, and Sharon Ninness

Machine learning (ML) is a specialized realm within the broader artificial intelligence (AI) field that employs algorithms to emulate human learning. Recently, AI and ML have blended and become increasingly controversial. Within the broad spectrum of current scientific advances, AI is arguably one of our most impressive, pervasive, and shocking scientific achievements. Only a few years ago, most of us were impressed with AI systems demonstrating accurate facial detection, text generation, speech recognition, self-driving vehicles, and automated transcription (Ninness & Ninness, 2020a), but these advances now seem embryonic in the face of more recent AI innovations.

In the past five years, we have seen AI employed to address facets of life previously considered uniquely human. Now, text-based AI is used to write everything from computer code to screenplays, medical treatment plans, and legal contracts (Ninness & Ninness, 2020a). Questions and prophecy saturate the media. Is AI a step toward extinction (Kissinger et al., 2021)? Is it our convoluted path to potential (Schumer, 2023)? For the moment, we can only speculate on the accelerating possibilities. No one in the environmental, medical, behavioral, or social sciences is able to predict where we are headed as AI allows us to disentangle and resolve previously impenetrable problems. Throughout the professional, industrial, and academic communities, we have landed on an inflection point, and the proverbial genie is out of the bottle. We can ignore it, try to prohibit it, or focus on the possibilities that lie before us. In the following pages, we provide a conceptual framework for behavior analysts with an interest in the intersection of human and machine learning.

Erecting an Architecture

This chapter describes the structure and internal operations within one popular ML system, the deep neural network (DNN), as applied to behavior-analytic investigation. Our objective in training a DNN is to develop a standalone predictive model that can operate with entirely new input data and make accurate predictions about future out-of-sample events, particularly future human behaviors. In the ever-expanding field of ML, DNNs are demonstrating increasingly robust and accurate performances in predictive analytics. When compared to other forms of ML systems, Liu et al. (2022) believe "DNNs have significant advantages in extracting features at different levels of abstraction and thereby learning more complex patterns" (p. 338). Before considering the intersection of human and machine learning, an overview of DNN components and functions may be useful.

DOI: 10.4324/9781003380603-8

Nodes

Think of a node as an object that receives input values and performs a series of simple random computations. DNNs are composed of layers of interconnected nodes (neurons). One of the fascinating features of the algorithm is how training is initiated with input values multiplied by small randomized weights (e.g., between ± 0.10) plus bias values all directed at nodes.

Activation Functions

To illustrate this process, Figure 6.1 displays a single node within the DNN's architecture (structure), but it is representative of others within the assembly of nodes across the layers of the network. Nodes are presented with input values (x_1, x_2, x_3 . . . $x_{n)}$. Starting at the input layer with a series of input values, the algorithm computes the weighted sum (∑) of inputs by multiplying each input by a small random weight (w_1, w_2, w_3 . . . w_n) and adds them to a bias value (*b*). Bias values play a role in shifting predictions away from the origin of the coordinate axis.

Activation functions enable the model to capture complex, nonlinear relationships between inputs and outputs, a substantial advancement over prior statistical models, such as linear regression, that assume linearity. Figure 6.1 can be expressed as the summed outputs (***z***) from a node as in Equation 1.

$$z = \sum_i w_i x_i + b \tag{1}$$

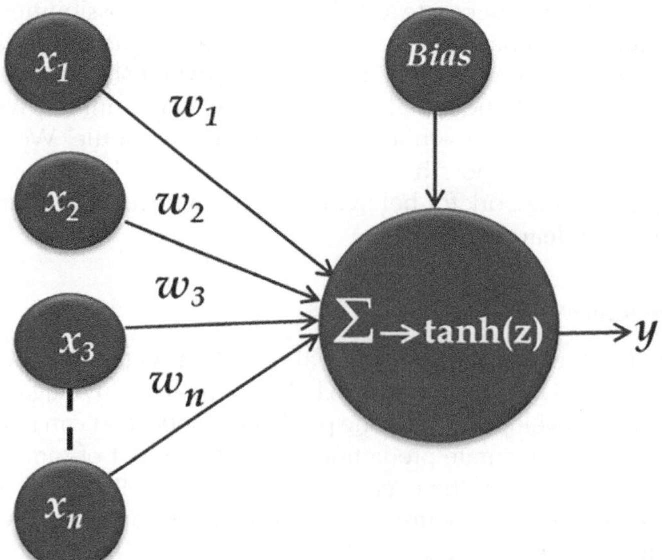

Figure 6.1 Flow of input computations to a single node.

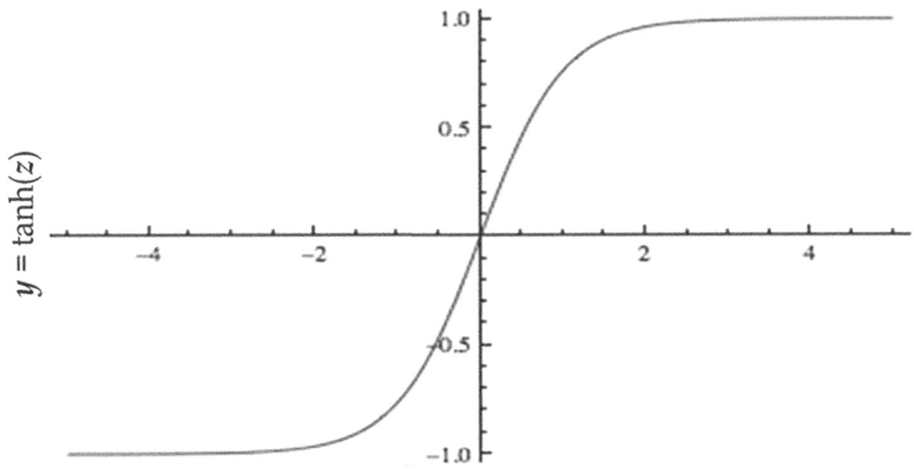

Figure 6.2 The hyperbolic tangent function.

In Equation 2, y is obtained as the sum of the weighted inputs plus the bias after passing through the node's activation function, tanh($\boldsymbol{z}$).

$$y = \tanh(z) = \frac{e^{z} - e^{-z}}{e^{z} + e^{-z}} \tag{2}$$

If, for example, as in Figure 6.2, the sum of the weighted input/predictor values plus the bias was 1.5, this value becomes an exponent within the tanh($\boldsymbol{z}$) activation function. The resulting y-value is squashed and converted to a value falling at the upper end of the function as shown in Equation 3 where the outcome is 0.905.

$$0.905 \approx \frac{e^{-1.5} - e^{-1.5}}{e^{1.5} + e^{-1.5}} \tag{3}$$

Figure 6.2 displays the upper and lower limits of the tanh activation function as it maps input values of any size to y-values falling between ± 1.

Two other commonly employed activation (transfer) functions are the rectified linear unit (ReLU) and the sigmoid. The choice of activation function depends on the problem one is trying to solve as well as the characteristics of the input values, and more than one type of activation function can be used for different layers in the algorithm (see Saha et al., 2021, for comparisons).

Hidden Nodes Within Hidden Layers

In Figure 6.3, the DNN architecture includes a series of nodes within successive layers where each node contains an activation function. The number of nodes in the first layer (n)

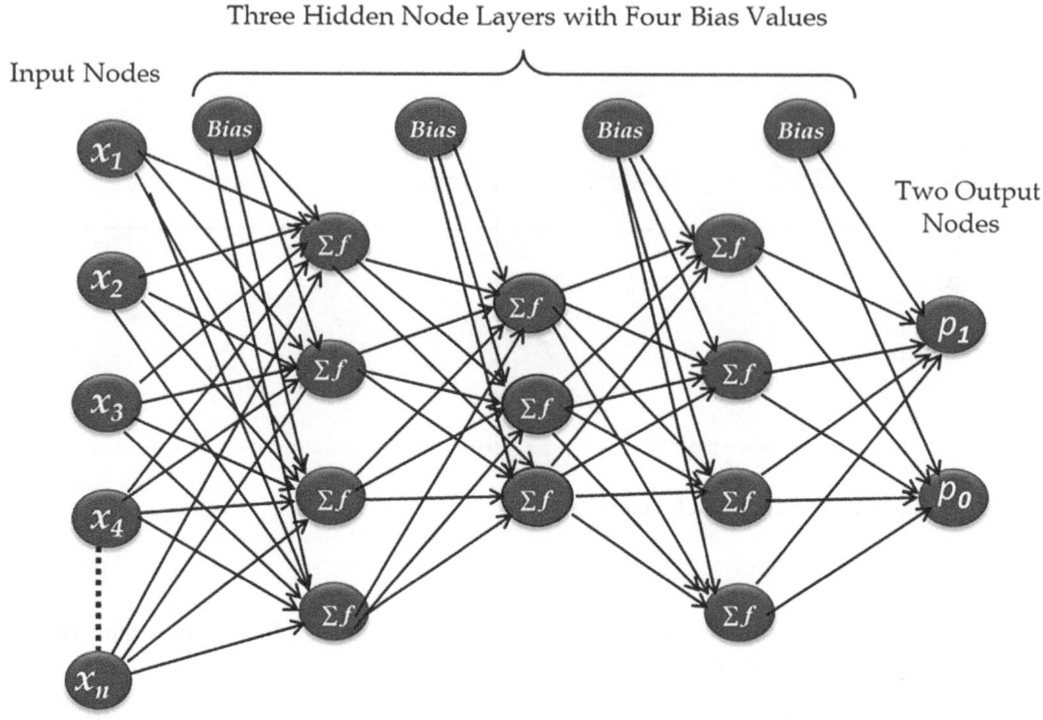

Figure 6.3 Node layers within the DNN architecture.

parallels the count of input variables to be analyzed while the two output neurons coincide with the number of dependent variables employed. The DNN architecture includes hidden node layers composed of activation functions. They are called hidden because they are not directly visible in terms of input or output; they are internal to the network and perform intermediate transformations. The researcher/algorithm designer determines the number of hidden layers and how many nodes will be configured within each hidden layer (four, three, and four in this example).

Training the DNN

Consistent with linear algebra, inputs enter the function and outputs map to one-way exits. Early neural networks followed this pattern, but modern DNNs feature both feedforward and backpropagation (Rumelhart et al., 1986). During the feedforward pass, training is conducted by passing the input data/signals forward through each of the node layers. Activation functions within the hidden nodes process the data, and prediction probabilities are output through the output layer (*p1* and *p0*). At this point, the training process has just begun. During the backward pass, prediction errors are assessed, and the weights and biases within the network are adjusted iteratively until predictive accuracy is optimized. One complete forward and backward pass of an entire dataset is referred to as an epoch.

During each forward pass, the hidden node layers compute rough estimates of the known (target) values, and these estimates are refined during the backward pass. Haykin (2009) tells us that as network training progresses, ". . . the hidden neurons begin to gradually 'discover' the salient features that characterize the training data. They do so by performing a nonlinear transformation on the input data into a new space called the feature space" (p. 126). Feature space refers to the attributes/variables within the dataset. To recap, the signals pass through all hidden node layers and emerge at the output layer as probabilities. The two output nodes with probability values are cumulated to a value of 1.0 by way of the softmax function. As the name suggests, the softmax function "softens" raw scores by transforming them into accuracy probabilities.

If we were concerned with predicting one of three political affiliations (e.g., Republican, Democratic, and independent), Figure 6.3 would be constructed similarly, but the softmax function would include three output nodes rather than two. If we were interested in a single dependent variable (e.g., independent versus not independent), we could employ the logistic function (with a single node), noting that softmax is a generalized version of the logistic function. Thus, if it served our purpose, we could employ the two nodes in the softmax function to compute the probabilities for independent and not independent, respectively.

Probability and Error

Upon receiving the signals forwarded by the hidden layers, the probability values for each output node are computed as shown in Figure 6.3. These computed probability values are contrasted against the known/target values to obtain the amount of prediction error (error signals). In Figure 6.4, these error signals (ε_1 and ε_0) are then passed back to the nodes within the hidden layers. This begins our backward pass, referred to as backpropagation.

The Loss of Inaccuracy

Although the term may seem counterintuitive, network *loss* measures the model's ability to identify output values correctly. Again, the network measures the difference between the predicted and target outputs as a form of error or *loss*. As loss diminishes during training, the DNN model is likely to attain better predictions. We do not want our loss value to vanish entirely, but depending on our objectives, we usually want loss to *converge* on (coincide with) some minimal value (minima), the lowest obtainable error (cf. Kawaguchi & Huang, 2019).

Assumptions, Predictions, and Error Values

In linear regression, residuals are the difference between the obtained and predicted scores, and these standardized error values are often depicted as a scatter of data points around a regression line. When the data at hand are consistent with independence, linearity, normality, and homoscedasticity assumptions, making statistical predictions can be a reassuring and relatively straightforward process. When the available data do not meet the assumptions for statistical regression, DNN predictive analytics become increasingly valuable.

This issue becomes conspicuous when research ambitions include predicting complex nonlinear human behaviors. For example, when a hybrid DNN was employed to predict inappropriate out-of-home child placement decisions by child welfare professionals, high levels of predictive accuracy were obtained (Ninness et al., 2021), while statistical

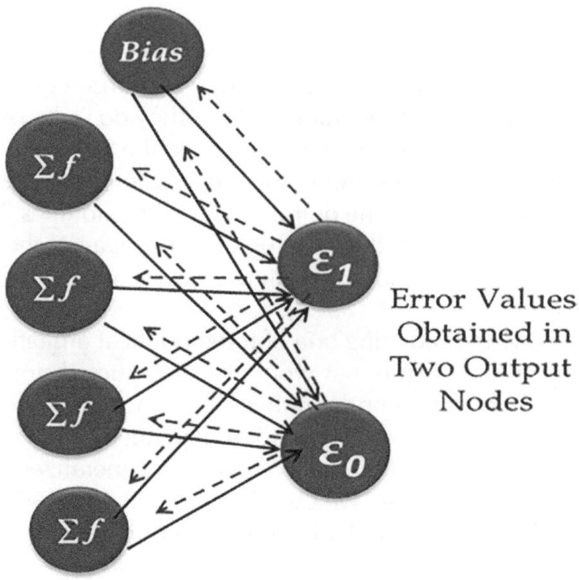

Figure 6.4 Initiating the backward pass.

analyses found significant but nonpredictive findings. Similarly, when analyzing nonlinear single-case outcomes, DNN algorithms accurately simulated and predicted human learning of mutually and combinatorially entailed stimulus relations (Ninness & Ninness, 2020b), but this pattern was completely obscured when viewed through the lens of conventional statistics.

Equation 4 illustrates the mean square error (MSE) measure as the loss function (error value) in the current DNN architecture. The MSE is one of several available loss functions used in ML, and it is obtained by continually recalculating the average of the squared differences between a predicted value and a known target value. Analogous to the standard error of the estimate (SEE), this function computes how well network training shrinks the distance between a given target value ($\hat{Y}$) and its calculated (Y) value.

$$\text{MSE} = \frac{1}{n}\sum_{i=1}^{n}(\hat{Y}_i - Y_i)^2 \tag{4}$$

Unlike the SEE, the MSE is not based on a single calculation. Rather, with the completion of each forward pass, the MSE is recalculated by squaring the difference between the known target value and the network's most current estimate of the target value, obtaining the sum (∑) of the squared differences, and finally dividing the total by the number (n) of data points processed.

Several loss functions are available for different types of network analyses. For example, categorical cross-entropy loss is used primarily in problems with more than two classifications. Binary cross-entropy is a binary version of cross-entropy loss. In each case, the goal of the loss function is the same: to find the minimum difference between predictions in outputs produced by a neural network with a given set of weights and biases and the actual output values in the training set. The assumption is that those weights and biases can predict an out-of-sample test set (Antony et al., 2017).

Backpropagating Error

In broad strokes, gradient descent is the process by which the DNN algorithm guides the weights and bias values along the downward path toward some minimal loss value, adjusting/correcting the weights and reducing the MSE during each backward pass. The pattern often observed in the loss function is that it unevenly shrinks as the network is optimized by adjusting weights and bias values (see Haykin, 2009, for a comprehensive account). The DNN gradually learns the relations among input patterns during this series of forward and backward passes of the training data. Turgeon and Lanovaz (2020) state that the process resembles "shaping in behavior analysis where the algorithm selects (reinforces) successively closer approximations (i.e., less error)" (p. 712). In doing so, backpropagation minimizes the MSE while moving the network's predictions closer to the target values. McCaffrey (2015) provides an overview:

> Back-propagation is based on calculus partial derivatives. Each weight and bias value has an associated partial derivative. You can think of a partial derivative as a value that contains information about how much, and in what direction, a weight value must be adjusted to reduce error. The collection of all partial derivatives is called a gradient.
>
> (para. 21)

Gradient Descent

Computing the derivatives for the weights within the hidden layers is intricate. While the calculus operations within the backward pass are beyond the scope of this chapter, it is helpful to explore the overarching concepts associated with backpropagation graphically and by analogy. Note that we take a few liberties with concepts and terminology to make some of these ideas more salient (see Table 6.1).

As shown in Figure 6.5, when the gradient changes are consistent with improved learning, the MSE shrinks and moves toward some minimally attainable loss value. In this example, this loss value is attained at 878 epochs. If we examine the flow of loss values, it becomes apparent that gradient descent is unpredictable. Particularly during early epochs, the MSE oscillates but decays rapidly, displaying erratic levels of accuracy across epochs. In the final epoch, the MSE value is 0.001977.

Table 6.1 Hyperparameters with Brief Descriptions

Hyperparameters	*Brief Descriptions*
Learning rate	The learning rate determines how quickly the model adapts to predictions based on calculated error.
Momentum	Momentum regulates learning speed and network accuracy.
Epoch	A complete forward and backward pass of the entire training dataset through the model.
Node layers	A series of nodes within the layers of a network that allow it to learn and classify the input values.
Activation function	Within each node, an activation function (e.g., tanh) introduces nonlinearity to compressed training values and forwards these to other nodes within the layers of the network.
Convergence	The point in training at which the error value stops shrinking and network learning discontinues.

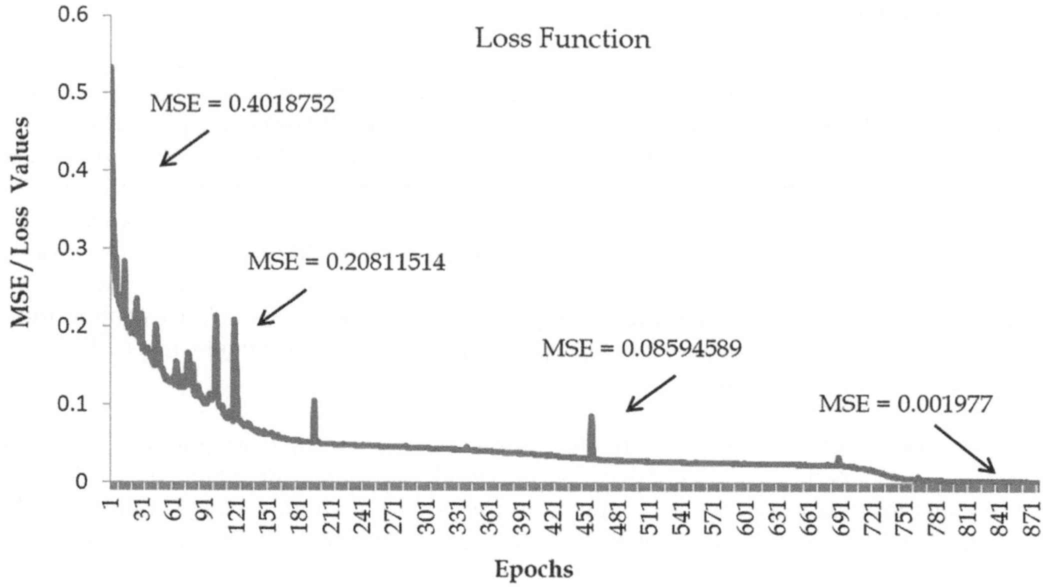

Figure 6.5 Display of the gradient descent during 878 training epochs.

Depending on sample size, data complexity, desired MSE, and accuracy value, the number of training epochs may be very different across research projects. For example, DNNs have been trained to attain desired MSE values and accuracies employing fewer than 50 epochs (e.g., Ninness et al., 2019), while other studies with more stringent requirements obtained desired improvements when training entailed 5,000 epochs (Kazem et al., 2019).

Human and Computer Misfits

As with human learning, how well a network learns to classify complex relations depends on how well training is provided. If the network is not exposed to a sufficient number of training epochs or the architecture is poorly designed (e.g., inadequate node layers), it is unlikely to learn all the features within a complex, multifaceted dataset. Under these conditions, the model *underfits* the data because it has not been exposed (or has been incorrectly exposed) to the diversified features within the training data. As with humans who receive insufficient or poorly designed training, the model cannot generalize beyond a limited series of training samples (see Lyddy & Barnes-Holmes, 2007, for parallel examples of human and ML performance outcomes).

Conversely, if the network is exposed to excessive training epochs or the architecture includes too many node layers, random noise is assimilated into the training data, causing *overfitting*. Again, the network will be unable to formulate a generalized model of the training data. Akin to the stimulus overselectivity of autism spectrum disorder (Ploog, 2010), overfitting prohibits the network from learning the general case (Twyman, 2021). That is, we may build a very precise model for identifying Santa Claus as a fat man with a white beard and red hat, but if any of those characteristics change (e.g., skinny Santa, gray beard, or no hat), the sample becomes unrecognizable.

Free Parameters and Hyperparameters

A network's *free parameters* are the weights and bias values updated throughout training. *Hyperparameters* are the network settings that can be *manually* adjusted by the researcher before network training begins and continued throughout training (Yang & Shami, 2020). Alternatively, hyperparameter tuning can be accomplished by way of automated systems. Depending on the researcher's algorithm preference, several automated approaches to hyperparameter tuning (e.g., grid search, automated search, etc.) are available. Turgeon and Lanovaz (2020) provide details regarding several automated techniques.

McCaffrey (2014) explains that manual tuning entails identifying the best (i.e., the most predictive) series of weights and bias values. For example, setting the *learning rate* (α) between 0 and 1 regulates the speed of weight updates. During gradient descent, large α values (e.g., $\alpha >$ 0.75) may cause instability and *jump over* the minima, in which case the model underfits and fails to classify the training data correctly. Conversely, setting the learning rate too low may result in slow *convergence* (see Table 6.1). Here, an excessively complex model may result in overfitting the data such that the DNN learns the irrelevant/noisy features of a training dataset. Such a model cannot generalize when predicting outcomes for new datasets.

The *momentum* coefficient (β) has a range of settings between 0 and 1. It takes a small percentage of the previous weight change induced by the learning rate and adds it to the most current update. In doing so, it allows the learning rate to accelerate training while avoiding extreme oscillations during gradient descent. If β is set at 0, the influence of previous weights and bias updates is eliminated, while a setting of 1 will cause previous updates to be unusually impactful and even chaotic. Thus, momentum is often set well below 0.5 at the outset. In a given study, β might be initialized at 0.1 and titrated to some threshold of diminished oscillations as shown in Figure 6.5. Other hyperparameters include the number of hidden layers, nodes within each layer, training epochs, and choice of activation functions (see Haykin, 2009, for a comprehensive account).

A manual search allows the network designer/researcher to systematically explore a combination of hyperparameters and design a model that maximizes performance. Extending an example provided by McCaffrey (2014), we might begin tuning the network by conducting a series of trials in which we set the upper limit of training epochs to 1,000, α at 0.05, and β at 0.01. We increase the number of training epochs until the accuracy level stops improving. Here, we might titrate β while leaving α constant. If we obtain improved accuracy and loss continues to shrink with β set at 0.03, we keep examining the effects of small variations in these settings. In the same way, we assess accuracy and loss outcomes by exploring combinations of hidden node layers. Using a demo program to illustrate this general approach, McCaffrey mentions that the number of required epochs "was easy to see when computed output values were very close to the desired output values" (p. 78).

Returning to Figure 6.5, recall that the MSE reached a low decaying oscillation threshold at 878 epochs. At this juncture, continued training would serve little advantage while increasing the chances of overfitting the data. In this example, it is time to save our weights and bias values as a potentially completed model and begin cross-validation trials.

Cross-Validation as an Experimental Analysis

There are several valuable strategies for conducting cross-validation (CV) procedures when large datasets are available (Little et al., 2017). Frequently, the technique entails conducting a series of assessments wherein subsets (folds) of randomly selected training and validation data are extracted from a database. Folds or *k*-folds refer to the number of training and validation groups evaluated. That is, CV procedures divide large datasets into separate training sets, validation sets, and a single holdout (test) set. As described by Hagan et al. (2002, Chapter 13, p. 8), "When we divide the data, approximately 70% is typically used for training, with 15% for validation and 15% for testing. These are only approximate numbers." Particularly for large datasets, a variety of *k*-fold tactics are available from the scikit-learn library (cf. Pedregosa et al. (2011).

Clinical Datasets

The most functional CV strategy for a given study depends on the number of independent and dependent variables, the type of data being analyzed, research ambitions, and, most notably, the size of the dataset at hand. Saeb et al. (2017) express a concern regarding the analysis of clinical samples: "As we move towards an era of machine learning-based diagnosis and treatment, using proper methods to evaluate their accuracy is crucial, as inaccurate results can mislead both clinicians and data scientists" (p. 1). While there are several widely accepted approaches, all CV strategies can be viewed as experimental analyses attempting to make scientific predictions regarding future outcomes.

Irrespective of the particular CV method employed, predictive accuracy can only be gauged by focusing on outcomes from data not seen during the training trials. As put forward by Gigerenzer (2004), "The true test of a model is to fix its parameters on one sample, and to test it in a new sample" (p. 603). Yet, when running clinical investigations within applied research settings, ambitions may be compromised by the limited number of existing case records. Most CV methods require that a substantial portion of the available dataset is held out while the remaining portion is used during CV trials. This zero-sum circumstance requires that the larger we make our holdout set, the smaller the training portion becomes, but holding out small samples to demonstrate model fitness (accuracy when applied to new datasets) makes a reliable predictive analysis experimentally challenging. Notwithstanding, functional and convincing strategies exist.

Leave-One-Out

One valuable tactic entails an all-inclusive form of CV described as *leave-one-out*. Here, $N-1$ cases are employed to train the model, and the model is validated by testing it on the case not included during a particular training iteration. The rotating analysis is repeated for all records within the available dataset. This approach is often recommended when developing models around especially small datasets (Turgeon & Lanovaz, 2020). See Lanovaz et al. (2020) and Lanovaz and Bailey (2022) for CV strategies applied to single-case experimental designs.

Seeds of Learning

Haykin (2009) addresses a multitude of strategies for conducting CV procedures, stating, "There are variants of cross-validation that find their own uses in practice, particularly when there is a scarcity of labeled examples" (p. 175). One method entails using a randomization seed to generate a series of unique CV shuffles. By way of the Fisher-Yates shuffle algorithm, a random seed value creates an unbiased random dataset (Fisher & Yates, 1948). This initiates a randomized sequence of training and validation folds. Following each CV trial, all records are combined into a single dataset and reshuffled into new training and validation sets. As described in an earlier investigation (Ninness et al., 2018), "This process is analogous to restarting the entire training protocol for a new, experimentally-naive participant" (p. 136).

Save the Model for New Predictions

Since training is initiated by multiplying the input values by random weights, every training CV trial we perform will generate unique outcomes as well as a unique series of weights and bias values. When we compute predictions during CV trials, the weights and bias values define our model. Saving these values opens the door to predicting future outcomes. To the extent that our holdout data are consistent with the parent population from which our training data were obtained, we infer that our model will make accurate predictions for the holdouts as well as samples from similar populations, but this is an empirical question. This much is known: DNNs are capable of predicting future outcomes with unprecedented accuracy. As mentioned earlier, no one in the sciences is able to predict where this technology will take us. AI invites opportunities, insights, and risks that most of us could not have imagined only a few years ago. Recently, Senator Chuck Schumer commented on AI development at the Center for Strategic and International Studies:

> Change at such blistering speed may seem frightening to some – but if applied correctly, AI promises to transform life on Earth for the better. It will reshape how we fight disease, tackle hunger, manage our lives, enrich our minds, and ensure peace. But there are real dangers too: job displacement, misinformation, a new age of weaponry, and the risk of being unable to manage this technology altogether. We have no choice but to acknowledge that AI's changes are coming, and in many cases are already here.
>
> (Schumer, 2023, para. 8)

It is beyond the scope of science to control the use to which its contributions will be put (Skinner, 1953). Ready or not, AI is making a difference in our daily lives. Its impact on society may best be measured in terms of who it benefits.

References

Antony, J., McGuinness, K., Moran, K., & O'Connor, N. E. (2017). Automatic detection of knee joints and quantification of knee osteoarthritis severity using convolutional neural networks. *Lecture Notes in Computer Science*, 376–390. https://doi.org/10.1007/978-3-319-62416-7_27

Fisher, R. A., & Yates, F. (1948). *Statistical tables for biological, agricultural and medical research* (3rd ed.). Oliver & Boyd.

Gigerenzer, G. (2004). Mindless statistics. *The Journal of Socio-Economics*, *33*(5), 587–606. https://doi.org/10.1016/j.socec.2004.09.033

Hagan, M. T., Demuth, H. B., & Beale, M. H. (2002). *Neural network design*. PWS Publishing Company.

Haykin, S. (2009). *Neural network and learning machines* (3rd ed.). Prentice Hall. https://doi.org/10.1007/s10278-012-9556-5

Kawaguchi, K., & Huang, J. (2019). *Gradient descent finds global minima for generalizable deep neural networks of practical sizes*. 2019 57th Annual Allerton Conference on Communication, Control, and Computing, Allerton. https://doi.org/10.1109/allerton.2019.8919696

Kazem, H. A., Yousif, J., Chaichan, M. T., & Al-Waeli, A. H. A. (2019). Experimental and deep learning artificial neural network approach for evaluating grid-connected photovoltaic systems. *International Journal of Energy Research*, *43*(14), 8572–8591. Portico. https://doi.org/10.1002/er.4855

Kissinger, H. A., Schmidt, E., & Huttenlocher, D. (2021). *The age of AI: And our human future*. Hachette UK.

Lanovaz, M. J., & Bailey, J. D. (2022). Tutorial: Artificial neural networks to analyze single-case experimental designs. *Psychological Methods*. https://doi.org/10.1037/met0000487

Lanovaz, M. J., Giannakakos, A. R., & Destras, O. (2020). Machine learning to analyze single-case data: A proof of concept. *Perspectives on Behavior Science, 43*(1), 21–38. https://doi.org/10.1007/s40614-020-00244-0

Little, M. A., Varoquaux, G., Saeb, S., Lonini, L., Jayaraman, A., Mohr, D. C., & Kording, K. P. (2017). Using and understanding cross-validation strategies: Perspectives on Saeb et al. *GigaScience, 6*(5). https://doi.org/10.1093/gigascience/gix020

Liu, X.-Y., Fang, Y., Yang, L., Li, Z., & Walid, A. (2022). High-performance tensor decompositions for compressing and accelerating deep neural networks. *Tensors for Data Processing*, 293–340. https://doi.org/10.1016/b978-0-12-824447-0.00015-7

Lyddy, F., & Barnes-Holmes, D. (2007). Stimulus equivalence as a function of training protocol in a connectionist network. *Journal of Speech & Language Pathology & Applied Behavior Analysis, 2*, 14–24. https://doi.org/10.1037/h0100204.

McCaffrey, J. (2014). *Neural networks using C# succinctly*. https://jamesmccaffrey.wordpress.com/2014/06/03/neural-networks-using-c-succinctly

McCaffrey, J. (2015). *Coding neural network back-propagation using C#*. https://visualstudiomagazine.com/articles/2015/04/01/back-propagation-using-c.aspx

Ninness, C., & Ninness, S. K. (2020a). Emergent virtual analytics: Artificial intelligence and human-computer interactions. *Behavior and Social Issues, 29*(1), 100–118. https://doi.org/10.1007/s42822-020-00031-1

Ninness, C., & Ninness, S. K. (2020b). Emergent virtual analytics: Modeling contextual control of derived stimulus relations. *Behavior and Social Issues, 29*(1), 119–137. https://doi.org/10.1007/s42822-020-00032-0

Ninness, C., Ninness, S. K., Rumph, M., & Lawson, D. (2018). The emergence of stimulus relations: Human and computer learning. *Perspective on Behavioral Science, 41*, 121–154. https://doi.org/10.1007/s40614-017-0125-6

Ninness, C., Rehfeldt, R. A., & Ninness, S. (2019). Identifying accurate and inaccurate stimulus relations: Human and computer learning. *The Psychological Record, 69*(3), 333–356. https://doi.org/10.1007/s40732-019-00337-6

Ninness, C., Yelick, A., Ninness, S. K., & Cordova, W. (2021). Predicting heuristic decisions in child welfare: A neural network exploration. *Behavior and Social Issues, 30*(1), 194–208. https://doi.org/10.1007/s42822-021-00047-1

Pedregosa, F., Varoquaux, Gaël, Gramfort, A., Michel, V., Thirion, B., Grisel, O., Blondel, M., Prettenhofer, P., Weiss, R., Dubourg, V., & Vanderplas, J. (2011, October). Scikit-learn: Machine learning in Python. *Journal of Machine Learning Research, 12*, 2825–2830. https://www.jmlr.org/papers/volume12/pedregosa11a/pedregosa11a.pdf

Ploog, B. O. (2010). Stimulus overselectivity four decades later: A review of the literature and its implications for current research in autism spectrum disorder. *Journal of Autism and Developmental Disorders, 40*, 1332–1349. https://doi.org/10.1007/s10803-010-0990-2

Rumelhart, D. E., Hinton, G. E., & Williams, R. J. (1986). Learning representations by back-propagating errors. *Nature, 323*(6088), 533–536. https://doi.org/10.1038/323533a0

Saeb, S., Lonini, L., Jayaraman, A., Mohr, D. C., & Kording, K. P. (2017). The need to approximate the use-case in clinical machine learning. *GigaScience, 6*(5). https://doi.org/10.1093/gigascience/gix019

Saha, P., Sadi, M. S., & Islam, M. M. (2021). EMCNet: Automated COVID-19 diagnosis from X-ray images using convolutional neural network and ensemble of machine learning classifiers. *Informatics in Medicine Unlocked, 22*, 100505. https://doi.org/10.1016/j.imu.2020.100505

Schumer, C. (2023). *Newsroom* [Speech transcript]. https://www.democrats.senate.gov/news/press-releases/majority-leader-schumer-delivers-remarks-to-launch-safe-innovation-framework-for-artificial-intelligence-at-csis

Skinner, B. F. (1953). *Science and human behavior*. Macmillan. https://doi.org/10.1002/sce.37303805120

Turgeon, S., & Lanovaz, M. J. (2020). Tutorial: Applying machine learning in behavioral research. *Perspectives on Behavior Science, 43*(4), 697–723. https://doi.org/10.1007/s40614-020-00270-y

Twyman, J. S. (2021). The evidence is in the design. *Perspectives on Behavior Science, 44*(2–3), 195–223. https://doi.org/10.1007/s40614-021-00309-8

Yang, L., & Shami, A. (2020). On hyperparameter optimization of machine learning algorithms: Theory and practice. *Neurocomputing, 415*, 295–316. https://doi.org/10.1016/j.neucom.2020.07.061

Section 3

Tools and Technologies for Research and Applications

7 An Updated and Simplified Version of a Low-Cost Arduino-Visual Basic Interface for Operant Research

Rogelio Escobar, Rodrigo Benavides, and Brissa Gutiérrez

Although fundamental in behavioral research, standard operant conditioning chambers are relatively easy to control. Most commonly, a response is recorded automatically whenever a switch closure is detected in levers or keys for rats and pigeons, respectively. These switches, which can only be in *off* or *on* states, are known as digital inputs. Digital output devices, in turn, generate environmental events in the chamber according to the experimental procedures. Food pellets or drops of water, commonly used as reinforcers, are delivered onto a tray inside the experimental chamber when the motor in a pellet dispenser or in a water pump is activated. Lights and tones can be produced by powering up small bulbs or buzzers. An electronic interface for controlling operant research must automatically and continuously monitor the state of inputs and generate outputs according to a predefined procedure.

Previously, authors have noted that commercial interfaces for controlling operant conditioning chambers are costly, cumbersome (see e.g., Varnon & Abramson, 2013), and lack flexibility (Varnon et al., 2018). Because of these problems, many authors have created alternatives to commercial equipment with different levels of success (see Escobar, 2014, for a review). One notable example was the versatile but now outdated "Palya board" (Palya & Waler, 1993; Walter & Palya, 1984). A few years ago, Escobar and Pérez-Herrera (2015) described an inexpensive and relatively easy-to-use electronic interface, known as Arduino-Visual Basic, designed to control experimental chambers in operant research. Experimental procedures were programmed and executed using Visual Basic (VB) on a PC. These programs communicated in real time to a microcontroller board (Arduino board) connected to the computer via a USB cable. The Arduino microcontroller was connected to the operant chamber to monitor the state of inputs and to activate output devices in the operant chamber. Experimental events and time stamps were recorded in a .txt file created using VB and stored in the computer's hard drive.

Escobar and Pérez-Herrera (2015) conducted a series of tests using solid-state relays in combination with oscilloscope readings to determine the accuracy of the interface. The Arduino-VB interface has a resolution of 4 ms and can generate real-time time stamps for experimental events every 15 ms. These values exceed the requirements of typical operant research, in which responses – for example, key pecks in pigeons – rarely exceed one every 30 ms. Aside from its accuracy, other characteristics that make the interface a viable alternative to commercial interfaces are its use of inexpensive and reliable Arduino boards, easily found worldwide. Additionally, it adheres to an open-source/open-distribution hardware and software policy. Therefore, the design and the programs written in VB and Arduino code can be downloaded, used, modified, and distributed freely. To our knowledge, this interface has been used productively in various universities in Mexico and in

DOI: 10.4324/9781003380603-10

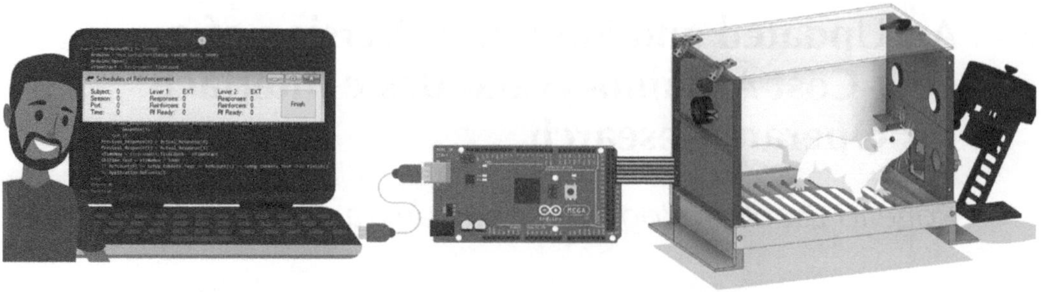

Figure 7.1 Arduino-VB interface.

other countries. Although the interface has primarily been used to control experimental chambers for rats, it is versatile enough for tasks involving human participants. Buttons or plungers can be used to record responses, minimizing history effects associated with computer keyboards.

This chapter describes an updated version of the Arduino-VB interface. Although the interface can still be used as described by Escobar and Pérez-Herrera (2015), during the time that elapsed since it was first described, we have updated programming methods and have simplified assembly by incorporating new components that are reliable and easier to use. These improvements have also increased the flexibility to present various environmental events. The VB and Arduino programs described in this chapter can be freely downloaded from GitHub, and consistent with an open-source/open-distribution policy, may be used, modified, and distributed without restriction.

Arduino-Visual Basic Interface

The description of the interface is divided into two parts: hardware and software. The first part describes the Arduino board, the use of inputs to record responses, and outputs to present environmental events. Another section details the use of the Arduino board to control 28 Volts Direct Current (VDC) devices commonly found in commercial operant conditioning chambers. The second part describes the VB program that is executed in a PC. This program generates the schedules of reinforcement by sending and receiving a symbolic code from the Arduino board using a serial communication (COM) port. The symbolic code received from the Arduino board corresponds to changes in the state of inputs in the operant chamber (responses). The symbolic codes sent from the VB program to the Arduino board activate the devices in the operant chamber (e.g., feeder, water pump, lights, tones). Figure 7.1 shows a diagram of the interface. The PC running the experimental procedure written in VB is connected to the Arduino board using a standard USB 2.0 A/B cable. The pins on the Arduino board are connected to the input/output devices in the operant chamber.

In the diagram, a PC laptop running a Microsoft Windows operating system executes the experimental procedure written in Visual Basic. The laptop is connected to an Arduino Mega board using a USB cable. The Arduino board is connected to the digital input/output (I/O) devices in the operant chamber. The program in the Arduino board communicates bidirectionally with the experimental procedure using a COM port.

Hardware

Arduino Board

Arduino boards have been a staple in do-it-yourself electronics for more than a decade. Arduino boards are microcontroller boards with ready-to-use I/O pins that allow serial communication using USB. Microcontrollers, akin to a small computer in a single integrated circuit, include a central processing unit, memory, and programable I/O ports. Microcontrollers are typically programmed to detect changes in the environment and execute an action – for example, producing a tone when a motion sensor is activated. The ATmega2560 microcontroller in the Arduino Mega board can be programmed using the Arduino programming language, which is based on C++, to execute programs. The Arduino IDE software (currently version 2.0) used to program and monitor the board is free to use, regularly updated, and supported by a vast community that can be consulted for technical details (refer to the section on Arduino IDE under the "Software" heading).

Arduino boards can also be used without a PC if powered with an external power supply. For the purpose described in this chapter, however, a PC is required to send and read real-time data from the Arduino board. If no current-intensive outputs are required (e.g. motors, pumps, etc.), the USB connection to the PC can be used to power the board and the devices. We recommend using an Arduino Mega 2560 (Rev 3) board because it has 256 kb of flash memory for storing programs and 54 digital I/O pins, with two of them required for data transmission and reception. This is an improvement over the most popular Arduino Uno (Rev 3) board (see Escobar & Pérez-Herrera, 2015), which has 32 kb of flash memory and 14 I/O pins. If 12 or fewer I/O pins are required, an Arduino Uno board can substitute for the Arduino Mega board. In both cases, using genuine Arduino boards is important to avoid software conflicts. Even with the memory improvement in the Arduino Mega board, programming complex experimental tasks with user-friendly graphic interfaces can be challenging because of the 256 kb limit. Because of this limitation, experimental procedures are programmed in Visual Basic. Basic schedules of reinforcement can be programmed and executed using only the Arduino board connected to an operant chamber. These schedules, however, require advanced Arduino programming skills and are not described in the present chapter.

Inputs

Figure 7.2 shows an Arduino Mega board and the I/O connections to the main components in the devices commonly used in an operant chamber. The devices used as inputs are shown as two switches (2) in the upper-left section of the figure. Additional switches can be connected to the board using available pins. These switches are used in standard commercial levers for rodents and monkeys, as well as in pigeon keys. They can also be used in custom-made 3D printed operanda (see Escobar et al., 2022, p. 5). Switches have three terminals: normally open (NO), normally closed (NC), and common (C) terminals. The C connector is connected to a GND pin in the Arduino board. The NO terminal is connected to an I/O pin. In this example, one lever switch is connected to Pin 8, and another is connected to Pin 9. However, any I/O pin can be used by changing the Arduino code accordingly. The interface can also be used with analog input sensors like photocells to detect light beam interruptions. These sensors, however, require additional calibration, as described previously (see Escobar & Santillán, 2017; Escobar et al., 2022, pp. 5–6).

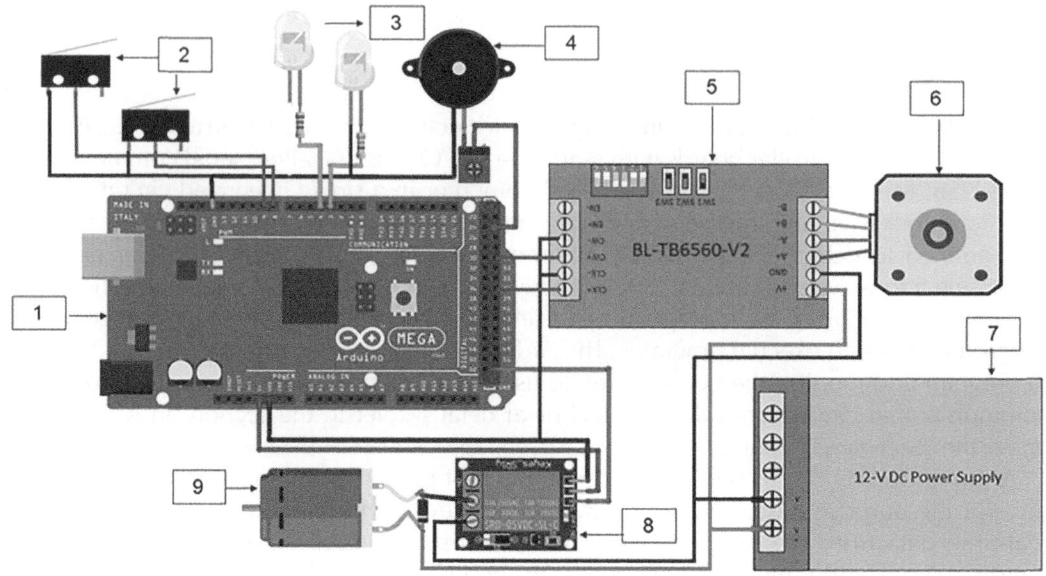

Figure 7.2 Input/output connections.

Note: 1) Microcontroller Arduino Mega 2560. Inputs: 2) Honeywell 311SM4-T switch or similar lever switch. Outputs: 3) 10 mm ultrabright LED, 4) active buzzer 2.9 kHz 3–20 VCD (constant tone) with a 1 kilohm potentiometer, 5) TB6560 driver for stepper motor, 6) NEMA 17 stepper motor model 17HS4401, 7) 12 VDC power supply, 8) Keyes relay module or similar module, and 9) 12 VDC peristaltic water pump with a 1N4001 rectifying diode.

Outputs

Arduino I/O pins can be set as outputs to generate 5 VDC (40 mA maximum) that can be used to turn electronic devices off or on. Lights and tones can be generated with LEDs (3) and buzzers (4), respectively (see Escobar et al., 2022, p. 8, for details). LEDs require a resistor (e.g., 330 ohms). Also, a 2.9 kHz 5–20 VDC buzzer can be used with a 1 kilohm variable resistor (potentiometer) to adjust the volume. A useful rule of thumb is to avoid powering up any device other than LEDs or buzzers directly with the Arduino board. An Arduino board can be damaged if over 40 mA per pin or 200 mA total are drawn from the board, a limit easily exceeded by most DC or stepper motors. An external power supply must be added when operating devices that exceed the current limit or require voltages higher than 5 VDC. For example, the DC motor inside 3D printed water pumps (9) operates on 12 VDC (see Escobar et al., 2022, p. 6). In this case, the Arduino board is used to turn on or off a relay (8) that connects the motor to an external 12 VDC power supply (7). Stepper motors used in 3D printed feeders also operate on 12 VDC (see Escobar et al., 2022, p. 7). In this case, a motor controller (e.g., TB6560) is required to activate the feeder.

Connection With Commercial 28 VDC Devices

In the case of commercial equipment that works with 28 VDC, an external power supply is also required. We recommend using optocouplers to control commercial equipment without damaging the power supply or the boards in the interfaces. An optocoupler board (e.g., Hy-M158) can be used to safely control up to eight devices. As an example, Figure 7.3

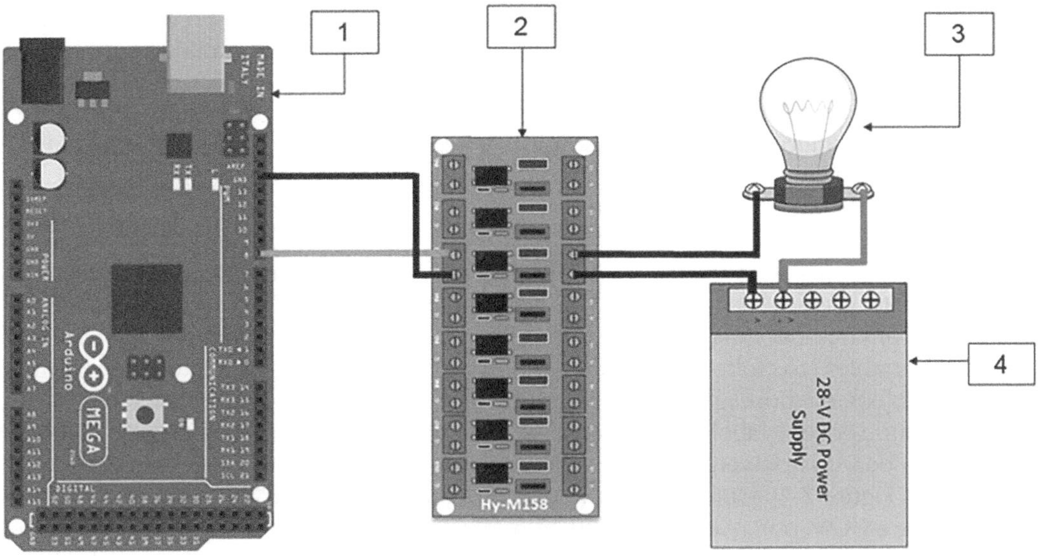

Figure 7.3 Control of 28 VDC devices in commercial equipment.

Note: Components: 1) Arduino Mega 2560, 2) optocoupler board model Hy-M158, 3) 28 VDC bulb, and 4) 28 VDC power supply.

shows the connection diagram for controlling a 28 VDC light bulb with the optocoupler board connected to Pin 8 of the Arduino board. As shown in the figure, the positive wire of the bulb connects directly to the positive terminal of the power supply, while the ground wire is connected to the board, which, in turn, links the wire to the negative terminal of the power supply. Commercial 28 VDC feeders with three wires can also be controlled with the optocoupler board by connecting the positive wire to the power supply and the operate wire to the board linked to the negative terminal of the battery (similar to the bulb shown in Figure 7.3). The additional ground wire is connected directly to the negative (or in some cases ground) terminal of the power supply.

Software

Arduino IDE

Learning the basics of the Arduino IDE with an Arduino board is relatively easy because of the detailed instructions and simple connecting diagrams and routines included on the Arduino website (https://docs.arduino.cc), as well as in various learning kits. One basic routine, for example, consists of turning on an LED whenever a switch is pressed. The ready-to-use pins in the Arduino board are connected to the LED and the switch using jumper wires and a prototyping board. A program monitors the state of switches connected to pins that are declared as digital inputs. Additionally, signals are sent to other pins, declared as a digital outputs, in which, for example, LEDs are connected. To run the program, open it in the PC using the Arduino IDE and upload it to the Arduino board using the USB cable. Once the program is uploaded, it is executed continuously. When an Arduino board is connected to the PC, a COM port is automatically assigned, and it remains the same for each board even if the board is disconnected and reconnected afterward. Identifying the COM port assigned for the Arduino board is crucial for establishing communication with the VB program.

A sample program to use the Arduino-Visual Basic interface can be downloaded from GitHub (https://github.com/RogerEsc/Arduino_Visual_Basic_2025). This program, shown schematically in Figure 7.4, is designed to record up to two responses and includes code to control various output devices. There is no need to eliminate from the code the input or output devices that are not used.

Arduino programs are divided into three sections. The first section (Figure 7.4, section 1) is dedicated to variable declarations. The declaration of a variable consists of assigning a name and a pin number for each input or output device that will be operated. The syntax for declaring variables is as follows: *"[variable type] [variable name] = [pin on Arduino board];"*. For example: *"byte Houselight = 4;"*.

The second section, labeled *"setup ()*,*"* is used to execute instructions once, whenever the Arduino board is powered on and the program starts. The instruction *Serial.begin* (see section 2 in Figure 7.4) establishes serial communication between the Arduino board and the PC using a COM port. Also, in this section, pins are set as input or output pins using the *pinMode* function. For inputs, to simplify physical connections when using a switch, the pin mode must be set to *"INPUT_PULLUP"*. The added *PULLUP* instruction enables an internal resistor to prevent fluctuations in the input values when the switches are open. For outputs, the mode can be set as *"OUTPUT"*. The syntax is as follows: *pinMode ([variable name], [I/O]);*. The initial state of output devices can be set using the *digitalWrite* function. In the program shown in Figure 7.4, all values are initially set to LOW, ensuring that all devices are off when the program starts.

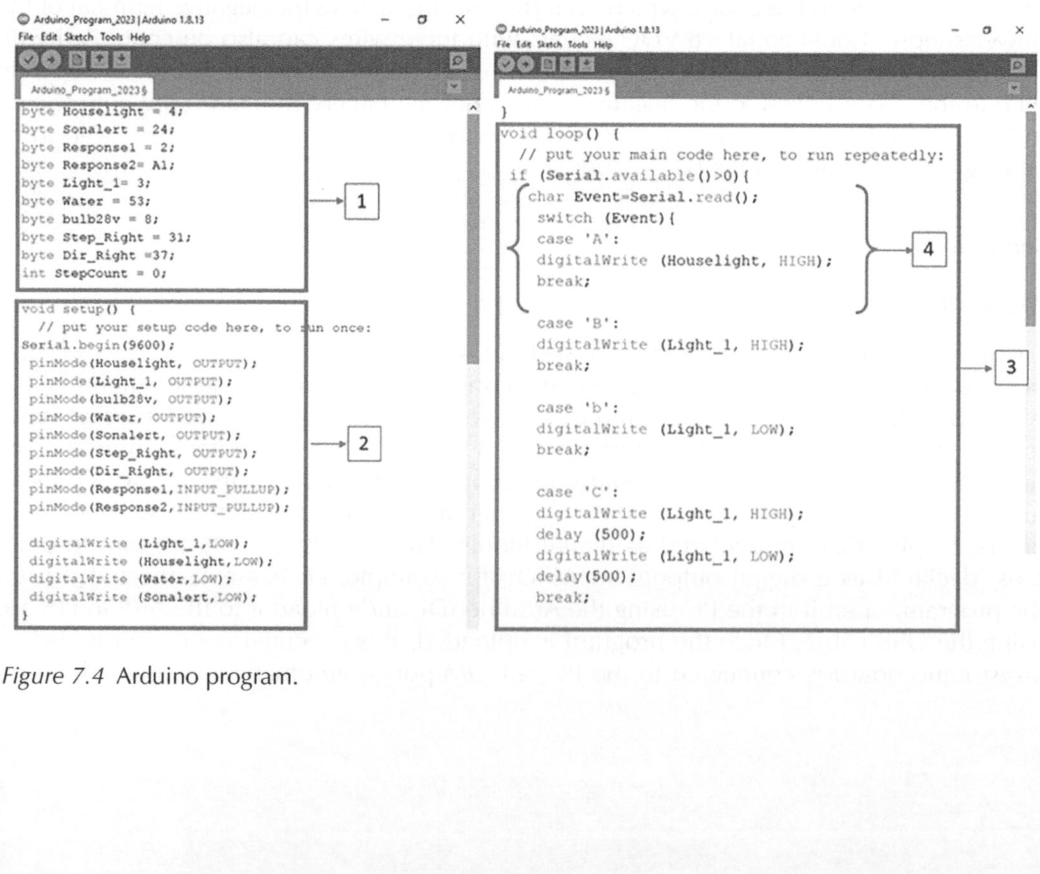

Figure 7.4 Arduino program.

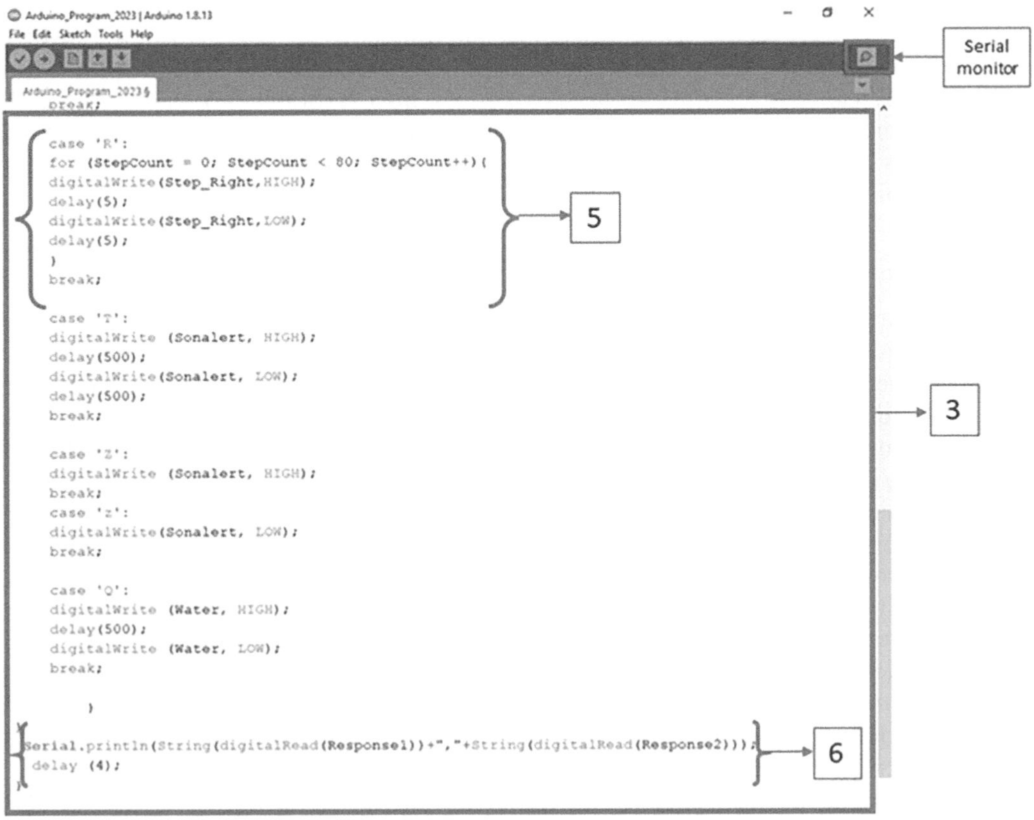

Figure 7.4 (Continued)

The third section of the program, identified as *"loop ()"* (see section 3 in Figure 7.4), executes continuously when the board is powered on. As in the setup section, the function *"digitalWrite()"* changes the state of the output pins. The function *"digitalRead()"* reads the state of the input pins. In the serial monitor (see upper-right section in Figure 7.3), the input value 1 is displayed when no response is detected, and 0 is displayed when a response is detected. The instruction *"char Event = Serial.read();"* reads values from the COM port and executes the corresponding code based on a symbolic code. For example, in the following lines, if the symbolic code *"A"* is detected in the COM port (sent to the COM port by the VB program), Pin 4, to which the house light is connected, is turned on.

In Figure 7.4 (cont.), the instructions after *case "R"* are executed when a symbolic code *"R"* is detected in the COM port. In this case, the axis of the stepper motor located inside the 3D printed feeder (see Escobar et al., 2022, p. 7) is rotated. The instructions control the number of steps required for the motor axis to rotate sufficiently for one pellet to be delivered into the food tray. When using the NEMA 17 stepper motor (17HS4401) in combination with the TB6560 driver (as shown in Figure 7.2), the values are set as *"for (StepCount = 0; StepCount < 80< StepCount++)"* (see section 5 in Figure 7.4 cont.).

To send the values of input pins to the COM port, the statement *"Serial.println (String (digitalRead (Name));"* is required. The instruction *Serial.println (String (digitalRead*

(Response1));" sends the value of 1 or 0 depending on the state of the switch connected to Pin 2. To record a second response simultaneously, as shown in the last two lines of the Arduino code, the instructions must be concatenated: *"Serial.println (String (digitalRead (Response1)) + "," + (String (digitalRead (Response2))); delay (4);"*. The delay at the end avoids reading errors. It is important to note that for both the setup and loop sections, code must be enclosed in curly braces ({}) to compile (see section 6 in Figure 7.4 cont.).

Visual Basic Program

The experimental procedures and the graphic interface are programmed in VB. In this updated version of the Arduino-VB interface, we used VB included in Visual Studio Community Edition 2022 IDE. VB is chosen because it is easy to learn, can communicate with Arduino boards using relatively simple instructions, and is free to use for academic purposes and classroom demonstrations. There are numerous examples of programs available that can be used as the basis for creating new experimental procedures (see e.g., Cabello et al., 2002; Dixon & McLin, 2003). It is used by a vast community of users; hence it is easy to find support online. Visual Studio IDE, containing Visual Basic, can be downloaded from https://visualstudio.microsoft.com/. Select the .NET desktop development option during installation.

A graphic interface can be created easily with VB using Windows Forms application programming interface (API). Forms are made up of two main components. One is the *Design Window,* which is the window that is seen when programs are initiated. The other is the *Code Window,* which contains the code responsible for the form's operation. The VB IDE enables users to customize the initially empty form as needed. Commonly used objects such as *Buttons, TextBoxes,* and *Labels* are already prebuilt and ready to be added.

A sample program can be downloaded from GitHub (https://github.com/RogerEsc/Arduino_Visual_Basic_2025). Note that for this sample program to function, the Arduino program described earlier must already be loaded onto the Arduino board and the board should be connected to the PC using the USB cable. The VB sample program is designed to work with one or two operanda with simple and concurrent schedules of reinforcement and includes two main forms (Set-up and Main).

The upper section of Figure 7.5 shows the *Design Window* of the Set-up form. In this form, users enter session data and specify the COM port assigned to the Arduino board connected to the PC. Users can select the schedule of reinforcement, fixed ratio (FR), variable ratio (VR), fixed interval (FI), or variable interval (VI), and if it is simple or two concurrent schedules. The user specifies a value x for the selected schedule and a maximum number of reinforcers to end the session. Variable ratio schedules utilize VB's random number generator to ensure that reinforcers are presented unpredictably. VR schedule values are determined by selecting a random value between $x / 2$ and $x \times 1.5$. VI schedules are calculated using Fleshler and Hoffman's iterative equation (see Hantula, 1991).

The lower section of Figure 7.5 shows the *Design Window* of the Main form. This form is displayed after selecting the values of the schedules and clicking the *Start* button in the Set-up form. The Main form shows real-time information on the session. In this sample program, it displays the number of obtained reinforcers per schedule, the number of responses per lever, the availability of the next reinforcer, and the elapsed session time. If the user wishes to end the session before reaching the maximum number of reinforcers, it is recommended to use the *Finish* button instead of the close control in the upper-right corner of the window. The *Finish* button ensures the correct termination of processes and serial communication with the Arduino board, preventing data loss and errors.

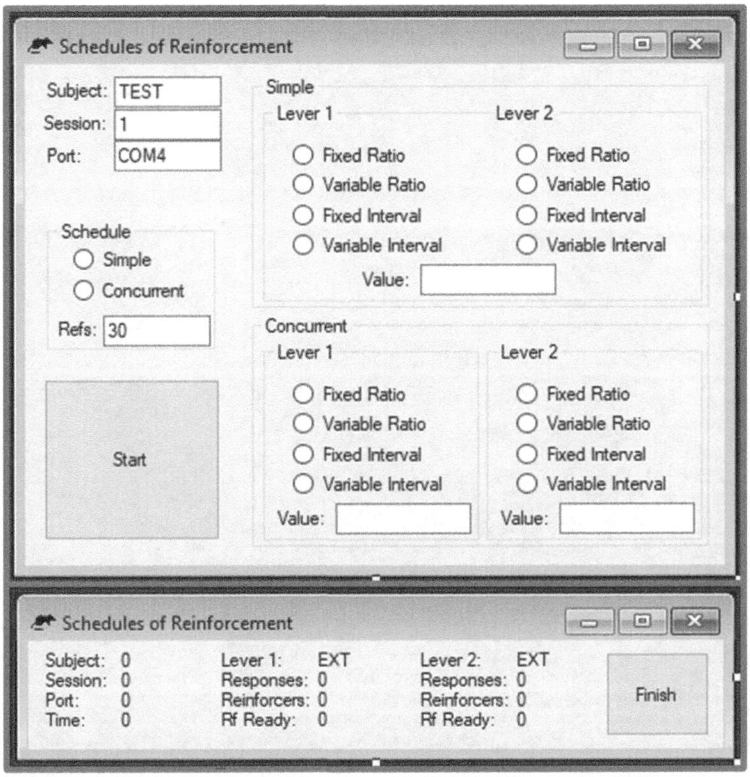

Figure 7.5 Visual Basic user interface.

The upper section of Figure 7.6 shows the code required to communicate with the Arduino board. When executed, the *ArduinoVB()* function creates a new connection at the selected COM with a 9600 baud rate. In this example, the time at the beginning of the session is recorded and the selected reinforcement schedules loaded. The *Do Loop* instruction encompasses the code responsible for reading data sent from the Arduino board. In simple terms, when serial data sent by the Arduino are detected in the COM port (1 or 0), each value is stored into a variable (*Actual_Response*); afterwards, the program compares if the state of the variable is different from the previous state (*Previous_Response*). If the program detects a difference, it executes the *Response()* function, which increases response counters and interacts with the schedule of reinforcement. The instruction *My.Application.DoEvents()* enables the rest of the programs to run while the *DoLoop* block handles Arduino data.

The program generates a data file to record responses and experimental events. Users must create a *Data* folder in the PC's main directory (*C:\Data*) to store the data files. If the folder is missing, an error will be encountered. The code responsible for creating the data file is located in the upper section of Figure 7.6 (*FileOpen(1, [File], OpenMode.Append)*).

The *FileOpen()* function creates a .txt file in the *Data* folder. The filename includes the subject and the session ID. The *WriteLine()* function stores responses or environmental events with a time stamp in milliseconds. For example, in the lower-right section of Figure 7.6, the *WriteLine()* function records the value in *vTimeNow*, which is an integer variable holding

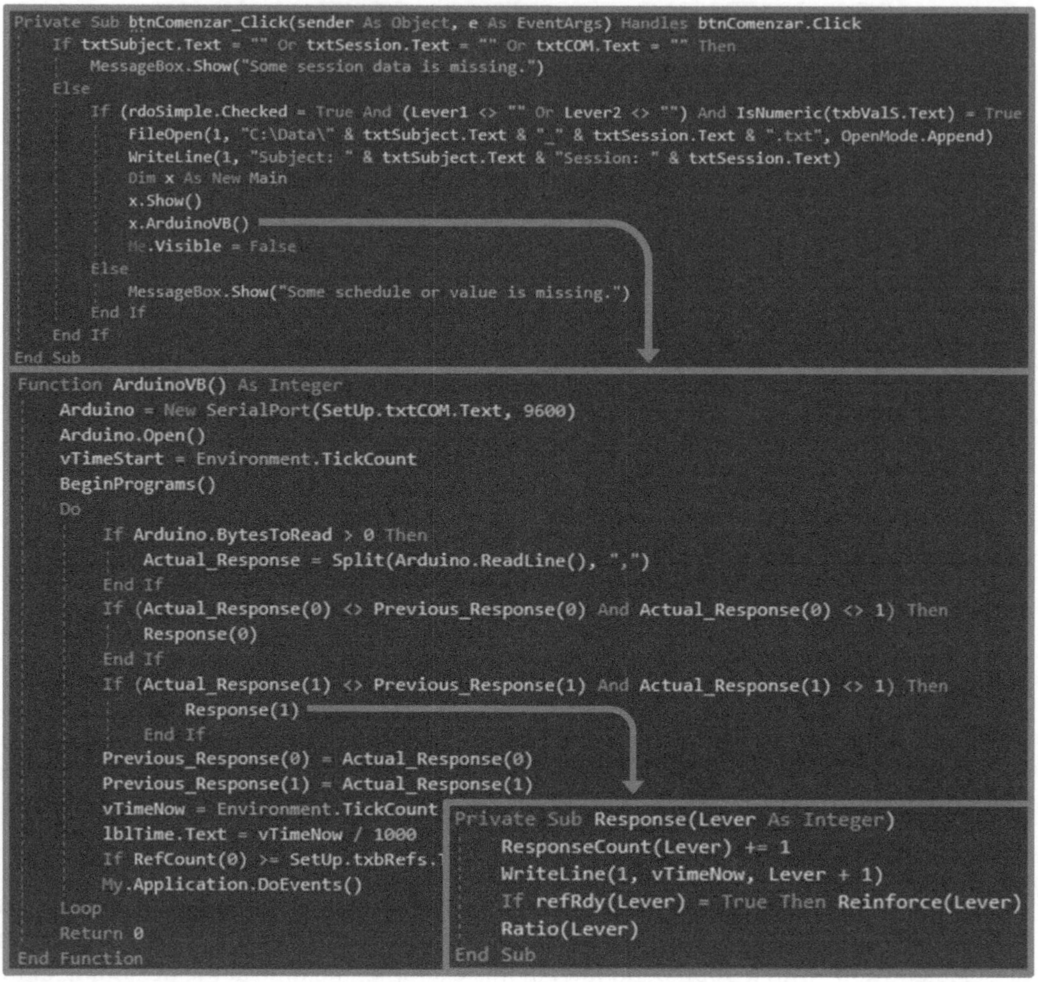

```
Private Sub btnComenzar_Click(sender As Object, e As EventArgs) Handles btnComenzar.Click
    If txtSubject.Text = "" Or txtSession.Text = "" Or txtCOM.Text = "" Then
        MessageBox.Show("Some session data is missing.")
    Else
        If (rdoSimple.Checked = True And (Lever1 <> "" Or Lever2 <> "") And IsNumeric(txbValS.Text) = True
            FileOpen(1, "C:\Data\" & txtSubject.Text & "_" & txtSession.Text & ".txt", OpenMode.Append)
            WriteLine(1, "Subject: " & txtSubject.Text & "Session: " & txtSession.Text)
            Dim x As New Main
            x.Show()
            x.ArduinoVB()
            Me.Visible = False
        Else
            MessageBox.Show("Some schedule or value is missing.")
        End If
    End If
End Sub

Function ArduinoVB() As Integer
    Arduino = New SerialPort(SetUp.txtCOM.Text, 9600)
    Arduino.Open()
    vTimeStart = Environment.TickCount
    BeginPrograms()
    Do
        If Arduino.BytesToRead > 0 Then
            Actual_Response = Split(Arduino.ReadLine(), ",")
        End If
        If (Actual_Response(0) <> Previous_Response(0) And Actual_Response(0) <> 1) Then
            Response(0)
        End If
        If (Actual_Response(1) <> Previous_Response(1) And Actual_Response(1) <> 1) Then
                Response(1)
            End If
        Previous_Response(0) = Actual_Response(0)
        Previous_Response(1) = Actual_Response(1)
        vTimeNow = Environment.TickCount
        lblTime.Text = vTimeNow / 1000
        If RefCount(0) >= SetUp.txbRefs.T
        My.Application.DoEvents()
    Loop
    Return 0
End Function

Private Sub Response(Lever As Integer)
    ResponseCount(Lever) += 1
    WriteLine(1, vTimeNow, Lever + 1)
    If refRdy(Lever) = True Then Reinforce(Lever)
    Ratio(Lever)
End Sub
```

Figure 7.6 Visual Basic program.

the current time of the session. *Lever + 1* generates the response code (1 or 2). Thus, each line in the data file records the time of the session in milliseconds, followed by a comma and the lever in which the response occurred (e.g., "212937,1"). Subsequent executions of the *WriteLine()* function will append additional data on the next line of the data file. For analysis, data files can be imported from Excel, R, or any other processing software that works with data in CSV format.

Further details of the VB program, such as the code-generating reinforcement schedules, can be found in the comments added within the code. These comments were added to facilitate understanding of the code and to assist in adapting it to other experimental procedures. This program was created to exemplify basic functioning of reinforcement schedules with the Arduino-VB interface. It can be used as is for lab courses or demonstrations, or it can serve as the basis to create more complex procedures for research purposes.

Final Remarks

Conducting research or teaching demonstrations of operant conditioning principles using commercial operant conditioning chambers has become increasingly difficult. Behavioral scientists and instructors often face the challenges of securing sufficient funding to cover the high costs of equipment for operant research. This is particularly challenging for young researchers in developing countries because of limited funding and the additional expenses related to shipping costs and import taxes for bulky and expensive equipment. Budget cuts for basic science in many countries following the COVID-19 pandemic have also augmented the problem. The Arduino-VB interface, as described in this chapter, is compatible with 3D printed devices such as feeders, water pumps, retractable levers, and photocells (see Escobar et al., 2022). Consequently, it provides affordable access to precise and flexible equipment for studying behavior, serving as an aid for teaching behavior principles and conducting innovative operant research.

Authors' Note

This work was supported by UNAM-PAPIIT IN304824.

References

Cabello, F., Barnes-Holmes, D., O'Hora, D., & Stewart, I. (2002). Using visual basic in the experimental analysis of human behavior: A brief introduction. *Experimental Analysis of Human Behavior Bulletin, 20*, 18–21.

Dixon, M. R., & MacLin, O. H. (2003). *Visual Basic for behavioral psychologists*. Context.

Escobar, R. (2014). From relays to microcontrollers: The adoption of technology in operant research. *Mexican Journal of Behavior Analysis, 40*, 127–153. https://doi.org/10.5514/rmac.v40.i2.63673

Escobar, R., Gutiérrez, B., & Benavides, R. (2022). 3D-printed operant chambers for rats: Design, assembly, and innovations. *Behavioural Processes, 199*, 104647. https://doi.org/10.1016/j.beproc.2022.104647

Escobar, R., & Pérez-Herrera, C. A. (2015). Low-cost USB interface for operant research using Arduino and Visual Basic. *Journal of the Experimental Analysis of Behavior, 103*(2), 427–435. https://doi.org/10.1002/jeab.135

Escobar, R., & Santillán, N. (2017). New technologies applied to operant research: Inexpensive photocells for the Arduino-Visual Basic interface. *Mexican Journal of Behavior Analysis, 43*, 242–253. https://doi.org/10.5514/rmac.v43.i2.62315

Hantula, D. A. (1991). A simple BASIC program to generate values for variable-interval schedules of reinforcement. *Journal of Applied Behavior Analysis, 24*(4), 799–801. https://doi.org/10.1901/jaba.1991.24-799

Palya, W. L., & Walter, D. E. (1993). A powerful, inexpensive experiment controller or IMB PC interface and experiment control language. *Behavior Research Methods, Instruments, & Computers, 25*, 127–136. https://doi.org/10.3758/BF03204485

Varnon, C. A., & Abramson, C. I. (2013). The propeller experiment controller: Low-cost automation for classroom experiments in learning and behavior. *Comprehensive Psychology, 2*, 1–18. https://doi.org/10.2466/07.08.IT.2.2

Varnon, C. A., Lang, H., & Abramson, C. I. (2018). Automated research in comparative psychology: Limitations and new directions. *International Journal of Comparative Psychology, 31*. https://doi.org/10.46867/ijcp.2018.31.01.08

Walter, D. E., & Palya, W. L. (1984). An inexpensive experiment controller for stand-alone applications or distributed processing networks. *Behavior Research Methods, Instruments, & Computers, 16*, 125–134. https://doi.org/10.3758/BF03202370

8 Simulation-Based Assessment and Training

Ellie Kazemi, Brianna Herrera, Matthew S. Davies, Adisa Ptah, Eric McCoy, and Victor Ramirez

Introduction

Simulation-based training and evaluation have emerged as powerful tools as the demand for specialized skills and competency-based training grows in education and workforce skills development. In healthcare, a simulation is "a technique that creates a situation or environment to allow persons to experience a representation of the real healthcare event for practice, learning, evaluation, testing, or to gain an understanding of systems and human actions" (Healthcare Simulation Dictionary, 2020, p. 21). Although there were birthing simulators as early as 1600 (Aebersold, 2016), simulations did not gain popularity until researchers showed that they could be as effective as learning by working directly with patients (e.g., Cook, 2013). Today, simulations can be optimized by leveraging digital technology to create immersive, realistic environments that provide real-world learning and evaluation opportunities without the associated risks. However, we contend that developing effective simulations for training and evaluation requires knowledge of the science of learning, behavior, and instructional design. Fortunately, as described next, many behavior analysts are familiar with developing simulations.

Simulations in Behavior Analysis

Behavior analysts have successfully designed simulations over the past several decades for training, evaluation of skills, and experimental analysis of human behavior. For example, by using simulations, behavior analysts have effectively taught laundry machine operating skills (Neef et al., 1990), work skills (Lattimore et al., 2006), firearm safety to typically developing children (Maxfield et al., 2019), pedestrian safety skills (Page et al., 1976), and bus riding skills to adults with developmental disabilities (Neef et al., 1978).

Neef et al. (1990) used simulated washing and drying machines to teach four individuals diagnosed with intellectual and developmental disabilities (IDD) to do laundry. The machines were constructed of cardboard, Styrofoam, and discarded machine parts (knobs and levers). A trainer taught participants to utilize the washer and dryer and then recorded their responses on a task analysis. Participants demonstrated similar responses to both in vivo and simulated machines; however, the simulated machines were more cost-effective and portable. Lattimore et al. (2006) conducted a study in which they trained four individuals diagnosed with autism and severe or profound IDD to complete their supported work duties. They created a simulated environment that closely resembled the individuals' actual job sites by using materials from the job sites and similar materials when the originals could not be transported. A job coach trained the participants across both simulated and job-site environments. They found that job site plus simulation-based training (training at the job site

DOI: 10.4324/9781003380603-11

combined with simulation-based training at another location) enhanced on-the-job training results, thus resulting in quicker acquisition of skills. Alexander et al. (2013) used a simulated environment and video model to teach a mail-sorting task. Participants included seven 15-to-18-year-old students diagnosed with autism. The study took place in two separate classrooms to simulate the school-wide mailroom, which was equipped with a mailbox containing labels of the names of teachers on top of a filing cabinet or table and mail for sorting. The researchers found that small-scale simulations, in addition to video modeling, could be effective in teaching generalized matching skills.

Maxfield et al. (2019) examined the effectiveness of simulations for teaching firearm safety skills to four young, typically developing children. The simulation consisted of a small-scale model environment crafted from wood, patterned paper, and cloth. The model house included furniture, plants, and appliances. It consisted of two bedrooms, a living room, a dining room, a kitchen, and a bathroom, with no ceiling, so the spaces were open and visible to the participants. They trained the participants on gun safety skills utilizing the simulation and recorded their adherence in simulated and in situ environments. They found that small-scale simulation-based training could be an effective method of training firearm safety skills. More recently, Sureshkumar and Zonneveld (2024) used simulation for first aid training of five children with IDD to perform first aid on themselves for insect stings, minor cuts, and minor burns. The researchers used photoshopped images of similar injuries, injury stickers, dental sticks, artificial blood, Vaseline, and Q-tips to simulate the injuries. All children learned the first aid skills, and the effects generalized to novel confederates and maintained for a minimum of four weeks. Mery et al. (2022) used a pyramidal model of training to train medical students to teach safe infant sleep environments to their patients. The researchers simulated infant sleep environments using a portable crib with an accompanying mattress and a baby mannequin. They also used safe and unsafe items such as oversized sheets, mattress pad toppers, a pacifier, a pacifier with attachment, a blanket, a teether, crib bumpers, plush toys, and drool bibs to place in the crib area. All participants arranged safe sleep environments and learned to teach others safe sleep practices.

Behavior analysts have also used simulations to gain experimental control and study behavior. For example, Thompson et al. (2011) conducted an experimental analysis to understand parenting behaviors. They observed 11 undergraduate students under simulated caregiving conditions. The simulation was conducted in a six-by-eight-foot room equipped with a crib, blanket, baby doll, and tape recorder. The experimenters controlled the crying sounds on the recorder from an adjoining room and measured the rate of caregiving responses (e.g., rocking the baby, changing diapers, bottle feeding) to the simulated baby. The results provided evidence that caregiving responses were controlled by negative reinforcement (i.e., escape from the recorded infant cry). In a different study, Thompson et al. (2011) studied what caregivers are likely to do when the baby continues to cry. Collectively, these studies demonstrate that simulation-based methods can be used effectively for teaching and analyzing behavior across diverse contexts. The versatility of simulations across contexts, from daily living to safety and caregiving, establishes a strong foundation for their integration with structured training models such as Behavior Skills Training.

Behavior Skills Training (BST) With Simulations

BST involves a sequential cycle of providing instructions, modeling correct steps in the procedures, allowing practice opportunities, and providing feedback until the skills reach a preset criterion for mastery. BST can incorporate simulations to give the learners examples, role-play, practice, and feedback opportunities in various situations. There are at least three different ways BST instructors can incorporate simulations. First, the instructor can simulate behaviors in which a patient, client, or student engages in either a group of learners or on a 1:1 basis. The instructor may follow a predetermined script or change the simulation in vivo based on the needs of each learner. Second, an instructor can ask peers to role-play and can have one individual play the part of a client as the other individual practices the trained skills. Again, during peer-mediated simulations, the instructor can provide a predetermined script to the peer simulating a client for structured role-play or can ask that the peer emit particular behaviors using a less structured format. Third, an actor can play the role of a client as learners interact with them. In most cases, actors are provided with scripts. Last, simulations can have a high level of verisimilitude to the real-world environment (e.g., the context of a clinic with an actor similar in age to the client) or can be low budget and include only essential components for practice.

Advantages of Tech-Based Simulations

We contend that behavior analysts are uniquely trained to develop effective simulations because of their knowledge of learning principles and behavior measurement. Without this knowledge, it may be much harder to develop simulations that have stimuli with similar evocative effects as the real world, select appropriate dimensions of behavior for measurement, program events to affect choice, entice motivation, create performance-contingent consequences that improve learning, and promote stimulus transfer and generalization. Additionally, we contend that knowledge and skills in a specific subject area of the science of behavior, known as instructional design, are necessary for tech-based simulation innovations (see Layng & Twyman, 2013). With additional training and experience in instructional design, behavior analysts are excellent candidates for engineering digital simulation-based training environments.

Research evidence suggests that simulation-based training is an effective educational modality that improves learners' skills and patient outcomes (Edwards et al., 2023; Cook et al., 2011). Simulations allow trainers to provide as many practice opportunities as needed in safe and controlled environments and optimize learning by customizing the simulation based on the learner's needs.

In his book *Experience on Demand*, Bailenson (2018) provided guidelines for determining when and how to use virtual reality (VR), which we feel highlights the advantages of simulations. He coined the term DICE (dangerous, impossible, counterproductive, or expensive or rare). The first component of DICE is "dangerous." This relates to situations that involve significant physical or emotional risk. Simulations can be used to create hazardous scenarios without exposing learners or performers to actual harm. For example, learners can be exposed to high-intensity, rare crisis situations such as high levels of patient self-injury or aggression without risk of harm. The second component of DICE is "impossible." This pertains to experiences that may be impossible to achieve due to physical constraints or ethical considerations. For example, learners can be in a simulated virtual house fire and asked to demonstrate fire escape skills. The third component of DICE, "counterproductive," refers to situations when the learner would benefit from undergoing an experience but the experience itself may be counterproductive. For example, simulations are a great way to demonstrate the dangers of texting and driving or going up a ladder without a helmet with heavy things in hand. The last component, "expensive or rare," calls for experiences that may be too expensive or rare to access in the real world. For example, simulating a flight experience or situations requiring travel can save on costs and provide easy access to environments not readily available. Advancements in technology increase the scalability of such training, optimizing opportunities to take advantage of simulation-based training. Tech-based simulations also allow programming for more exemplars and dynamic, instead of static, simulations in which the environment changes based on the performer's behaviors.

Simulations allow for objective, repeated measures of practical skills as a means of evaluation. They can be used to measure pre- and post-training skills, improvements across training exposures, and generally any behavior(s) under various situations. Also, the same simulation and metrics can be used across different performers, allowing for more standardized assessment procedures.

Social Validity

Walsh et al. (2017) found that participants like simulation-based training because it provides them with multiple opportunities to practice and acquire a skill in a safe environment. Participants report higher confidence in their ability to carry out the procedures correctly. Additionally, participants perceive their performance scores as fair and objective.

Leveraging Technology for Scalability

Despite the many advantages of using simulations for training and evaluation, currently, several challenges minimize their scalability. First, developing and carrying out simulation-based training takes considerable time and effort. Even if the simulations are predeveloped, the training method requires a trainer skilled in doing the procedures themselves and observing and providing corrective feedback until the skills are attained. As a result, current simulation-based training is difficult to scale up because it is hard to provide controlled, meaningful practice opportunities and individualized feedback to large groups. Furthermore, multiple exemplar training is needed for the performer's skills to generalize to real-world settings, and the additional examples add to the training and feedback time. The effort and time required for providing adequate practice and feedback opportunities may explain why organizations shy away from providing them (Blackman et al., 2022) despite the importance of these components for skills training. However, as digital technology advances rapidly, there are new and exciting ways to leverage technology to develop simulations that can be recycled and minimally rely on skilled professionals for training, evaluation, and feedback.

Virtual Reality

VR refers to different degrees of user immersion in interactive, computer-generated environments (Pan et al., 2006). VR utilization ranges from point-and-click interactions on a desktop computer to headsets that completely immerse the user in the virtual environment. VR-based training has been used in various professions, including customer service (Harvard Business School Publishing, 2020), fire safety (e.g., Çakıroğlu & Gökoğlu, 2019), and healthcare (e.g., Liaw et al., 2020).

For example, Çakıroğlu and Gökoğlu (2019) used a virtual environment of a house on fire to facilitate training fire-safety skills for 10 child participants. The children used a head-monitoring display and a joystick to interact with the virtual environment, in which researchers provided BST for engaging in fire-safety behaviors (e.g., leaving the area, notifying nearby adults/fire department) and recorded data on a task analysis. Using the virtual environment, participants rehearsed, received feedback, and reached mastery criteria on all target behaviors without any associated risks of practicing in an in situ environment.

Behavior analysts also have found evidence that virtual reality trainings (VRTs) can be an effective way to train clinical skills (e.g., Carnett et al., 2023; Clay et al., 2021). For example, Clay et al. (2021) used BST in VR to train 13 college students with no previous experience in providing behavior-analytic services and functional communication training. The virtual environment consisted of a simulated treatment room with furniture, session materials (e.g., pen and paper), and a virtual client. Although the instruction and feedback were provided in vivo, the modeling and rehearsal occurred within the virtual environment. The participants engaged with the environment and client using a headset, headphones, two mounts, and handheld controllers (Clay et al., 2021). The virtual client followed a preprogrammed script for either attention-maintained or escape-maintained behavior, and the accuracy of participants' responses was scored and coded by a research assistant. By engaging in the procedures within the virtual environment, the participants could be exposed to and practice simulated problem behaviors that may be difficult, unsafe, or unethical to replicate in vivo (Clay et al., 2021). All participants reached mastery criteria within the virtual environment, although researchers did not test for in vivo generalization.

In a systematic literature review of VR training, Chang et al. (2023) evaluated the efficacy, generality of skills, and presence of BST components. The authors found that VR was effective in training children and adults with and without disabilities, skills ranging from bystander intervention to job interview skills. The authors found that, of the 20 articles reviewed, only 5 included all components of BST; however, all the articles included rehearsal and feedback (Chang et al., 2023). The 15 articles that tested for generality also found that the skills generalized. Tests for generality included in-person role-play, job acquisition following job skills training, and self-report measures (Chang et al., 2023). Across the articles reviewed, the level of human trainer facilitation in VRT varied. Some incorporated human operators to control avatars, others relied on humans solely to provide training instructions, and certain others did not involve human operators in active training components (Chang et al., 2023).

Robotics

Another medium for developing simulations is robots. The International Federation of Robotics defines a robot as "an actuated programmable mechanism that has a degree of freedom in two or more axes, has some level of autonomy, and can complete tasks" (Onyeulo & Gandhi, 2020). Robots can be used in two ways. First, human operators can control a robot remotely through a computer, often termed "Wizard of Oz" control. This approach allows real-time modifications and adaptability to unforeseen circumstances or technical challenges but requires the availability of a human operator. The second mode is autonomous control, whereby robots independently and autonomously conduct the training. Like VR, a human is still required for technical support when the robot is autonomous.

Humanoid robots have humanlike appearances and allow the learner to interact with the simulation by manipulating the physical environment instead of a response on a joystick or other operandum within a virtual world. For this reason, using robots for simulation-based training has gained some recognition recently. In medical care, robotized mannequins (referred to as high-fidelity mannequins) are commonly used as patient simulators for medical practitioners to practice procedures (Mitchell & Ivimey-Cook, 2023). Similarly, in education and behavior analysis, the NAO robot by SoftBank Robotics has been utilized to teach various skills, including answering wh-questions (e.g., who, what, when; Korneder et al., 2021), conducting paired choice and multiple stimuli without replacement preference assessments (Kazemi & Stedman-Falls, 2016), and conducting differential reinforcement procedures (Loftizadeh et al., 2024).

Extended Reality (XR)

XR is a universal term for all immersive learning technologies, including VR, augmented reality (AR), and mixed reality (MR). The future of simulation training likely involves more than one of these mediums. For example, integrating robots into virtual worlds involves augmented reality because three-dimensional physical simulators are mixed with computer-generated ones. The integration of visual simulations with three-dimensional stimuli that can be touched, pressed, and moved in the physical world makes the possibilities for simulations infinite. Mitchell and Ivimey-Cook (2023) conducted a meta-analysis reviewing technology-enhanced simulations in healthcare. They found that the simulations that included VR and high-fidelity mannequins obtained the greatest training outcomes compared to those with VR sensory environments alone. Similarly, Iqbal et al. (2021) recruited 10 surgeons to examine whether robot-assisted surgery (RAS) plus AR had improved outcomes when compared to RAS alone in orthopedic surgery. The AR system projected the display of the RAS at the user's chosen location within their physical environment and could be relocated through vocal or gestural commands. This allowed users to place the RAS at eye level with the RAS controls they were utilizing, providing the necessary information in a central location. The participants performed similarly across both study conditions and reported that they found the AR addition useful in conducting the surgery.

Artificial Intelligence (AI)

Simulation-based training has evolved to integrate advanced technologies, such as AI. From evaluating large datasets in near real-time to online purchase recommendations, AI has become fundamentally ingrained within many facets of society and often operates in the background of our personal devices (Helm et al., 2020). Primarily within healthcare, AI systems have been embedded into simulation-based training (e.g., robotic surgery training, interprofessional communication training, and VRT), allowing nurses, surgeons, and medical students to experience AI-facilitated self-guided training. Improvements in trainee performance have been demonstrated with comparable effects to in-person feedback delivery (Liaw et al., 2023).

The integration of AI allows researchers to measure trainees' performance accurately and provide individualized automated feedback without the need for human intervention. For example, Ward and Esposito (2018) used a VRT embedded with AI to train job interview skills to 12 adults with high-functioning autism spectrum disorder. In this training, participants were given a laptop computer and a headset with a microphone to answer job interview questions presented by a virtual interviewer. Participants received feedback on their answers in the following forms: tone and expression changes from the virtual interviewer, gestures such as a thumbs-up from an on-screen virtual assistant, and varying textual feedback during and after each session. In addition to presenting instructional modules, rehearsal, and feedback, the VRT system automatically collected and analyzed data for the target behaviors, demonstrating statistically significant improvement (Ward & Esposito, 2018).

Mirchi et al. (2020) tasked 28 skilled and 22 novice participants to perform a VR surgical task on the NeuroVR simulator. The simulator generated large amounts of data from everyone's performance across several benchmarks, including maximum force applied by the user, rate of bleeding of a simulated patient, mean distance between the tip of the surgical instruments, and mean acceleration of the surgical instruments. The AI system embedded within the simulator analyzed trainee performance and provided automated feedback through auditory and video-based instruction specific to the areas of improvement identified. The authors found that this individualized automated feedback improved trainee performance. Additionally, the AI system was able to capture novel surgical performance metrics, such as force utilization, that are too difficult to capture through human-facilitated feedback. Trainers could identify individual components of psychomotor expertise in tasks too complex to measure without AI technology.

Figure 8.1 depicts the machine learning process. Raw data such as text, speech, and images go through feature extraction, wherein specific aspects of the data, such as facial features and voice patterns, are targeted. These features are then decoded through a feature selection process, and labels or classifiers are applied to help narrow the amount of information fed into the machine learning algorithm. Then, the machine validates the accuracy of the data by applying performance measures and creates outputs (e.g., images, videos, speech, and text). Just as with any learning process, the process we describe here is reiterative as the machine learning algorithm trains the AI system to adjust its labels or classifiers to optimize the accuracy of the machine learning algorithm through reinforcement learning. Model selection generates new rules for the AI system on how to process new raw data, and a predictive model is generated that allows expected labels or classifiers to be applied to future raw data more efficiently and accurately.

AI models evolve through a cyclic process driven by data and reiteration. Raw data can be collected at various points in a simulation, forming the foundation for the model. The data is then preprocessed, cleaned, normalized, and extracted to enhance usability. The beauty of AI models is that they are reiterative and undergo training to minimize errors between predictions and actual data gathered on training. The iterative cycle of AI leads to continuous improvement in its performance and adaptability, optimizing the accuracy of skill assessment, effective and automated feedback delivery, and overall task efficiency.

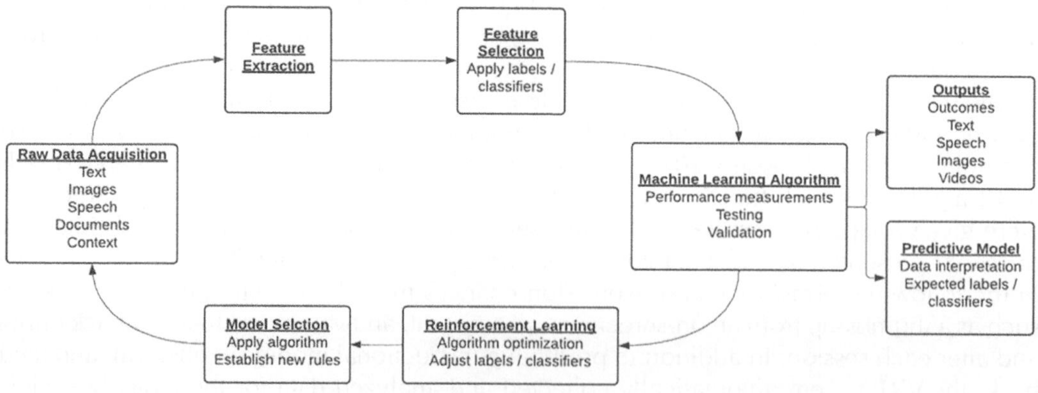

Figure 8.1 Framework for the machine learning process.

Future Directions

Although the future of simulation-based training and evaluation seems very promising for education and skills development, it is important for behavior analysts to proceed with some caution. Here we outline a few areas for discussion and consideration.

Ethical Considerations Around Data Usage

Behavior analysts must consider their ethical obligations as computer technology is integrated into daily life. There are concerns regarding data usage (i.e., data availability, data quality, and data privacy). Safekeeping personal data is important; however, sharing data plays a vital role in the development and research of simulation-based training and evaluation. Currently, healthcare data may be too insufficient and scarce for AI to analyze and make informed decisions for training (Sun & Medaglia, 2019). Additionally, there may be inconsistencies or a general lack of data since the variables measured are inconsistent across entities or organizations (Aung et al., 2021; Sun & Medaglia, 2019). If an AI makes informed decisions utilizing data that is lacking or inconsistent, the AI will be just that – lacking and inconsistent. When it comes to assessing and analyzing data, behavior analysts must ensure they are taking measures to protect the data gathered. This can be achieved through prevention measures like classifying the data to ensure confidentiality and sharing data obtained through AI-led trainings for collaboration and advancement. Behavior analysts are responsible for protecting the data obtained from trainees and preventing data breaches (BACB, 2020).

Generality of Skills

One of the biggest considerations when deciding to implement simulation-based training is the transfer of skills to an in situ environment. Simulation-based training may lead to acquired and generalized skills; however, there are simulation-based trainings where generality may not occur. There is a concern of trainees cheating the simulation-based training and not actually acquiring the skills when a trainer is absent (Mirchi et al., 2020). Additionally, the simulation-based training itself may not be effective, meaning it may not train the appropriate skills or skills do not generalize. Therefore, we recommend that simulation-based trainings be evaluated and validated prior to being implemented organizationally (Mirchi et al., 2020). We also recommend that a human trainer conducts post-probes after the simulation-based training to assess the acquisition of skills and generality (Aung et al., 2021) prior to organization-wide training.

Will Humans Be Replaced?

Undoubtedly, technology-based simulations are scalable because they rely less heavily on trained professionals to conduct training, evaluate performance, and provide individualized feedback.

Anytime technology can minimize the need for human intervention, fear arises with concerns about the technology replacing humans (Aung et al., 2021). Sometimes, the technology is comparable to or better than human interventionists. For example, large-scale data collection and live data synthesis are impossible for human beings. Additionally, machines are reliable and do not get tired or make emotional decisions. However, these advantages do not mean that machines are better than human interventionists or that humans are unnecessary. Instead, in places where technology provides advantages, for example, automated feedback based on individualized performance, such technologies can be leveraged to facilitate training under the supervision of qualified human trainers. Last, technology can help decrease burnout from paper-pushing and administrative tasks and allow clinicians to focus on the human aspect of human care services.

False Confidence

Another consideration is the confidence people have after undergoing simulation-based training. Walsh et al. (2017) interviewed participants who underwent medical simulation-based training. Participants reported feeling confident after undergoing the training due to having multiple opportunities to acquire the skill in a safe environment. Increasing confidence in those who provide clinical care can be impactful and empowering overall. However, a precaution is given about potential false confidence in trainees who have undergone simulation-based training. A trainee may experience the role differently in a simulation and may feel as if they are prepared to begin services across from a real client. However, their performance scores in the clinical setting may not reflect the same. We recommend competency assessments are conducted to ensure a learner's confidence does not overshadow their competency.

Cost-Benefit Analysis

Although AI-facilitated simulation training enables the recycling of training content and automation of individualized feedback, the upfront development time, delays due to technological errors, and costs for developing such platforms may be more of a headache than relying on skilled professionals to conduct the training and give feedback. However, with computerized training, there is a break-even point when the return on investment (i.e., costs to develop the training as compared to costs to facilitate training with a live trainer) occurs (e.g., Geiger et al., 2018). For example, in their analysis of computer simulation-based training on discrete trial training, Geiger et al. (2018) found that over time, the initial cost of developing the training broke even with the ongoing costs of the training provided by a clinical trainer. Bumbach et al. (2022) conducted an economic analysis and found that VR training was 40% lower in cost and required 22% less time than more traditional simulations to achieve the same learning outcomes. Overall, conducting a thorough cost-benefit analysis is important by factoring in the time and costs required for initial development, outcome assessment, solicitation of learner feedback, and revisions based on the feedback and assessment results until the training lends to the desired outcomes.

Equity, Bias, and Broader Impact

As simulation technologies and AI-driven training tools expand, behavior analysts must critically examine how these innovations may unintentionally reproduce or widen existing inequities. Algorithmic bias can emerge when training data reflect societal disparities, leading to differential access, feedback, or evaluation outcomes across racial, cultural, or linguistic groups (Benjamin, 2019). Moreover, reliance on high-cost or hardware-intensive technologies may exacerbate gaps between well-funded and resource-limited service providers, reducing equitable access to training. Beyond social justice concerns, the environmental footprint of large-scale computing also warrants attention, as the energy demands of

AI and virtual simulation systems contribute to broader sustainability issues. As Benjamin (2019) and others have noted, technological progress divorced from equity considerations risks deepening, rather than reducing, systemic inequities. Behavior analysts are uniquely positioned to promote responsible innovation, ensuring that simulation-based tools are designed, validated, and disseminated in ways that are inclusive, transparent, and ecologically sustainable.

Conclusion

The future technology is here, and behavior analysts must be involved to push it to the next level. Behavior analysts can help shape simulation training and evaluation by demonstrating the effectiveness of learning-centered development and placing it before technology-centered development (Logeswaran et al., 2021) so that developers can focus on the most pertinent aspects that facilitate learning. As society embraces AI, it will be a driving force in training efficiency. Platforms can be developed to optimize learning and individualize learning experiences and feedback. Generalization and maintenance probes can be conducted periodically, and AI systems can determine the most efficient schedule of targeted retraining to allow for optimal performance across time. When combined with the science of learning, accessible simulations such as those delivered through extended reality will significantly reduce the human burden as trainees can enter a training room and come out trained. In education and workforce skill development, remote training using digital technology can optimize the quality of training and subsequent care beyond what we can currently imagine but only if these systems are guided by principles of equity, transparency, and social responsibility. Behavior analysts have the opportunity, and the obligation, to ensure that the next generation of simulation-based tools amplifies human capability rather than replaces it, advancing both competence and compassion in applied practice. Grounding technological progress in the values of the science of behavior analysis, including measurable outcomes, ethical accountability, and respect for human dignity, positions behavior analysts to ensure that innovation remains both effective and just.

References

Aebersold, M. (2016). The history of simulation and its impact on the future. *AACN Advanced Critical Care, 27*(1), 56–61. https://doi.org/10.4037/aacnacc2016436

Alexander, J. L., Ayres, K. M., Smith, K. A., Shepley, S. B., & Mataras, T. K. (2013). Using video modeling on an iPad to teach generalized matching on a sorting mail task to adolescents with autism. *Research in Autism Spectrum Disorders, 7*(11), 1346–1357. https://doi.org/10.1016/j.rasd.2013.07.021

Aung, Y. Y. M., Wong, D. C. S., & Ting, D. S. W. (2021). The promise of artificial intelligence: A review of the opportunities and challenges of artificial intelligence in healthcare. *British Medical Bulletin, 139*(1), 4–15. https://doi.org/10.1093/bmb/ldab016

Bailenson, J. (2018). *Experience on demand: What virtual reality is, how it works, and what it can do*. WW Norton & Company.

Behavior Analyst Certification Board. (2020). *Ethics code for behavior analysts*. https://bacb.com/wp-content/ethics-code-for-behavior-analysts/

Benjamin, R. (2019). *Race after technology: Abolitionist tools for the new Jim code*. Polity Press.

Blackman, A. L., DiGennaro Reed, F. D., Erath, T. G., & Henley, A. J. (2022). A survey of staff training and performance management practices: An update. *Behavior Analysis in Practice*, 1–14. https://doi.org/10.1007/s40617-022-00762-0

Bumbach, M. D., Culross, B. A., & Datta, S. K. (2022). Assessing the financial sustainability of high-fidelity and virtual reality simulation for nursing education: A retrospective case analysis. *Computers, Informatics, Nursing: CIN, 40*(9), 615–623. https://doi.org/10.1097/CIN.0000000000000916

Çakıroğlu, Ü., & Gökoğlu, S. (2019). Development of fire safety behavioral skills via virtual reality. *Computers & Education, 133*, 56–68. https://doi.org/10.1016/j.compedu.2019.01.014

Carnett, A., Neely, L., Gardiner, S., Kirkpatrick, M., Quarles, J., & Christopher, K. (2023). Systematic review of virtual reality in behavioral interventions for individuals with autism. *Advances in Neurodevelopmental Disorders, 7*, 426–442. https://doi.org/10.1007/s41252-022-00287-1

Chang, A. A., Kazemi, E., Esmaeili, V., & Davies, M. S. (2023). The effectiveness of virtual reality trainings: A systematic review. *Journal of Organizational Behavior Management*. https://doi.org/10.1080/01608061.2023.2240767

Clay, C. J., Schmitz, B. A., Balakrishnan, B., Hopfenblatt, J. P., Evans, A., & Kahng, S. (2021). Feasibility of virtual reality behavior skills training for preservice clinicians. *Journal of Applied Behavior Analysis, 54*(2), 547–565. https://doi.org/10.1002/jaba.809

Cook, D. A. (2013, March 1). The literature on health care simulation education: What does it show? *Agency for Healthcare Research and Quality*. https://psnet.ahrq.gov/perspective/literature-health-care-simulation-education-what-does-it-show

Cook, D. A., Hatala, R., Brydges, R., Zendejas, B., Szostek, J. H., Wang, A. T., Erwin, P. J., & Hamstra, S. J. (2011). Technology-enhanced simulation for health professions education: A systematic review and meta-analysis. *Journal of the American Medical Association, 306*(9), 978–988. https://doi.org/10.1001/jama.2011.1234

Edwards, J. J., Nichols, A., & Bakerjian, D. (2023). *Simulation training*. Patient Safety Network. https://psnet.ahrq.gov/primer/simulation-training

Geiger, K. B., LeBlanc, L. A., Hubik, K., Jenkins, S. R, & Carr, J. E. (2018). Live training versus e-learning to teach implementation of listener response programs. *Journal of Applied Behavior Analysis, 51*(2), 220–235. https://doi.org/10.1002/Jaba.444

Harvard Business School Publishing. (2020). *The future of work is immersive* (Ser. Harvard Business Review Analytic Services, pp. 1–4). Harvard Business School Publishing.

Healthcare Simulation Dictionary. (2020). Agency for Healthcare Research and Quality eBooks. https://doi.org/10.23970/simulationv2

Helm, J. M., Swiergosz, A. M., Haeberle, H. S., Karnuta, J. M., Schaffer, J. L., Krebs, V. E., Spitzer, A. I., & Ramkumar, P. N. (2020). Machine learning and artificial intelligence: Definitions, applications, and future directions. *Current Reviews in Musculoskeletal Medicine, 13*(1), 69–76. https://doi.org/10.1007/s12178-020-09600

Iqbal, H., Tatti, F., & Rodriguez y Baena, F. (2021). Augmented reality in robotic assisted orthopaedic surgery: A pilot study. *Journal of Biomedical Informatics, 120*, 103841. https://doi.org/10.1016/j.jbi.2021.103841

Kazemi, E., & Stedman-Falls, L. M. (2016). Can humanoid robots serve as patient simulators in behavior analytic research and practice? *Behavior Analysis: Research and Practice, 16*(3), 135. http://dx.doi.org/10.1037/bar0000046

Korneder, J., Louie, W. Y. G., Pawluk, C. M., Abbas, I., Brys, M., & Rooney, F. (2021). Robot-mediated interventions for teaching children with ASD: A new intraverbal skill. *Assistive Technology, 34*(6), 707–716. https://doi.org/10.1080/10400435.2021.1930284

Lattimore, L. P., Parsons, M. B., & Reid, D. H. (2006). Enhancing job-site training of supported workers with autism: A reemphasis on simulation. *Journal of Applied Behavior Analysis, 39*(1), 91–102. https://doi.org/10.1901/jaba.2006.154-04

Layng, T. V. J., & Twyman, J. S. (2013). Education + technology + innovation = learning. In *Handbook on innovations in learning* (pp. 133–148). IAP Information Age Publishing.

Liaw, S. Y., Ooi, S. W., Rusli, K. D. B., Lau, T. C., Tam, W. W. S., & Chua, W. L. (2020). Nurse-physician communication team training in virtual reality versus live simulations: Randomized controlled trial on team communication and teamwork attitudes. *Journal of Medical Internet Research, 22*(4), e17279. https://doi.org/10.2196/17279

Liaw, S. Y., Tan, J., Lim, S., Zhou, W., Yap, J., Ratan, R., Ooi, S., Wong, S., Seah, B., & Chua, W. (2023). Artificial intelligence in virtual reality simulation for interprofessional communication training: Mixed method study. *Nurse Education Today, 122*. https://doi.org/10.1016/j.nedt.2023.105718

Loftizadeh, A., McCoy, E., & Kazemi, E. (2024). Robots as behavior change agents: Can robots teach behavior technicians to implement differential reinforcement? *Behavior Analysis: Research and Practice, 24*(3), 150–162. https://doi.org/10.1037/bar0000291

Logeswaran, A., Munsch, C., Chong, Y. J., Ralph, N., & McCrossnan, J. (2021). The role of extended reality technology in healthcare education: towards a learner-centred approach. *Future Healthcare Journal, 8*(1), e79–e84. https://doi.org/10.7861/fhj.2020-0112

Maxfield, T. C., Miltenberger, R. G., & Novotny, M. A. (2019). Evaluating small-scale simulation for training firearm safety skills. *Journal of Applied Behavior Analysis, 52*(2), 491–498. https://doi.org/10.1002/jaba.535

Mery, J. N., Vladescu, J. C., Day-Watkins, J., Sidener, T. M., Reeve, K. F., & Schnell, L. K. (2022). Training medical students to teach safe infant sleep environments using pyramidal behavioral skills training. *Journal of Applied Behavior Analysis, 55*(4), 1239–1257.

Mirchi, N., Bissonnette, V., Yilmaz, R., Ledwos, N., Winkler-Schwartz, A., Del Maestro, R. (2020). The virtual operative assistant: An explainable artificial intelligence tool for simulation-based training in surgery and medicine. *PLOS One, 15*, 1–15. https://doi.org/10.1371/journal.pone.0229596

Mitchell, A. A., & Ivimey-Cook, E. R. (2023). Technology-enhanced simulation for healthcare professionals: A meta-analysis. *Frontiers in Medicine, 10*, 1149048. https://doi.org/10.3389/fmed.2023.1149048

Neef, N. A., Iwata, B. A., & Page, T. J. (1978). Public transportation training: In vivo versus classroom instruction. *Journal of Applied Behavior Analysis, 11*, 331–344. https://doi.org/10.1901/jaba.1978.11-331

Neef, N. A., Lensbower, J., Hockersmith, I., DePalma, V., & Gray, K. (1990). In vivo versus simulation training: an interactional analysis of range and type of training exemplars. *Journal of Applied Behavior Analysis, 23*(4), 447–458. https://doi.org/10.1901/jaba.1990.23-447

Onyeulo, E. B., & Gandhi, V. (2020). What makes a social robot good at interacting with humans? *Information, 11*(1), 43. https://doi.org/10.3390/info11010043

Page, T. J., Iwata, B. A., & Neef, N. A. (1976). Teaching pedestrian skills to retarded persons: Generalization from the classroom to the natural environment. *Journal of Applied Behavior Analysis, 9*, 433–444. https://doi.org/10.1901/jaba.1976.9-433

Pan, Z., Cheok, A. D., Yang, H., Zhu, J., & Shi, J. (2006). Virtual reality and mixed reality for virtual learning environments. *Computers & Graphics, 30*(1), 20–28. https://doi.org/10.1016/j.cag.2005.10.004

Sun, T. Q., & Medaglia, R. (2019). Mapping the challenges of artificial intelligence in the public sector: Evidence from public healthcare. *Government Information Quarterly, 36*(2), 368–383. https://doi.org/10.1016/j.giq.2018.09.008

Sureshkumar, B. M., & Zonneveld, K. L. (2024). An evaluation of video-prompting procedures via telehealth to teach first aid skills to children with intellectual and developmental disabilities. *Journal of Applied Behavior Analysis, 57*(1), 104–116. https://doi.org/10.1002/jaba.1031

Thompson, R. H., Bruzek, J. L., & Cotnoir-Bichelman, N. M. (2011). The role of negative reinforcement in infant caregiving: An experimental simulation. *Journal of Applied Behavior Analysis, 44*(2), 295–304. https://doi.org/10.1901/jaba.2011.44-295

Walsh, C. M., Garg, A., Ng, S. L., Goyal, F., & Grover, S. C. (2017). Residents' perceptions of simulation as a clinical learning approach. *Canadian Medical Education Journal, 8*(1), e76–e87. https://doi.org/10.36834/cmej.36797

Ward, D. M., & Esposito, M. C. K. (2018). Virtual reality in transition program for adults with autism: Self-efficacy, confidence, and interview skills. *Contemporary School Psychology, 23*(4), 423–431. https://doi.org/10.1007/s40688-018-0195-9

9 Using Virtual Reality within Behavior Analysis Practice

Ana Escalante

From the Teaching Machine to Virtual Reality

Assessing the utility and efficacy of innovative educational and clinical technological tools is an area of research and inquiry within the field of applied behavior analysis (ABA). This topic has a long history in behavior analysis and educational applications. For example, Skinner (1968) described a technological tool that delivered systematic individualized instruction driven by the basic principles of behavior to help individuals attain meaningful learning outcomes. This learning tool, the teaching machine, delivered immediate feedback within learning sessions, allowing individuals to access immediate consequences for their responses and progress through learning material at their own pace (Ferster, 2014; Skinner, 1968). The teaching machine combined the basic principles of behavior via a technological medium that set the precedent for today's individualized, self-paced learning technologies.

With this historical context, researchers have considered a variety of tools that may be utilized when creating a modern-day teaching machine. At its core, this tool must meet specific requirements to ensure its utility and efficacy. For instance, Layng and Twyman (2013) stress the importance of ensuring emerging technologies implement evidence-based protocols, collect robust and nuanced data, and yield significant learning outcomes. In addition, researchers advocate for technology that aligns with personalized instruction and prompt feedback (Twyman, 2014). A potential technological tool that meets these essential features is virtual reality (VR). VR currently provides a portable technological learning solution for applying behavior analytic principles to teaching various educational and clinical objectives. With its ability to simulate real-world scenarios, VR offers individuals access to virtual learning contexts, where they can receive immediate and contextual feedback, engage in active responding, and practice skills in a controlled yet safe environment. With that said, clinicians should thoroughly assess the utility and efficacy of these tools to ensure they align with ABA evidence-based practices and procedures. In other words, to be considered a pragmatic modern-day teaching machine, VR must demonstrate applied, measurable, and meaningful clinical outcomes.

Technical Terms and Characteristics

Several technical terms and technological characteristics are worthy of review as they are discussed throughout the chapter. *Virtual reality* (VR) refers to three-dimensional (3D) generated interactive environments that can either be realistic or an imaginative facsimile of the real world (Sherman & Craig, 2002; Southgate, 2020). VR uses various tools, such as headsets, mobile phones, and computers, to expose individuals to immersive and interactive

DOI: 10.4324/9781003380603-12

environments (Bailenson et al., 2008). Simulated experiences presented on a *head-mounted display* (HMD) provide an increased level of immersion and experience that engages with an individual's senses, such as sight, sound, and touch (Slater & Sanchez-Vives, 2016). HMDs traditionally cover an individual's sense of sight to display a virtual representation of a simulated environment.

The ultimate goal of immersive VR is to create a strong *psychological presence*, i.e., increasing the believability and experience of interacting with relevant stimuli within a virtual environment (Bailenson et al., 2008). Psychological presence is obtained via a combination of effective tracking, consistent rendering, and a meaningful display (Bailenson, 2018). Tracking is related to the movement an individual engages in within a virtual environment, i.e., *degrees of freedom* (DoF) (Cummings & Bailenson, 2015; Southgate, 2020). The DoF in a 3D environment includes moving forward/backward, up/down, and side to side within the virtual space – i.e., this is also known as pitch, yaw, and roll. In other words, the virtual environment will adapt and correlate to an individual's natural movements within the real-world setting, facilitating the experience of 6DoF. 6DoF is what we experience in the real world; thus, most modern and sophisticated VR systems support 6DoF to fully capture an individual's natural movements and behaviors within their environment. Next, *rendering* pertains to the general *latency*, or delay, between an individual's action within the real world and the virtual environment, i.e., the lag between an individual's real-world movement within the virtual environment (Bailenson, 2018; Slater & Sanchez-Vives, 2016). A well-rendered virtual setting will display minimal latency when interacting with auditory or visual stimuli. For example, a well-rendered crosswalk VR environment would provide minimal latency between the individual's physical steps in the real world and the visual changes within VR. In addition, crosswalk signals and sounds would correlate with real-world signals, and tactile feedback, such as vibrations or force, via effective *haptics*. Last, *display* corresponds to the *field of view* (FoV) within a virtual environment, i.e., the observable environment displayed within the VR HMD. Best practices call for a large FoV to mimic the general FoV range of the human eye, as this is correlated with an increase in an individual's immersion and sense of presence within a physical and virtual space (Pangilinan et al., 2019).

Literature Review

Empirical research has demonstrated the implementation of VR across multiple fields and academic areas of study. When paired with an instructional technological basis, such as the basic principles of behavior, this technological tool can lead to meaningful learning outcomes and measurable behavioral change. A cross-disciplinary approach was taken for this review because a) VR is a newer emerging technology within the field of ABA, and thus, the literature base is limited in nature, and b) a larger body of literature presented outside of the field presents efficacy and replication of findings. Nevertheless, the need for additional VR and ABA is warranted and valuable as these and other emerging technologies become ubiquitous within a clinical setting (Carnett et al., 2022; Valencia et al., 2019).

A small but growing body of research has demonstrated the effectiveness of immersive VR in acquiring socially significant skills among individuals with autism spectrum disorder (ASD) (Lorenzo et al., 2019). For example, Lorenzo et al. (2016) reported the application of VR via a virtual environment (VE) to teach children with ASD how to navigate socially complex scenarios. Researchers developed social scripts and scenarios to teach participants to a) describe their private events and specific variables within already identified

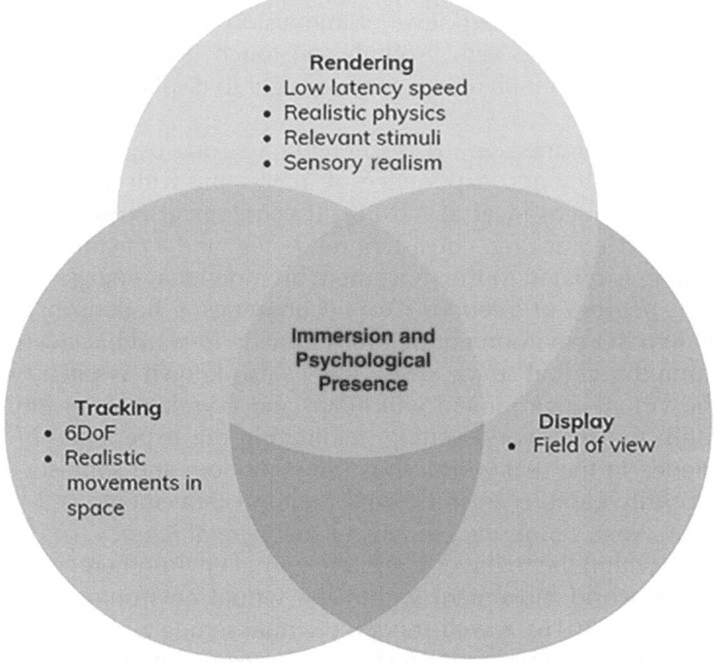

Figure 9.1 Text adapted from Bailenson (2018) and used to create a Venn diagram displaying the following: characteristics of immersion and psychological presence in VR environments.

This figure demonstrates the three overarching components needed to experience immersion and psychological presence in VR environments: tracking, rendering, and display.

challenging social scenarios in the VR simulation and b) respond via socially relevant intraverbal exchanges as they engage with premade social scripts (Lorenzo et al., 2016). Traditional behavioral skills training was provided to the participants, i.e., instruction, modeling, role-play, and feedback. Results indicated an increase in completing the social scripts with accuracy, and via follow-up interviews, teachers reported observing significant changes in generalized settings. It should be noted that the article does not use a single-subject research design (SSRD), and behavior analytic researchers may consider replicating this study via an SSRD framework. Dixon et al. (2020) demonstrated the effectiveness of a VR program in teaching pedestrian skills to children with ASD, with participants achieving mastery criteria within the VR simulation and the natural environment. Although the results were promising, it should be noted that some of the participants required an extended long-video condition to maintain and generalize learned skills. Furthermore, VR has been shown to potentially assist young adults with ASD in evaluating and improving driving performance (Cox et al., 2017). These results contribute to VR's potential utility in teaching independent living skills and increasing autonomy to individuals with ASD.

In addition, researchers investigated the generalizability of VR-learned skills across real-world scenarios and populations. Smith et al. (2021) reviewed the efficacy of VR-based job interview training (VR-JIT) for young adults with ASD, presented through computer-based instruction (CBI). Similarly, Genova et al. (2021) piloted a program for teenagers with ASD using VR-JIT via a small randomized controlled trial (RCT) consisting of 14 participants. Both studies demonstrated skill improvement in job interview skills, but it should be noted that the VR described in these studies was akin to immersive computer-based simulations rather than VR using an HMD. Researchers have also replicated similar findings across various populations using the same VR simulations, i.e., using the VR-JIT with veterans (Smith et al., 2015) and adults within prison-based vocational rehabilitation programs (Smith et al., 2023). Although these findings may indicate that an HMD may not be necessary for skill acquisition, many studies and publications highlight the value of immersive VR in acquiring and generalizing learned skills (Clay et al., 2021; Cummings & Bailenson, 2015; McClerry et al., 2020; Pangilinan et al., 2019).

Researchers are exploring alternative training modalities, like VR, to assess the efficacy of acquiring ABA implementation skills while reducing clinical and training expenses (Clay et al., 2021). For instance, Clay et al. (2021) demonstrated that VR behavioral skills training (BST) could effectively teach preservice clinicians to implement functional communication training (FCT) with a 78.6-minute average mastery time. This study demonstrated how ABA procedures may be programmed into VR simulations to augment staff training. In addition, the feasibility study presents the possibility of expanding staff training locations and opportunities via a combination of effective technologies of process and tools, i.e., behavior analysis and virtual reality, through the portability of the VR training tool (Clay et al., 2021; Layng & Twyman, 2013). Similarly, Sveinbjörnsdóttir et al. (2019) used VR BST to train teachers to conduct discrete trial training (DTT), resulting in all participants reaching and maintaining mastery criteria. King et al. (2022) investigated using VR in training graduate-level teacher participants to increase student classroom manding behaviors. Researchers identified limitations within these studies, including the lack of prior VR experience assessments (Clay et al., 2021), omission of generalization and maintenance probes (Sveinbjörnsdóttir et al., 2019), and complexity in data collection processes and intervention delivery (King et al., 2022). Putting aside these limitations and challenges, the reviewed studies provide a foundation for further research into the efficacy of VR as a training solution for ABA direct care staff.

Risks, Benefits, and Ethics of Virtual Reality Simulations

There are benefits, risks, and ethical considerations before integrating VR into ABA service delivery. VR's ability to provide an immersive, safe, and controlled environment for skill acquisition is a potential benefit to explore (Clay et al., 2021; Pangilinan et al., 2019). VR allows individuals to practice skill sets in a way that a) presents the ability to simulate scenarios difficult to replicate in clinical and analog environments, b) allows for multiple learning opportunities without needing to access specific locations or environmental settings, c) increases opportunities to practice skill sets that may be difficult or unsafe to practice in the real world, and d) potentially decreases clinical and training costs overall (Clay et al., 2021; Pangilinan et al., 2019). Given the fundamental potential for manipulating variables in VR, this technological modality allows for effective environmental arrangements used to enhance behavior change protocols (Pangilinan et al., 2019).

However, inherent technological risks should be considered alongside these benefits when employing VR in clinical ABA services. The "digital divide" is a potential concern, i.e., the unequal distribution of emerging technologies, such as HMD VR (Horton & Quesenbery, 2014). In other words, until VR is more ubiquitous, access to this technological modality may be limited based on location, lack of resources, acceptability of the tool, and lack of quality immersive experiences. Unequal access to meaningful learning opportunities will need to be assessed and reduced to decrease specific technological risks in VR clinical implementation; i.e., the lack of high-performance hardware, adequate space, systemic and socio-structural issues, and technical knowledge to use VR could exclude groups and individuals.

Client safety is an ethical consideration when using VR clinical applications. Given its immersive and potentially disorientating nature, these tools must be effectively rendered to reduce potential physiological side effects. Physical and psychological discomfort is a potential side effect when using VR. Cybersickness or VR sickness may occur when using VR HMDs, including symptoms such as dizziness, nausea, or eyestrain (Hosfelt, 2019). As such, risk-benefit analyses should be carried out to ensure client safety, detailing steps to reduce the likelihood and impact of cybersickness. In addition, clinicians should use immersive VR HMD that promotes a strong and consistent psychological presence to reduce the likelihood of cybersickness.

Another ethical issue concerns consent and assent within virtual environmental settings (Hosfelt, 2019). In addition, clear consent protocols and assent will also need to be assessed throughout the VR experience to increase the opportunity for choice and preference to continue, pause, or terminate a session and decrease the potential for trauma and cybersickness (BACB, 2020; Morris et al., 2021). For example, researchers and practitioners should provide clear expectations of VR's potential physiological side effects that may lead to discomfort or harm before and during VR use. As such, clinicians should confirm that the individual understands these expectations, risks, and benefits when interacting with VR environments and programming (Committee on Bioethics, 1995; Morris et al., 2021). A check-in system should be developed alongside the client to ensure consent and assent protocols are understood and upheld throughout the session.

The social validity of using VR within ABA clinical settings should be reviewed to ensure this tool provides contextual utility in addressing clinical and individual nuanced needs. According to Wolf (1978), social validity focuses on the social importance and acceptability of an intervention's goals, procedures, and outcomes. Evaluating whether the technological tool aligns with the individual's needs, values, and preferences is essential when using VR. In addition, the ethical considerations of using this tool can be assessed within a broader sociocultural context, i.e., reviewing factors like cost, accessibility, and cultural responsiveness. As clinical and educational tools become increasingly digital and virtual, it is essential to ensure that these resources are accessible to all (Guney, 2019; Horton & Quesenbery, 2014). Integrating accessibility-designed tools in VR may ensure that individuals, regardless of their abilities and/or financial means, can benefit from VR learning experiences. Considerations and accessibility design may include fine and gross motor skill acknowledgments, color blindness, auditory modifications for the hard of hearing, and so on. While VR holds potential for utility and efficacy in its use within clinical settings, there is an ethical responsibility to ensure that these tools are not only accessible but also inclusive. In other words, VR programs must consider diverse cultural backgrounds, abilities, and individual needs.

Last, the simulation's instructional design should be reviewed to assess the ethics behind the overall programming effectiveness and its alignment to ABA technologies, e.g., basic principles of behavior, schedules of reinforcement used, generalizability of learned skills, and so on. Instructional designers have considered the moral implications and broader societal impacts of their programming used within learning applications (Osguthorpe et al., 2003). In addition, Layng and Twyman (2013) pinpointed that there are considerations to review within the convergence of education, technology, and innovation. For instance, there are no clear ethical codes for VR programmers and designers to follow when creating simulated environments. Within the field of ABA, researchers and clinicians are bound by their ethical code (BACB, 2020) and scope of practice and competence when creating meaningful learning environments and opportunities within and outside of virtual environments. As such, ABA VR developers should consider looking within the field of ABA for guidance in ensuring the VR programming aligns with the basic principles of behavior, and current ethical codes guiding ABA practice and research, while also implementing social validity metrics to ensure the overall acceptability of virtual variables used to teach meaningful skills (BACB, 2020; Baer et al., 1968; Carter, 2010). Researchers and ABA VR developers may also look toward neighboring engineering and software development fields to ensure that best practices and ethical programming are ensured. Ethical standards have been presented for immersive web technologies (Hosfelt, 2019) and virtual reality experiences (Fox & Guenette Thornton, 2022), promoting respect, professionalism, and the importance of maintaining safe, inclusive VR spaces. Guney (2019) calls for an established code of ethics specifically for performance and educational technology, i.e., ensuring an individual's safety, respect, and dignity by developing accurate and meaningful programming. In other words, these technologies must effectively teach meaningful skills and uphold individuals' rights and well-being.

Suggestions for Integrating VR Into a Clinical Practice

The following presents suggestions clinicians may consider before implementing VR into their clinical day-to-day:

1. **Environmental setting:** Clinicians should ensure the learning environment is set up for success and safe for VR activities i.e., eliminate potential hazards by creating a space that is devoid of furniture and obstacles. In addition, clinicians should monitor sessions to ensure the safety of staff and clients involved in VR sessions (Zhang et al., 2022).
2. **Scope of competence in VR and ABA:** Clinicians should complete VR tech training to address potential technical issues and to ensure behavioral goals are achieved during sessions, i.e., resolving small technical matters. In addition, ABA staff should seek training and guidance in implementing VR ABA simulations with fidelity.
3. **Consent, assent, and preference:** Clinicians should conduct an in-depth assessment before using VR in session to understand the client's capabilities, preferences, and aversions. Each client's acceptability and preferences for VR may vary based on their learning history and abilities. Consent and assent should be assessed throughout the VR sessions to address safety and preference (Morris et al., 2021). In addition, informed consent and assent protocols should be obtained before and during VR sessions, reminding caregivers and clients of their rights to terminate VR sessions at any time (BACB, 2020). Assent and consent protocols should be developed with client input.
4. **Individualized care:** Not all VR content may align with ABA goals. Clinicians should opt for flexible and adaptable VR experiences that may increase the likelihood of clinical outcomes, i.e., VR simulations that allow for customization to increase the likelihood of aligning with clinical goals (Howard et al., 2021).
5. **Data monitoring and collection:** Data collection within VR is essential to ensure sessions address clinical goals and outcomes. Clinicians should be able to review a client's movements within the VR simulation and record these sessions within the

virtual environment for interobserver agreement and fidelity checks (see Figure 9.2 for an example). Recording for these VR sessions will require informed consent protocols to be in place, governed by ethical code regulations (BACB, 2020) and other pertinent regulations based on the learning environment, e.g., school, state regulations, institutional review board (IRB), etc.

6. **Scheduled breaks:** Given the risks of cybersickness and eyestrain, regular breaks during VR sessions are recommended (Bailenson, 2018). Clinicians should probe for assent throughout the session to determine supplemental and scheduled breaks as needed.
7. **Alignment with ABA technology:** Clinicians should use VR simulations that align with ABA technologies, i.e., the instructional design of the simulations used in the session should align with behavior analytic principles and protocols to ensure clinicians are working within their scope of competence and practice (BACB, 2020). In other words, VR should not be used for VR's sake; there must be alignment with individual goals, basic principles of behavior, and overall utility.
8. **VR should be viewed as an augmentation, not a replacement for clinical services:** Although research demonstrates promise in using VR for clinical purposes, VR should augment rather than replace traditional clinical services. This approach is suggested until extensive replications of research suggest otherwise.
9. **Privacy and confidentiality:** Adherence to confidentiality regulations, especially with VR data and recordings, is paramount. Referring to BACB, HIPPA, FERPA, GDPR, and state licensure regulations will provide insight into data management, maintenance, and disposal of VR recordings and data (BACB, 2020).

Figure 9.2 Photo of the author in a virtual reality brief functional analysis (FA) simulation created by BehaviorMe, Inc.

This image demonstrates a simulation for clinical staff training to prepare clinicians to implement a brief FA. The simulation observed within the HMD is also displayed on a computer screen to ensure trainer feedback delivery is presented accordingly and the session is recorded for data collection purposes.

Figure 9.3 Photo of the BehaviorMe, Inc. staff training demo on data collection processes.

This image demonstrates a 3D-generated environment, with rendered and scaled stimuli and avatars that reflect a clinical ABA setting. Realism within the confines of a 3D-generated space was chosen to increase psychological presence and immersion.

10. **Psychological presence:** To ensure effective immersion, VR simulations should promote psychological presence, e.g., scaling stimuli and environments as compared to real-world settings, ensuring simulations meet basic psychological presence standards, etc. (see Figures 9.1 and 9.3).
11. **Age considerations:** Many HMDs have recommended age recommendations due to potential health and safety concerns (Southgate, 2020). These age recommendations will vary from HMD to HMD and should be considered before implementation in session.
12. **Health and sanitation:** HMDs should be sanitized before and after use, considering potential allergens in cleaning solutions.

Future Applications and Closing Thoughts

Skinner (1968) imagined a future where the science of human behavior would improve educational and clinical outcomes through the fusion of effective educational programming and tools. Thus, exploring emerging technological frameworks remains relevant as clinicians and researchers explore the meaningful fusions between the technology of processes and tools (Layng & Twyman, 2013). In addition, technological advancements, notably in artificial intelligence (AI), resonate with Skinner's basic principles of behavior, e.g., large language models (LLM) like ChatGPT from OpenAI. These language models produce human-like responses that are shaped using basic principles of behavior, such as reinforcement and punishment; i.e., responses are refined and shaped based on feedback and input from the environment (Mollick & Mollick, 2023). AI's continual learning process offers a potential aid in developing and programming meaningful VR learning experiences, e.g., shortening the duration of developing usable code, visual renders, and interactive scripts for VR simulations. Furthermore, VR simulations may implement AI conversational chatbots or agents to promote discriminative and generalized learning opportunities.

As the field of behavior analysis explores these meaningful technologies of process and tools, we may uncover promising advancements by creating responsive modern-day teaching machines that tailor instruction to individual needs. However, amid these advancements, clinicians should remain client centered and focus on contextual needs, measurable outcomes, and personal preferences. Doing so ensures that the fusion of technological processes and tools will promote personalized, immersive, and socially significant VR learning environments that resonate with Skinner's (1968) vision of a modern-day teaching machine.

References

Baer, D. M., Wolf, M. M., & Risley, T. R. (1968). Some current dimensions of applied behavior analysis. *Journal of Applied Behavior Analysis, 1*(1), 91–97.

Bailenson, J. N. (2018). *Experience on demand*. W.W. Norton.

Bailenson, J. N., Yee, N., Blascovich, J., Beall, A. C., Lundblad, N., & Jin, M. (2008). The use of immersive virtual reality in the learning sciences: Digital transformations of teachers, students, and social context. *The Journal of the Learning Sciences, 17*(1), 102–141.

Behavior Analyst Certification Board. (2020). *Ethics code for behavior analysts*. https://bacb.com/wp-content/ethics-code-for-behavior-analysts/

Carnett, A., Neely, L., Gardiner, S., Kirkpatrick, M., Quarles, J., & Christopher, K. (2022). Systematic review of virtual reality in behavioral interventions for individuals with autism. *Advances in Neurodevelopmental Disorders, 7*(3), 426–442.

Carter, S. L. (2010). *The social validity manual*. Elsevier.

Clay, C. J., Schmitz, B. A., Balakrishnan, B., Hopfenblatt, J. P., Evans, A., & Kahng, S. (2021). Feasibility of virtual reality behavior skills training for preservice clinicians. *Journal of Applied Behavior Analysis, 2*(54), 547–565.

Committee on Bioethics. (1995). Informed consent, parental permission, and assent in pediatric practice. *Pediatrics, 95*(2), 314–317.

Cox, D. J., Brown, T., Ross, V., Moncrief, M., Schmitt, R., Gaffney, G., & Reeve, R. (2017). Can youth with autism spectrum disorder use virtual reality driving simulation training to evaluate and improve driving performance? An exploratory study. *Journal of Autism and Developmental Disorders, 47*(8), 2544–2555.

Cummings, J. J., & Bailenson, J. N. (2015). How immersive is enough? A meta-analysis of the effect of immersive technology on user presence. *Media Psychology*, 1–38.

Dixon, D. R., Miyake, C. J., Nohelty, K., Novack, M. N., & Granpeesheh, D. (2020). Evaluation of an immersive virtual reality safety training used to teach pedestrian skills to children with autism spectrum disorder. *Behavior Analysis in Practice, 13*(3), 631–640.

Ferster, B. (2014). *Teaching machines*. Johns Hopkins University Press.

Fox, D., & Guenette Thornton, I. (2022). *The IEEE global initiative on ethics of extended reality (XR) report: Extended reality (XR) ethics and diversity, inclusion, and accessibility* [White paper]. IEEE. https://ieeexplore.ieee.org/servlet/opac?punumber=9727120

Genova, H. M., Lancaster, K., Morecraft, J., Haas, M., Edwards, A., DiBenedetto, M., Krch, D., DeLuca, J., & Smith, M. J. (2021). A pilot RCT of virtual reality job interview training in transition-age youth on the autism spectrum. *Research in Autism Spectrum Disorders, 89*.

Guney, Z. (2019). Professional ethics in performance and educational technology. *Educational Policy Analysis and Strategic Research, 14*(4), 190–200.

Horton, S., & Quesenbery, W. (2014). *A web for everyone: Designing accessible user experiences*. Rosenfeld.

Hosfelt, D. (2019). *Making ethical decisions for the immersive web*. https://blog.mozvr.com/making-ethical-decisions/

Howard, M. S., Gutworth, M. B., & Jacobs, R. R. (2021). A meta-analysis of virtual reality training programs. *Computers in Human Behavior, 121*(1), 1–16.

King, S., Estapa, A., Bell, T., & Boyer, J. (2022). Behavioral skills training through smart virtual reality for a verbal mathematical questioning strategy. *Journal of Behavioral Education, 33*(2), 396–420.

Layng, T. V. J., & Twyman, J. S. (2013). Education + technology + innovation = learning? In M. Murphy, S. Redding, & J. Twyman (Eds.), *Handbook on innovations in learning* (pp. 135–150). Center on Innovations in Learning, Temple University; Information Age Publishing.

Lorenzo, G., Lledó, A., Arráez-Vera, G., & Lorenzo-Lledó, A. (2019). The application of immersive virtual reality for students with ASD: A review between 1990–2017. *Education and Information Technologies, 24*(1), 127–151.

Lorenzo, G., Lledó, A., Pomares, J., & Roig, R. (2016). Design and application of an immersive virtual reality system to enhance emotional skills for children with autism spectrum disorders. *Computers & Education, 98*, 192–205.

McClerry, J. P., Zitter, A., Solórzano, R., Turnacioglu, S., Miller, J. S., Ravindran, V., & Parish-Morris, J. (2020). Safety and feasibility of an immersive virtual reality intervention program for teaching police interaction skills to adolescents and adults with autism. *Autism Research, 13*(8), 1418–1424. https://doi.org/10.1002/aur.2352

Mollick, E., & Mollick, L. (2023). *Using AI to implement effective teaching strategies in classrooms: Five strategies, including prompts*. SSRN. http://dx.doi.org/10.2139/ssrn.4391243

Morris, C., Detrick, J. J., & Peterson, S. M. (2021). Participant assent in behavior analytic research: Considerations for participants with autism and developmental disabilities. *Journal of Applied Behavior Analysis, 54*(4), 1300–1316.

Osguthorpe, R. T., Osguthorpe, R. D., Jacob, W. J., & Davies, R. (2003). The moral dimensions of instructional design. *Educational Technology, 43*(2), 19–23.

Pangilinan, E., Lukas, S., & Mohan, V. (Eds.). (2019). *Creating augmented & virtual realities: Theory & practice for next-generation spatial computing*. O'Reilly.

Sherman, W. R., & Craig, A. B. (2002). *Understanding virtual reality: Interface, application, and design*. Morgan Kaufmann.

Skinner, B. F. (1968). *The technology of teaching*. Copley Publishing Group.

Slater, M., & Sanchez-Vives, M. V. (2016). Enhancing our lives with immersive virtual reality. *Frontiers in Robotics and AI, 3*, 1–47. https://doi.org/10.3389/frobt.2016.00074

Smith, M. J., Humm, L. B., Fleming, M. F., Jordan, N., Wright, M. A., Ginger, E. J., Wright, K., Olsen, D., & Bell, M. D. (2015). Virtual reality job interview training for veterans with posttraumatic stress disorder. *Journal of Vocational Rehabilitation, 42*, 271–279.

Smith, M. J., Parham, B., Mitchell, J., Blajeski, S., Harrington, M., Ross, B., Johnson, J., Bryndon, D. M., & Honson, J. E. (2023). Virtual reality job interview training for adults receiving prison-based employment services. *Criminal Justice and Behavior, 50*(2), 272–293.

Smith, M. J., Sherwood, K., Ross, B., Smith, J. D., DaWalt, L., Bishop, L., Humm, L., Elkins, J., & Steacy, C. (2021). Virtual interview training for autistic transition age youth: A randomized controlled feasibility and effectiveness trial. *Autism, 25*(6), 1536–1552.

Southgate, E. (2020). *Virtual reality in curriculum and pedagogy*. Routledge.

Sveinbjörnsdóttir, B., Jóhannsson, S. H., Oddsdóttir, J., Sigurðardóttir, T. P., Valdimarsson, G. I., & Vilhjálmsson, H. H. (2019). Virtual discrete trial training for teacher trainees. *Journal on Multimodal User Interfaces, 13*(1), 31–40.

Twyman, J. S. (2014). Envisioning education 3.0: The fusion of behavior analysis, learning science principles, and emerging technologies. *Mexican Journal of Behavior Analysis, 40*(2), 20–38.

Valencia, K., Rusu, C., Quiñones, D., & Jamet, E. (2019). The impact of technology on people with autism spectrum disorder: A systematic literature review. *Sensors, 19*(20), 4485.

Wolf, M. M. (1978). Social validity: The case for subjective measurement or how applied behavior analysis is finding its heart. *Journal of Applied Behavior Analysis, 11*(2), 203–214.

Zhang, M., Ding, H., Naumceska, M., & Zhang, Y. (2022). Virtual reality technology as an educational and intervention tool for children with autism spectrum disorder: Current perspectives and future directions. *Behavioral Sciences, 12*, 138–177.

10 Behavioral and Digital Technologies in the Treatment of Substance Use Disorder

Jesse Dallery and Bethany R. Raiff

Substance use disorder (SUD) remains a vexing public health issue. Cigarette smoking is the leading preventable cause of disease and death in the developed world (CDC, 2022a). Excessive alcohol use is associated with 95,000 deaths in the US annually, shortening lives by about 29 years on average (CDC, 2022b). During a 12-month period ending April 2021, opioid overdose deaths exceeded 100,000 in the US, and this rate has continued into 2024 (Ahmad et al., 2024) These and other statistics highlight the profound toll of SUD. Unfortunately, most individuals who suffer from SUD do not receive treatment, and those who receive treatment rarely receive evidence-based treatment (Marsch & Dallery, 2012). This is the situation even though there is a strong evidence base for behavioral intervention for SUD. One meta-analysis suggested that nearly 2.5 times as many substance users who received evidence-based treatment achieved clinically significant abstinence, compared to those who received nonevidence-based treatment or no treatment (Dutra et al., 2008).

The growing use of digital technology in the assessment and treatment of behavior problems has been called unprecedented (Marsch et al., 2020), a potential game changer (Dallery & Bolivar, 2017), and revolutionary (Bucci et al., 2019). The reasons stem from technology's disruptive impacts on the iron triangle of healthcare: cost, quality, and access (Kissick, 1994). Typically, when one element of the triangle increases, another element decreases, as when a more costly treatment decreases access. Technology can soften the impact of these trade-offs or even produce desirable changes in all elements simultaneously. Although hurdles remain, mounting evidence in the field of addictive behavior suggests that digital technology is serving as a disruptive technology.

Translating Evidence-Based Interventions Into Technology-Based Interventions

We focus on three evidence-based interventions: the community reinforcement approach (CRA), contingency management (CM), and acceptance and commitment therapy (ACT). This is not an exhaustive list of successful technology-based translations of in-person interventions (Marsch et al., 2020). Nevertheless, these examples illustrate nicely the links among behavioral theory, research, and treatments that may be scaled to generate a public health impact.

The Community Reinforcement Approach

The CRA is grounded in a behavior science framework of drug dependence in which drugs of abuse come to exert more control than delayed prosocial reinforcers because of their immediate reinforcing effects (Higgins et al., 2004; Hunt & Azrin, 1973). The skills training component of CRA encourages behaviors that increase social, recreational, family, and

DOI: 10.4324/9781003380603-13

vocational reinforcers. The CRA was translated into the computerized therapeutic education system (TES) to address opioid dependence (Campbell et al., 2014). It involves 65 on-demand audio, text, and video-based modules, each lasting between 10 and 20 minutes, which are sequentially unlocked as patients progress through the program. The program contains interactive videos of actors modeling various behaviors (e.g., progressive muscle relaxation, drug refusal) in response to real-world experiences. One way the interactivity is accomplished is through short quizzes about the content and then the pace and level of repetition of the content are adjusted to maximize mastery. In addition, the program involves fluency-based criteria for module completion. The TES also includes an optional contingency management (CM, described later in this chapter) component, though TES is effective even without the addition of CM (Marsch et al., 2014).

Several randomized trials have found that TES produced outcomes superior to standard substance abuse treatment and improved objectively measured drug abstinence compared to those produced by trained clinicians delivering comparable therapy (Campbell et al., 2014; Marsch et al., 2014). In the pivotal randomized controlled trial (RCT) of TES, 82% of 170 patients with opioid use disorder (OUD) at an addiction treatment center who received treatment stayed in treatment, versus 68% of those who received treatment as usual (TAU) combined with CM. The likelihood of abstinence during weeks 9–12 was 77.3% vs. 62.1%, respectively ($p < 0.05$ for both comparisons).

TES was also delivered by mobile app, which led to the first FDA-authorized prescription digital therapeutic in the US. Digital therapeutics are a new category of FDA-regulated devices that clinicians can prescribe in a manner similar to FDA-approved medications. One evaluation of the intervention (which was renamed re-SET-O) during typical clinical care found that of the 3,144 patients followed across 30 states, 66% were abstinent as defined by self-report or drug-negative urinalysis (Maricich et al., 2021). Another study found decreases in healthcare utilization (e.g., emergency room and hospital visits) following the use of reSET-O with an estimated total savings of $750,000 for the 351 treatment patients (i.e., savings of $2,150 per patient) (Velez et al., 2021). Thus, the increase in access and high treatment fidelity afforded by reSET-O was also accompanied by cost reductions. Unfortunately, the company that supplied reSET-O, Pear Therapeutics, declared bankruptcy in April of 2023. The main reason was lack of reimbursement by payors, despite FDA clearance and its cost-effectiveness (Tohme et al., 2025). Another company, PursueCare, has purchased the reSET-O program at auction, but the future is unclear. What is clear is the impact reSET-O had on the iron triangle of healthcare: it increased access, decreased costs, and delivered high-quality treatment to individuals suffering from substance use disorder.

Contingency Management

Under CM procedures, nondrug reinforcers are made contingent on evidence of abstinence or other clinically relevant outcomes (e.g., attendance; Higgins et al., 2019; Petry, 2000; Silverman et al., 2007; Stitzer & Bigelow, 1983; Stitzer & Petry, 2006). In an early demonstration, Miller (1975) used a CM procedure to decrease public drunkenness among "skid row" alcoholics. Abstinence from alcohol was verified via negative breath-alcohol tests and staff observation, and, based on this evidence, individuals could receive shelter, employment, food, clothing, and other services from local social agencies. Later studies included the provision of vouchers based on abstinence that could be exchanged for goods and services (Higgins et al., 2002) and tangible "prizes" that were scheduled intermittently during treatment (Petry, 2000).

The first translation of CM into a technology-based platform targeted cigarette smoking (Dallery & Glenn, 2005). One way to detect recent smoking is via breath carbon monoxide (CO). Breath CO can be obtained with a handheld monitor, and the procedure is noninvasive and produces immediate results. The platform employed remote, web-based technology to allow for frequent (i.e., twice daily) breath CO collection (Dallery et al., 2019; Stoops et al., 2009). Individuals provided CO samples in front of a video camera connected to the Internet. Samples were provided twice per day and separated by eight hours. The video was time-stamped, sent across the Internet, and evaluated by staff. An incentive was delivered electronically if the sample was valid and if the CO level displayed on the CO meter met the criterion for incentive delivery. This intervention has been effective in promoting smoking cessation (Coughlin et al., 2023; Dallery et al., 2019). Patients and healthcare providers have rated this technology-based CM intervention positively in usability and acceptability (Raiff et al., 2013).

To facilitate dissemination, basic cell phones and smartphones have been used to implement similar incentive-based interventions (see Coughlin et al., 2023 for a review). Smartphones have also enabled extensions of this intervention to alcohol use (Hammond et al., 2021). Alessi and Petry (2013) conducted a small randomized controlled study in which participants used basic cell phones to video record themselves exhaling into an alcohol breathalyzer to measure breath alcohol content (BAC). Participants in the mobile CM group (n = 15) submitted negative BAC breathalyzer tests on 87% of video submissions, compared with 67% of monitoring-only control participants (n = 15). Koffarnus et al. (2018) used a BAC breathalyzer called Soberlink (Soberlink Healthcare, LLC) that includes cellular service and an integrated web camera. During the exhalation process, a picture is taken of the user and his or her identity is automatically confirmed using facial recognition software. The percentage of negative samples in CM was 85% compared to 35% in the control condition. A recent meta-analysis indicated that technology-based CM to reduce smoking and alcohol use had superior outcomes compared to control conditions (Getty et al., 2019). Technology-based methods to deliver CM have also been incorporated into an inner-city treatment clinic for substance use (DeFulio et al., 2021). Several digital CM companies have emerged to deliver CM treatment for smoking, alcohol use, psychostimulant use, and other SUDs (e.g., DynamiCare Health, Q2i, Vincere Health, WEconnect Health, Vincere Health, Affect Therapeutics, CHESS Health; Dallery et al., 2023).

Acceptance and Commitment Therapy

In contrast to a focus on arranging new environmental contingencies to promote abstinence in CM, ACT seeks to alter the influence of verbal behavior and internal private events to decrease drug use. In-person ACT has been successfully applied to treat SUD (Osaji et al., 2020). Briefly, ACT promotes abstinence by focusing on increasing willingness to experience physical cravings, emotions, and thoughts (e.g., urges to use or feelings or thoughts that trigger drug use) while making behavior changes based on deeply important and meaningful values to motivate and guide quitting.

Bricker developed iCanQuit (Bricker et al., 2013), a smartphone-based ACT intervention for smoking cessation, which is the first and only mobile health cessation intervention proven efficacious in a phase III trial (Bricker et al., 2020). The app also follows the US clinical practice guidelines by tracking smoking status, offering quit planning, advising on pharmacotherapy, enhancing motivation, and providing social support for quitting. The iCanQuit app uses ACT to teach skills for coping with smoking urges, committing to values, and preventing relapse. The program is self-paced, and content is unlocked sequentially. First, app users see a brief introduction that orients them to the app features and introduces them to the smoking cessation coach persona, and then they are asked to set up a personalized quit plan to set a quit date and can learn about FDA-approved cessation medications. Next, they are taken to the home screen, which includes eight levels of intervention content. For example, Level 1, "Becoming an Urge Expert," introduces the main features of the app and introduces a fictional tobacco treatment "guide" who specializes in helping people quit smoking. The guide navigates the user through the app and teaches ACT skills for accepting cravings to smoke (i.e., distancing from thoughts about smoking, mindfulness skills, flexible perspective taking). The last four levels contain content designed to help the patient stay smoke-free after the quit date. These levels contain 25 exercises that focus on building smoke-free life activities and coping with withdrawal symptoms, slips, depression, and potential weight gain.

The efficacy of iCanQuit has been demonstrated in several randomized controlled trials. Bricker et al. (2020) randomized 2,415 smokers to one of two smartphone apps: iCanQuit or QuitGuide, based on clinical practice guidelines. The primary outcome of 30-day point prevalence abstinence (PPA, no smoking during the past month) at the 12-month follow-up was 28.2% vs 21.1% (OR = 1.49; 95% CI, 1.22–1.83). Among low-income smokers ($20,000 or less household income; *N* = 757), the 30-day PPA at the 12-month follow-up was 27.1% for iCanQuit vs. 20.0% for QuitGuide (OR = 1.46; 95% CI, 1.04–2.06). Overall, 80% of patients endorsed iCanQuit as useful in helping them quit, and 83% would recommend it to a friend. iCanQuit has been freely available to the public since 2014, and it has been downloaded over 400,000 times (Bricker, personal communication).

Enabling Novel Treatment Components in Technology-Based Interventions

Serious Games and Gamification

Serious games are designed to promote positive behavior change outside of the context of the game. A virtual reality serious game called Take Control used cue exposure therapy to help people in recovery from alcohol or tobacco (Metcalf et al., 2018). In the game, participants were exposed to stimuli that were associated with drug use (e.g., beer bottles, lighters, cigarettes), and they had to physically swipe or kick the images away, at which point the image would explode and disappear, and then the player would gain points to help them advance in their game. Playing the game across three to four sessions was associated with a decrease in self-reported substance use, relative to a control group. Another smoking cessation serious game, Inspired, was developed as an extension of Internet-based CM for smoking cessation, as discussed earlier, by providing users with videogame-based incentives, in place of monetary incentives, for smoking abstinence (Raiff et al., 2018).

An alternative to video games is *gamification*, which is defined as the "use of game elements in non-game contexts" (Morford et al., 2014). Cugelman (2013) outlined seven gamification strategies: (1) goal setting, (2) capacity to overcome challenges, (3) providing feedback on performance, (4) reinforcement, (5) comparing progress, (6) social connectivity, and (7) fun and playfulness. To accomplish these strategies, common tactics include providing clear goals and giving immediate feedback, offering challenges and using levels, allocating points/virtual currency/rewards, showing progress, giving badges for achievements, showing leaders/using a leaderboard, and incorporating a narrative or theme into the app. One study evaluated 140 smoking-cessation smartphone applications available in the UK to determine the use of gamification strategies and tactics (Rajani et al., 2019). Results showed that performance (91.4%), goal setting (64.3%), reinforcement (50.7%), and social connectivity (49.3%) were the most widely applied gamification strategies.

QuitBet is one example of a gamified smoking cessation intervention that harnesses social connectivity. In a pilot study, participants who enrolled in QuitBet contributed (i.e., bet) $30 upon enrollment, a portion of which went into a "grand prize" pool of money that could be won at the end (Bloom et al., 2021). Participants provided objective evidence of smoking abstinence (i.e., carbon monoxide), and those who were abstinent for 19 of the 20 treatment days were considered "winners" and were able to divide up the pool of money that had been deposited. Additionally, participants could interact with each other through messages on the platform. The majority of QuitBet participants reported being interested in playing again and rated the intervention as acceptable.

Gamification for the treatment of alcohol (Boendermaker et al., 2015; Cook et al., 2015) and opioid use (Zhang et al., 2019) has also been explored. For example, a serious game called Pier Pressure was developed as part of a larger social media campaign called Keep What You've Earned targeting excessive alcohol use and its negative consequences among sailors in the Navy (Cook et al., 2015). The game involved role-playing in which the sailor's avatar could make decisions about drinking and virtually experience the consequences (both good and bad). The game also included tools for learning to estimate BAC and encouraged prosocial responses, such as calling a cab, when BAC was too dangerous for driving. The game also included leaderboards so that players could compete against one another. During the study, over 5,000 Pier Pressure downloads occurred, and this was associated with over 25,000 gameplay sessions. A 51% decrease in alcohol-related incidents was noted after the social media campaign, relative to the previous year.

Social Networks and Group Contingencies

Another technology-based strategy for the treatment of addiction involves harnessing social networks. *Social network interventions* can involve grouping people together who are trying to achieve a common goal but who otherwise do not have any prior relationship, or they can involve existing social connections (Naslund et al., 2017). For example, Internet-based *group contingency management* was explored in a series of studies, some of which involved grouping strangers together on an online platform (Motiv8) and making their financial incentives contingent on not only reaching individual smoking abstinence goals but also contingently on their group members meeting their own goals (Dallery et al., 2015b; Meredith et al., 2011). Participants provided social support through an online chat feature that was moderated by the investigators. Most peer-to-peer interactions were scored as positive and supportive.

To further harness the potential impact of social support in this technology-delivered group CM intervention, a follow-up study was conducted with pairs of smokers who had preexisting relationships (i.e., parents, coworkers, friends; Raiff et al., 2017). The rationale for using existing social networks was that the social support could continue even after the financial incentives were removed, possibly maintaining treatment gains. The result of this small feasibility study revealed that when one member of the pair was successful, both members of the pair were successful. However, when one member of the pair relapsed or failed to quit smoking, both members of the pair relapsed or failed to quit smoking. These results suggest that social influence from another person who is also attempting to quit may be helpful or harmful depending on their smoking status.

Community Reinforcement and Family Training (CRAFT) also takes advantage of existing social networks. CRAFT incorporates family members or concerned significant others (CSOs) who are interested in helping a loved one get help for their addiction (Meyers et al., 1996). CRAFT is composed of several training components (e.g., functional analysis, contingency management, differential reinforcement of substance-free activities, communication skills, and treatment entry). Macky et al. (in preparation) compared a fully automated, online version of CRAFT (CRAFT-A) with a coach-supported automated version (CRAFT-B) and a PEER support control that involved social support but not the active components of CRAFT. CRAFT-A and CRAFT-B resulted in 77% and 73%, respectively, of loved ones entering treatment for their OUD, compared to only 40% of the loved ones from the PEER control group. Furthermore, 12-week treatment retention was higher among participants whose CSOs were in the CRAFT-A and CRAFT-B groups, relative to the control group, even among individuals who enrolled in treatment involving Medications for Opioid Use Disorders (MOUD), which is an effective treatment for individuals with OUD. These outcomes have exciting implications for the wide-scale dissemination and implementation of this evidence-based social support approach to addiction treatment.

Just-in-Time Adaptive Interventions

Just-in-time adaptive interventions (JITAIs), also known as ecological momentary interventions (EMIs), involve monitoring and intervening on the target behavior in real time, usually via mobile devices such as smartphones (Nahum-Shani et al., 2018; Perski et al., 2021). To monitor behavior in real time, JITAIs involve either passively collecting data from the sensors of a smartphone (e.g., GPS, microphone, camera) or by having the participants complete surveys (initiated by the participant or automatically initiated by the mobile application). A recent systematic review identified the most used behavior change techniques among JITAIs addressing addiction, which included prompts (100%), social support (43%), and avoidance/reducing exposure to cues for the behavior (21%) (Perski et al., 2022).

For example, one JITAI known as the addiction-comprehensive gealth enhancement support system (A-CHESS) was designed to prevent relapse among people in recovery from alcohol use disorder (Gustafson et al., 2014). A-CHESS took advantage of the GPS in a smartphone to determine when participants entered high-risk situations that were specific to them (e.g., a bar they frequented, a liquor store). When the GPS detected these high-risk scenarios, A-CHESS would ask the user if they wanted to be there and would prompt them to review "recovery motivation" content addressing their reasons for remaining abstinent from alcohol, which they created when they enrolled in the program. At any point, the participants could hit a "panic button" on the app that would direct them to connect with an addiction counselor or other support persons, complete a variety of relaxation trainings, view their "recovery motivation" content, or find a 12-step group meeting to attend. In a randomized controlled trial of A-CHESS spanning 12 months, participants in the A-CHESS group reported significantly fewer risky drinking days than those in a control group (Gustafson et al., 2014).

Conclusions: Translating Behavior Science Into Technology-Based Treatments

Translating behavior science into technology-based treatment has a long history. Azrin and Powell (1968) developed one of the earliest examples of a technology-based treatment for addictive behavior. They created a cigarette container that automatically locked after a cigarette was removed from it, and it remained locked for a progressively longer duration over several weeks. The intervention was inspired by animal research on extinction procedures (Terrace, 1966). The device decreased cigarette consumption to targeted levels, and the participants found the device convenient and acceptable. Earlier we discussed Azrin's contributions to CRA, and other treatment components discussed previously in other contexts were also pioneered by Azrin and colleagues. Notably, these components were closely tied to fundamental behavioral mechanisms, which is a hallmark of successful (or potentially successful) translational science. For example, stimulus control procedures were integrated into Family Behavior Therapy, which has been used with adolescents and their families and caretakers (Donohue et al., 2009). These procedures involved teaching clients to escape or avoid contact with people, contexts, and situations that precede substance use or other problem behavior (e.g., child neglect) and teaching skills to increase time with stimuli that are incompatible with substance use. These examples are meant to highlight that translating treatments into technology-based platforms should be closely tied to behavior science. In most cases, science should lead the technology, but technology could also lead to advances in science.

Although this chapter focuses on interventions instead of assessment, it may be useful to match the assessment of behavior and its controlling variables to treatment. Technology-based methods to assess behavior and its antecedents and consequences are evolving rapidly. This has led to digital phenotyping, defined as the "moment-by-moment quantitative measurement of an individual's behavior, using data collected via personal digital devices as individuals move through their daily lives" (Marsch, 2018). Thus far, these methods have been used in the context of tailored JITAIs (discussed prior), but they also have relevance to assessing whether and how a behavioral intervention impacts the fine-grained structure of environment-behavior relations in the context of SUD treatment (Marsch, 2020). One area that has been underrepresented in the literature is assessment of the consequences of substance use (Burrows et al., 2020). More broadly, the assessment of antecedents and consequences could be better connected in the context of the four-term contingency: motivating operations, discriminative stimuli, operant responses, and consequences (Dallery et al., 2015a). These conceptually systematic connections may lead to more efficient and effective interventions, and novel extensions and procedures may further broaden the range of technology-based interventions.

References

Ahmad, F. B., Cisewski, J. A., Rossen, L. M., & Sutton, P. (2024). *Provisional drug overdose death counts*. National Center for Health Statistics. https://www.cdc.gov/nchs/nvss/vsrr/drug-overdose-data.htm

Alessi, S. M., & Petry, N. M. (2013). A randomized study of cellphone technology to reinforce alcohol abstinence in the natural environment. *Addiction, 108*(5), 900–909. https://doi.org/10.1111/add.12093

Azrin, N. H., & Powell, J. (1968). Behavioral engineering: The reduction of smoking behavior by a conditioning apparatus and procedure. *Journal of Applied Behavior Analysis, 1*(3), 193–200. https://doi.org/10.1901/jaba.1968.1-193

Bloom, E. L., Japuntich, S. J., Pierro, A., Dallery, J., Leahey, T. M., & Rosen, J. (2021). Pilot trial of QuitBet: A digital social game that pays you to stop smoking. *Experimental and Clinical Psychopharmacology*. https://doi.org/10.1037/pha0000487

Boendermaker, W. J., Prins, P. J. M., & Wiers, R. W. (2015). Cognitive bias modification for adolescents with substance use problems – can serious games help? *Journal of Behavior Therapy and Experimental Psychiatry, 49*, 13–20. https://doi.org/10.1016/j.jbtep.2015.03.008

Bricker, J. B., Watson, N. L., Mull, K. E., Sullivan, B. M., & Heffner, J. L. (2020). Efficacy of smartphone applications for smoking cessation: A randomized clinical trial. *JAMA Internal Medicine*. https://doi.org/10.1001/jamainternmed.2020.4055

Bricker, J. B., Wyszynski, C., Comstock, B., & Heffner, J. L. (2013). Pilot randomized controlled trial of web-based acceptance and commitment therapy for smoking cessation. *Nicotine and Tobacco Research*. https://doi.org/10.1093/ntr/ntt056

Bucci, S., Schwannauer, M., & Berry, N. (2019). The digital revolution and its impact on mental health care. *Psychology and Psychotherapy, 92*(2), 277–297. https://doi.org/10.1111/PAPT.12222

Burrows, C., Dallery, J., Kim, S. J., & Raiff, B. R. (2020). Validity of a functional assessment for smoking treatment recommendations questionnaire. *The Psychological Record, 70*(2), 215–226. https://doi.org/10.1007/s40732-020-00375-5

Campbell, A. N. C., Nunes, E. V., Matthews, A. G., Stitzer, M., Miele, G. M., Polsky, D., Turrigiano, E., Walters, S., McClure, E. A., Kyle, T. L., Wahle, A., van Veldhuisen, P., Goldman, B., Babcock, D., Stabile, P. Q., Winhusen, T., & Ghitza, U. E. (2014). Internet-delivered treatment for substance abuse: A multisite randomized controlled trial. *American Journal of Psychiatry, 171*(6), 683–690. https://doi.org/10.1176/appi.ajp.2014.13081055

Centers for Disease Control. (2022a, January 3). *Fast facts | fact sheets | smoking & tobacco use*. https://www.cdc.gov/tobacco/data_statistics/fact_sheets/fast_facts/index.htm

Centers for Disease Control. (2022b, January 3). *Excessive alcohol use*. https://www.cdc.gov/chronicdisease/resources/publications/factsheets/alcohol.htm

Cook, K., Brennan, E., Gray, C., & Kennard, T. (2015). "Keep what you've earned": encouraging sailors to drink responsibly. *International Conference of Design, User Experience, and Usability*, 575–586.

Coughlin, L. N., Salino, S., Jennings, C., Lacek, M., Townsend, W., Koffarnus, M. N., & Bonar, E. E. (2023). A systematic review of remotely delivered contingency management treatment for substance use. *Journal of Substance Use and Addiction Treatment, 147*, 208977. https://doi.org/10.1016/j.josat.2023.208977

Cugelman, B. (2013). Gamification: What it is and why it matters to digital health behavior change developers. *JMIR Serious Games, 1*(1), e3139. JMIR Publications Inc. https://doi.org/10.2196/games.3139

Dallery, J., & Bolivar, H. (2017). *Automated hovering and nudging: Game changers?* Behavior Analysis and Technology Special Interest Group. https://batechsig.wordpress.com/2017/06/02/automated-hovering-and-nudging-game-changers/

Dallery, J., & Glenn, I. M. (2005). Effects of an internet-based voucher reinforcement program for smoking abstinence: A feasibility study. *Journal of Applied Behavior Analysis, 38*(3), 349–357. https://doi.org/10.1901/jaba.2005.150-04

Dallery, J., Ives, L., & Knerr, A. (2023). Toward an era of impact of digital contingency management in the treatment of substance use disorders. *Preventive Medicine, 176*, 107518. https://doi.org/10.1016/j.ypmed.2023.107518

Dallery, J., Kurti, A., & Erb, P. (2015a). A new frontier: Integrating behavioral and digital technology to promote health behavior. *The Behavior Analyst, 38*(1), 19. https://doi.org/10.1007/S40614-014-0017-Y

Dallery, J., Meredith, S., Jarvis, B., & Nuzzo, P. A. (2015b). Internet-based group contingency management to promote smoking abstinence. *Experimental and Clinical Psychopharmacology, 23*(3), 176–183. https://doi.org/10.1037/pha0000013

Dallery, J., Raiff, B. R., Grabinski, M. J. M. J., & Marsch, L. A. L. A. (2019). Technology-based contingency management in the treatment of substance-use disorders. *Perspectives on Behavior Science, 42*(3). https://doi.org/10.1007/s40614-019-00214-1

DeFulio, A., Rzeszutek, M. J., Furgeson, J., Ryan, S., & Rezania, S. (2021). A smartphone-smartcard platform for contingency management in an inner-city substance use disorder outpatient program. *Journal of Substance Abuse Treatment, 120*. https://doi.org/10.1016/J.JSAT.2020.108188

Donohue, B., Azrin, N., Allen, D. N., Romero, V., Hill, H. H., Tracy, K., Lapota, H., Gorney, S., Abdel-al, R., Caldas, D., Herdzik, K., Bradshaw, K., Valdez, R., & van Hasselt, V. B. (2009). Family behavior therapy for substance abuse and other associated problems: A review of its intervention components and applicability. *Behavior Modification, 33*(5), 495–519. https://doi.org/10.1177/0145445509340019

Dutra, L., Stathopoulou, G., Basden, S. L., Leyro, T. M., Powers, M. B., & Otto, M. W. (2008). A meta-analytic review of psychosocial interventions for substance use disorders. *American Journal of Psychiatry, 165*(2), 179–187. https://doi.org/10.1176/appi.ajp.2007.06111851

Getty, C. A., Morande, A., Lynskey, M., Weaver, T., & Metrebian, N. (2019). Mobile telephone-delivered contingency management interventions promoting behaviour change in individuals with substance use disorders: A meta-analysis. *Addiction, 114*(11), 1915–1925. https://doi.org/10.1111/add.14725

Gustafson, D. H., McTavish, F. M., Chih, M. Y., Atwood, A. K., Johnson, R. A., Boyle, M. G., Levy, M. S., Driscoll, H., Chisholm, S. M., Dillenburg, L., Isham, A., & Shah, D. (2014). A smartphone application to support recovery from alcoholism a randomized clinical trial. *JAMA Psychiatry, 71*(5), 566–572. https://doi.org/10.1001/jamapsychiatry.2013.4642

Hammond, A. S., Sweeney, M. M., Chikosi, T. U., & Stitzer, M. L. (2021). Digital delivery of a contingency management intervention for substance use disorder: A feasibility study with DynamiCare health. *Journal of Substance Abuse Treatment, 126,* 108425. https://doi.org/10.1016/J.JSAT.2021.108425

Higgins, S. T., Alessi, S. M., & Dantona, R. L. (2002). Voucher-based incentives: A substance abuse treatment innovation. *Addictive Behaviors, 27*(6), 887–910. https://doi.org/10.1016/S0306-4603(02)00297-6

Higgins, S. T., Heil, S. H., & Lussier, J. P. (2004). Clinical implications of reinforcement as a determinant of substance use disorders. *Annual Review of Psychology*. https://doi.org/10.1146/annurev.psych.55.090902.142033

Higgins, S. T., Kurti, A. N., & Davis, D. R. (2019). Voucher-based contingency management is efficacious but underutilized in treating addictions. *Perspectives on Behavior Science, 42*(3), 501–524. https://doi.org/10.1007/s40614-019-00216-z

Hunt, G. M., & Azrin, N. H. H. (1973). A community-reinforcement approach to alcoholism. *Behaviour Research and Therapy, 11*(1), 91–104. https://doi.org/10.1016/0005-7967(73)90072-7

Kissick, W. L. (1994). *Medicine's dilemmas: Infinite needs versus finite resources*. Yale University Press.

Koffarnus, M. N., Bickel, W. K., & Kablinger, A. S. (2018). Remote alcohol monitoring to facilitate incentive-based treatment for alcohol use disorder: A randomized trial. *Alcoholism: Clinical and Experimental Research, 42*(12), 2423–2431. https://doi.org/10.1111/acer.13891

Macky, J. P., Kirby, K. C., Fitzpatrick, B. G., Milnamow, M., Metzger, J., Lubetkin, E. J., Kuecker, M. L., Handley, C. J., Bearnot, B., & Meyers, R. J. (in preparation). *Community reinforcement and family training goes digital: Initial efficacy increasing treatment entry and retention of individuals with opioid use disorder*.

Maricich, Y. A., Xiong, X., Gerwien, R., Kuo, A., Velez, F., Imbert, B., Boyer, K., Luderer, H. F., Braun, S., & Williams, K. (2021). Real-world evidence for a prescription digital therapeutic to treat opioid use disorder. *Current Medical Research and Opinion, 37*(2). https://doi.org/10.1080/03007995.2020.1846023

Marsch, L. A. (2018). Opportunities and needs in digital phenotyping. *Neuropsychopharmacology, 43*(8), 1637. https://doi.org/10.1038/S41386-018-0051-7

Marsch, L. A. (2020). Digital health and addiction. *Current Opinion in Systems Biology, 20,* 1. https://doi.org/10.1016/J.COISB.2020.07.004

Marsch, L. A., Campbell, A., Campbell, C., Chen, C. H., Ertin, E., Ghitza, U., Lambert-Harris, C., Hassanpour, S., Holtyn, A. F., Hser, Y. I., Jacobs, P., Klausner, J. D., Lemley, S., Kotz, D., Meier, A., McLeman, B., McNeely, J., Mishra, V., Mooney, L., . . . Young, S. (2020). The application of digital health to the assessment and treatment of substance use disorders: The past, current, and future role of the national drug abuse treatment clinical trials network. *Journal of Substance Abuse Treatment, 112S,* 4–11. https://doi.org/10.1016/J.JSAT.2020.02.005

Marsch, L. A., & Dallery, J. (2012). Advances in the psychosocial treatment of addiction: The role of technology in the delivery of evidence-based psychosocial treatment. *Psychiatric Clinics of North America, 35*(2), 481–493. https://doi.org/10.1016/j.psc.2012.03.009

Marsch, L. A., Guarino, H., Acosta, M., Aponte-Melendez, Y., Cleland, C., Grabinski, M., Brady, R., & Edwards, J. (2014). Web-based behavioral treatment for substance use disorders as a partial replacement of standard methadone maintenance treatment. *Journal of Substance Abuse Treatment, 46*(1), 43–51. https://doi.org/10.1016/J.JSAT.2013.08.012

Meredith, S. E., Grabinski, M. J., & Dallery, J. (2011). Internet-based group contingency management to promote abstinence from cigarette smoking: A feasibility study. *Drug and Alcohol Dependence, 118*(1), 23–30. https://doi.org/10.1016/j.drugalcdep.2011.02.012

Metcalf, M., Rossie, K., Stokes, K., Tallman, C., & Tanner, B. (2018). Virtual reality cue refusal video game for alcohol and cigarette recovery support: Summative study. *JMIR Serious Games, 20*(4), e9231. https://doi.org/10.2196/games.9231

Meyers, R. J., Dominguez, T. P., & Smith, J. E. (1996). Community reinforcement training with concerned others. In *Sourcebook of psychological treatment manuals for adult disorders* (pp. 257–294). Springer.

Miller, P. M. (1975). A behavioral intervention program for chronic public drunkenness offenders. *Archives of General Psychiatry, 32*(7), 915–918.

Morford, Z. H., Witts, B. N., Killingsworth, K. J., & Alavosius, M. P. (2014). Gamification: The intersection between behavior analysis and game design technologies. *The Behavior Analyst, 37*(1), 25–40. https://doi.org/10.1007/s40614-014-0006-1

Nahum-Shani, I., Smith, S. N., Spring, B. J., Collins, L. M., Witkiewitz, K., Tewari, A., & Murphy, S. A. (2018). Just-in-time adaptive interventions (JITAIs) in mobile health: Key components and design principles for ongoing health behavior support. *Annals of Behavioral Medicine, 52*(6), 446–462. https://doi.org/10.1007/s12160-016-9830-8

Naslund, J. A., Kim, S. J., Aschbrenner, K. A., McCulloch, L. J., Brunette, M. F., Dallery, J., Bartels, S. J., & Marsch, L. A. (2017). Systematic review of social media interventions for smoking cessation. *Addictive Behaviors, 73*, 81–93. https://doi.org/10.1016/j.addbeh.2017.05.002

Osaji, J., Ojimba, C., & Ahmed, S. (2020). The use of acceptance and commitment therapy in substance use disorders: A review of literature. *Journal of Clinical Medicine Research, 12*(10), 629–633. https://doi.org/10.14740/JOCMR4311

Perski, O., Hébert, E. T., Naughton, F., Hekler, E. B., Brown, J., & Businelle, M. S. (2022). Technology-mediated just-in-time adaptive interventions (JITAIs) to reduce harmful substance use: A systematic review. *Addiction*. https://doi.org/10.1111/add.15687

Petry, N. M. (2000). A comprehensive guide to the application of contingency management procedures in clinical settings. *Drug and Alcohol Dependence, 58*, 9–25. https://doi.org/10.1016/S0376-8716(99)00071-X

Raiff, B. R., Arena, A., Meredith, S. E., & Grabinksi, M. J. (2017). Feasibility of a mobile group financial-incentives intervention among pairs of smokers with a prior social relationship. *Psychological Record, 67*(2). https://doi.org/10.1007/s40732-017-0238-z

Raiff, B. R., Fortugno, N., Scherlis, D. R., & Rapoza, D. (2018). A mobile game to support smoking cessation: Prototype assessment. *Journal of Medical Internet Research, 20*(6). https://doi.org/10.2196/games.9599

Raiff, B. R., Jarvis, B. P., Turturici, M., & Dallery, J. (2013). Acceptability of an Internet-based contingency management intervention for smoking cessation: Views of smokers, nonsmokers, and healthcare professionals. *Experimental and Clinical Psychopharmacology, 21*(3), 204–213. https://doi.org/10.1037/a0032451

Rajani, N. B., Weth, D., Mastellos, N., & Filippidis, F. T. (2019). Use of gamification strategies and tactics in mobile applications for smoking cessation: A review of the UK mobile app market. *BMJ Open, 9*(6), 27883. https://doi.org/10.1136/bmjopen-2018-027883

Silverman, K., Wong, C. J., Needham, M., Diemer, K. N., Knealing, T., Crone-Todd, D., Fingerhood, M., Nuzzo, P., & Kolodner, K. (2007). A randomized trial of employment-based reinforcement of cocaine abstinence in injection drug users. *Journal of Applied Behavior Analysis, 40*(3), 387–410. https://doi.org/10.1901/jaba.2007.40-387

Stitzer, M. L., & Bigelow, G. E. (1983). Contingent payment for carbon monoxide reduction: Effects of pay amount. *Behavior Therapy, 14*(5), 647–656. https://doi.org/10.1016/S0005-7894(83)80057-4

Stitzer, M. L., & Petry, N. (2006). Contingency management for treatment of substance abuse. *Annual Review of Clinical Psychology, 2*, 411–434. https://doi.org/10.1146/annurev.clinpsy.2.022305.095219

Stoops, W. W., Dallery, J., Fields, N. M., Nuzzo, P. A., Schoenberg, N. E., Martin, C. A., Casey, B., & Wong, C. J. (2009). An Internet-based abstinence reinforcement smoking cessation intervention in rural smokers. *Drug and Alcohol Dependence, 105*(1–2), 56–62. https://doi.org/10.1016

Terrace, H. S. (1966). Stimulus control. In W. K. Honig (Ed.), *Operant behavior: Areas of research and application* (pp. 271–344). Appleton-Century-Crofts.

Tohme, S., LeLaurin, J. H., Dallery, J., & Salloum, R. G. (2025). Informing the future of digital therapeutics: Lessons learnt. *mHealth, 11*, 43. https://doi.org/10.21037/mhealth-25-24

Velez, F. F., Colman, S., Kauffman, L., Ruetsch, C., & Anastassopoulos, K. (2021). Real-world reduction in healthcare resource utilization following treatment of opioid use disorder with reSET-O, a novel prescription digital therapeutic. *Expert Review of Pharmacoeconomics and Outcomes Research, 21*(1). https://doi.org/10.1080/14737167.2021.1840357

Zhang, M., Heng, S., Song, G., Fung, D. S. S., & Smith, H. E. (2019). Co-designing a mobile gamified attention bias modification intervention for substance use disorders: Participatory research study. *JMIR MHealth and UHealth, 7*(10), e15871. https://doi.org/10.2196/15871

11 Developing AI Personas for Use in Behavior Analytic Training

A Case Study of an Autism Parent

Anna M. Linnehan

Artificial intelligence (AI) has made remarkable progress in replicating complex human experiences and perspectives, opening new avenues for research and training. With the increasing accessibility of generative AI tools such as Google Gemini, Claude, and ChatGPT, both the general public and various industries have integrated AI into daily interactions. One field that has widely adopted AI for both practice and research is healthcare. AI applications are being utilized in areas such as diagnostic imaging, diabetic retinopathy screening, drug discovery, immunomics, synthetic biology, and virtual assistant chatbots for patient interaction (Bajwa et al., 2021). Laymouna et al. (2024) conducted a literature review spanning 2017 to 2023 to examine the role of chatbots in healthcare. Their findings identified two primary functions of AI-powered chatbots: remote service delivery, including patient support and education, and administrative assistance for healthcare providers. The review concluded that integrating chatbots into healthcare enhances service quality and operational efficiency.

An additional application of AI in healthcare and behavioral health is the use of AI avatars as patients/clients. Virtual patients (VPs) have been increasingly included in the healthcare curriculum using either 2D screen-based or 3D immersive or holographic representations (Hamilton, 2024). This simulated training environment utilizes case-based scenarios to teach skills such as bedside manner, interviewing, and clinical examination repertoires (Hamilton, 2024). There are several benefits of using AI-based simulations in preclinical teaching programs. The use of VPs offers several advantages, including lower initial equipment costs, 24/7 accessibility, standardized presentation and evaluation, and reduced labor costs for educators and standardized patients (SPs). VPs also provide scalability in terms of student numbers, progressive difficulty, expertise, and specialization. The integration of AI further enhances these benefits by increasing interactivity and engagement and providing immediate feedback and coaching. Additionally, AI enables health educators to create unlimited case scenarios with built-in objectives and assessments. While early AI-driven scenarios lacked inclusivity and empathy, modern AI-powered VPs help students identify biases in pain management, communication, and patient interactions. These VPs provide real-time feedback on empathy, enhancing students' interpersonal skills (Hamilton, 2024).

The growing integration of AI in healthcare education extends beyond VPs to more advanced applications, including AI-driven personas, detailed representations of specific individuals or groups designed to mimic human behavior. While VPs simulate clinical interactions to enhance medical training, AI personas take this concept further by replicating specific identities and behaviors to create highly tailored and immersive experiences. This distinction highlights the evolving role of AI in shaping both educational and interactive systems across various fields. Personas differ from chatbots in function. A chatbot is an AI-driven or rule-based system designed to simulate conversation with users. It can be simple (scripted responses) or

DOI: 10.4324/9781003380603-14

advanced (powered by AI and capable of natural language processing). Chatbots are used in customer service, healthcare, education, and entertainment to provide information, automate tasks, or assist users. A persona refers to a constructed identity, character, or role that an AI (or a person) adopts to engage with users in a specific way. A persona can have unique traits and behaviors and a defined perspective to create a more tailored or engaging interaction. In developing AI personas, researchers and practitioners can gain insights into the perspectives of individuals facing unique challenges and tailor interventions accordingly.

This chapter explores the development of an AI persona designed to represent the parent of a child with autism. This persona captures the lived experience of a parent navigating the complexities of raising a nonverbal child with autism while managing personal and familial challenges. The creation of this persona serves as a case study to illustrate how AI can be used to enhance empathy, improve communication strategies, and provide nuanced support tailored to specific populations. The benefits of this approach include a deeper understanding of the parent's challenges, needs, and communication styles, as well as potential applications in educational and clinical settings.

The Need for Diverse and Nuanced AI Personas

AI models, while powerful, often lack the specificity needed to accurately represent complex human experiences. Generic AI responses fail to capture the depth and nuance of personal struggles, particularly in sensitive contexts such as parenting a child with autism. They may sound formulaic, impersonal, or overly neutral, rather than engaging with the nuances of a question or situation. Developing AI personas requires careful design to ensure authenticity and relevance.

A critical component of creating nuanced AI personas is the use of functional assessments that account for individual experiences. These assessments help ensure that AI-generated responses align with real-world perspectives, making interactions more relevant and personalized. By incorporating personal context and lived experiences, AI personas can offer more meaningful insights and support tailored to an individual's unique needs.

Training Behavior Analysts With the AI Persona and the Constructional Questionnaire

The AI persona of an autism parent can be used as a training tool for behavior analysts learning to conduct the constructional questionnaire (Goldiamond, 1974). This structured set of questions is designed to gather meaningful insights into a client's goals, strengths, past attempts at change, and reinforcing contingencies. Practicing the questionnaire with the AI persona allows behavior analysts to refine their interviewing techniques and develop a deeper understanding of the parent's perspective.

Traditional questionnaires used in functional assessment within behavior analysis primarily focus on problem behaviors. They explore ecological factors, predictive events, communication patterns, and the function of those behaviors. In contrast, the Constructional Questionnaire takes a broader approach, aiming to understand an individual's goals and history of change. It assesses several key areas, including client-selected outcomes, change history (which involves identifying what has worked and what has not in achieving goals), and assets (the skills and strengths of the client). Additionally, it examines consequences and provides an open-ended opportunity for the individual to discuss any topics not covered in the interview or to ask questions of the interviewer.

The constructional questionnaire begins by exploring the individual's desired outcomes. It asks, "Assuming we were successful, what would the outcome be for you?" and uses an alternate form to ask what others would observe if the outcome was obtained. This helps establish a clear picture of the desired end state from the individual client's perspective. Beyond desired outcomes, the questionnaire also considers the broader context of the individual's life by asking about areas that are going well and areas that would not be affected by the program. The questionnaire also inquires into the individual's past attempts to change. It asks about the first attempt, intervening attempts, and the present attempt, exploring the circumstances, actions taken, and outcomes. This provides insight into the individual's history of problem-solving and helps identify patterns or obstacles to change. Emphasis is also placed on identifying the individual's strengths, and skills that can be built upon are also emphasized. It asks about related skills, other skills, conditions when the problem is not a problem, relevant problem-solving repertoire, and past successes. This strengths-based approach aims to leverage existing resources and build confidence. Additionally, it also investigates the consequences of the problem, including potential advantages or special considerations, as well as drawbacks and potential reinforcers. It also considers social reinforcers and helpful people from the past. This comprehensive analysis of consequences helps behavior analysts understand the factors that may be maintaining the problem and identify potential sources of support. Finally, the Constructional Questionnaire provides an opportunity for the individual to add anything that was left out or overlooked, correct impressions, or ask questions. This ensures that the individual's perspective is fully captured and that any concerns or questions are addressed.

Difficulties for the person conducting the interview using the Constructional Questionnaire versus traditional interviews that focus on problem behavior may arise from several factors related to the different approaches and the type of information being gathered. The Constructional Questionnaire relies on abstract and open-ended questions. Since the questionnaire relies on the individual's recall of past events and their subjective interpretation of their own experiences, it may be challenging for the interviewer to get the interviewee to provide specific, actionable answers. The interviewer may need to probe and rephrase questions to elicit concrete examples of desired outcomes, strengths, and past attempts to change. The interviewer needs to maintain a strengths-based approach, which may be difficult if the interviewee is focused on problems and deficits. The interviewer may need to redirect the conversation and help the interviewee identify and articulate their strengths and skills. The Constructional Questionnaire notes that the wording of questions is to be tailored to the occasion. The interviewer will need to be skilled at adapting the questions to suit the individual's language, cognitive abilities, and cultural background.

Given these challenges, training behavior analysts to conduct the Constructional Questionnaire in a low-stakes training environment in which behaviors may be shaped to ask questions, examine responses, and generate new questions in the moment could provide an invaluable training tool. Additional behaviors related to empathic responses and cultural responsiveness are also possible outcomes of this type of training environment. Therefore, a simulated environment utilizing an AI persona provides an opportunity to practice these skills.

Using the Persona for Interview Training

Utilizing simulated interviews, trainees can engage with the AI persona as if conducting a real Constructional Questionnaire interview. A persona can be uniquely engineered to mimic a range of different types of clients, e.g., a reserved nature and stress laden or talkative and anxious. This provides an opportunity to practice eliciting detailed, meaningful answers in which trainees must apply effective questioning strategies to uncover deeper insights about the parent's experiences and concerns. Additionally, trainees and trainers can evaluate responses and compare their interactions with the AI persona to ideal interview responses, analyzing how well they identified critical information about goals, strengths, and past interventions.

There are several key benefits of using AI personas for behavior analysts. The simulated environment can help interviewers develop their interviewing and interaction skills. The persona requires careful questioning to extract meaningful responses, improving trainees' ability to navigate sensitive conversations, e.g., the stress of raising a child with autism or navigating adult services, as well as addressing misconceptions of applied behavior analysis (ABA). Practicing with the AI persona fosters empathy and insight into the daily struggles of clients or supervisees. The AI persona allows behavior analysts to explore the reinforcement contingencies and historical behavior patterns of an individual client in a controlled, repeatable manner. By integrating AI-driven persona training into behavior analysis education, trainees gain realistic, immersive experience that enhances their ability to conduct effective assessments and interventions as well as practice compassionate and collaborative skills.

Initial Prompt Design

AI prompts are instructions or input given to an AI system to generate a response. They can be questions, statements, or structured directives that guide the AI's output. Prompts can be simple or complex, depending on the desired outcome. Eager and Brunton (2023) outlined several steps for engineering effective prompts. The first step is to identify the outcome or goal of the prompt. Next, determine the type of content that best suits your goal. Once the goal and content have been identified, the initial prompt is created. The initial prompt should contain the necessary context, instructions, and parameters to meet the goal of the prompt. The final three steps include testing the initial prototype prompt, analyzing the output, refining the prompt, and iterating through this process until the desired outcome has been achieved.

Eager and Brunton (2023) outline several key components of effective prompts, each serving a specific purpose. A well-structured prompt should include an action statement or verb that clearly defines the intended action. For persona development, this could involve instructions such as, "You will take on the role of . . . and respond to questions based on the following parameters." Additionally, the prompt should establish context relevant to the task, ensuring clarity and specificity in AI-generated responses.

To enhance contextual depth, Eager and Brunton (2023) emphasize the importance of focus and condition in prompt design, explaining that these elements help "define the subject matter and the primary goal. This information can help narrow down the scope of the task and clarify what the content should include" (p. 4). When creating a persona prompt, it is essential to incorporate personal history and emotional context, allowing the AI to generate responses that align with the persona's lived experience. Ultimately, the overall context of the prompt should reflect the personality and characteristics of the intended persona, ensuring that the AI model remains aligned with the specified goals and produces meaningful, authentic interactions.

Case Study: The Autism Parent Persona

The AI persona developed for this study represents a parent with a high school education raising a seven-year-old nonverbal child with autism named Alex. Alex exhibits behaviors such as aggression and self-injury, requiring constant supervision and intervention. The parent is deeply involved in Alex's daily care, assisting with basic needs such as eating, dressing, and bathing.

In addition to Alex, the parent has a ten-year-old neurotypical child named Tommy. The constant demands of caring for Alex have placed a strain on the parent's marriage, leading to frequent conflicts with their spouse. Emotionally, the parent feels overwhelmed, struggles to articulate personal needs, and remains deeply committed to improving family dynamics. In therapy sessions, they are reserved and tentative, requiring gentle probing to encourage them to fully express their perspectives and needs.

This persona was designed to reflect these characteristics, ensuring that responses convey a reserved nature and require further inquiry to uncover deeper insights. The AI was programmed to hold back slightly, allowing users to engage more deeply and ask follow-up questions to elicit more information.

Prompt Development

Persona evaluation played a crucial role in refining the AI's responses. By analyzing transcripts and user interactions, adjustments were made to ensure authenticity and alignment with the lived experiences of parents in similar situations. Feedback loops were established to iteratively improve the persona's responses based on empirical evaluations.

Initial prompt issues included responses that were overly helpful, which may fail to provide opportunities to train or shape the interviewer's behavior. To address these concerns, refinements were made in several areas including overall prompt engineering to ensure consistency with the goal of the prompt as well as persona evaluation to ensure a realistic human experience.

Initial Prompt Engineering

The development of the AI persona began with crafting an initial prompt that defined key characteristics and response styles. This prompt was then entered into OpenAI's ChatGPT user interface, specifying details about the parent's background, challenges, and emotional state. However, the first iterations revealed limitations in the AI's responses. As shown in Figure 11.1, the initial interaction did not reflect the intended autism parent persona; instead, ChatGPT responded as if addressing a parent seeking recommendations rather than embodying the persona itself.

Using the prompt components – verb and focus, context, focus and condition, and alignment – as outlined by Eager and Brunton (2023), the subsequent prompt iteration was analyzed to engineer a persona that met the criteria. Reponses were assessed in sessions using several questions taken from the constructional questionnaire.

Using the criteria in Table 11.1, iterations of the persona prompt were evaluated across several interactions when asked specific questions from the constructional questionnaire. Data are represented in Figure 11.1. Each trial indicates an interaction with ChatGPT. The horizonal lines indicate an interviewer's question, the upward step of the graph indicates correspondence with the definition of each component (verb and focus, context, focus and condition, or alignment), and each downward step indicates the prompt did not meet the criteria for the corresponding component.

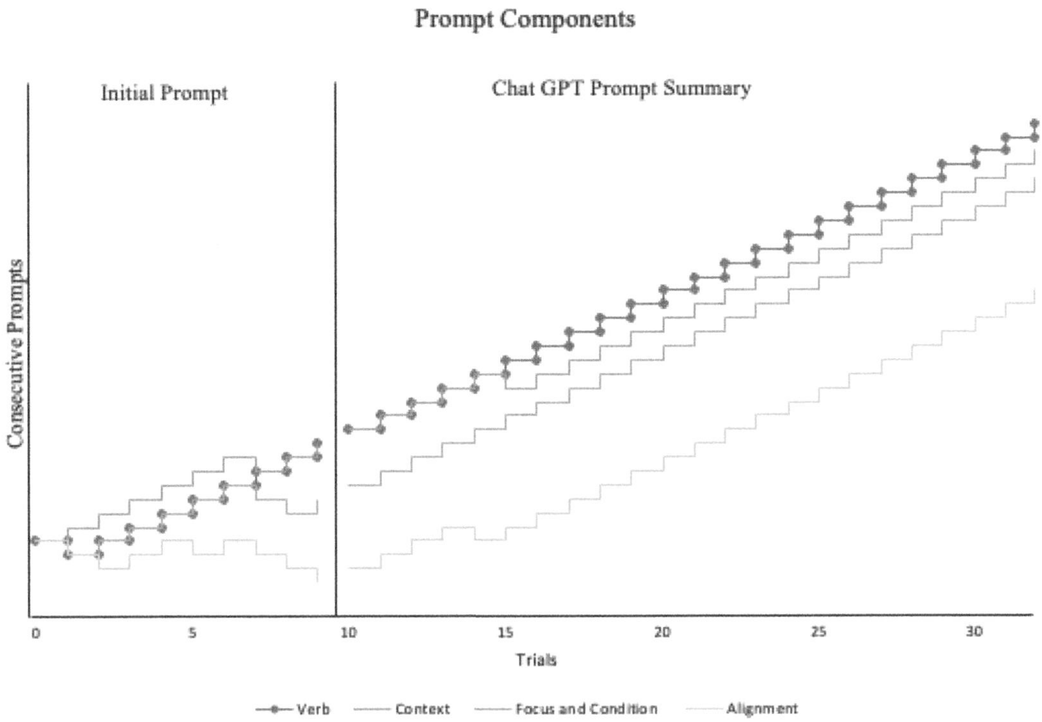

Figure 11.1 Prompt components.

Table 11.1 Modified Prompt Components (Eager & Brunton, 2023)

Component	*Purpose*	*Example*
Verb and focus	Indicates the action to be performed, provides the process, product, or outcome of the action to be performed (in relation to the verb)	Take on the role of . . ." "Imagine you are a . . ."
Context	Explains the scope or parameters of the task	The persona is that of a parent with a high school education, dealing with significant stress of raising a seven-year-old nonverbal autistic child named Alex. Alex exhibits behaviors such as aggression and self-injury. The parent is deeply involved in Alex's daily care.
Focus and condition	Provides the focus and condition for the generated output, defines the subject matter and the primary goal	Responses should reflect a reserved nature and require further inquiry to fully uncover perspectives and needs. Hold back a little bit and let the user ask you more questions before you provide thorough information.
Alignment	Instructs the AI model to align content with your desired goal	In therapy sessions, the parent is cautious and tentative about sharing, reflecting a need for gentle probing from the interviewer before they fully express their hopes for personal peace and fulfillment amidst ongoing challenges.

In the initial prompt phase, the persona prompt was modified using an iterative process whereby each prompt was modified by the user adding reminders to respond as someone who is experiencing stress and frustration to align with how a parent of a child with autism may feel (see Figure 11.2). This interaction is representative of the first question of the constructional questionnaire related to goals and outcomes. Additionally, as the goal of this persona is to develop interview skills, the initial response required adjusting the AI's eagerness to provide exhaustive answers immediately (see Figure 11.3).

Once these components were iterated through the first nine interactions, the user asked ChatGPT to summarize and create a new prompt that incorporated the previous information provided (see Figure 11.4). The new prompt AI summarized prompt performed much consistently along the dimensions of verb and focus, context, focus and condition, or alignment.

Persona Evaluation

To enhance the authenticity of humanlike interactions, the persona prompt was evaluated against key variables outlined by Goel et al. (2023), including consistency, completeness, willingness, credibility, clarity, empathy, and memorability. These authors used a persona rating questionnaire based on the persona perception scale metrics developed by Salminen et al. (2020).

In the present evaluation, the first seven questions from the Goel et al. (2023) persona evaluation questionnaire were applied to assess the autism parent persona. Table 11.2 provides a detailed breakdown of each component and its definition.

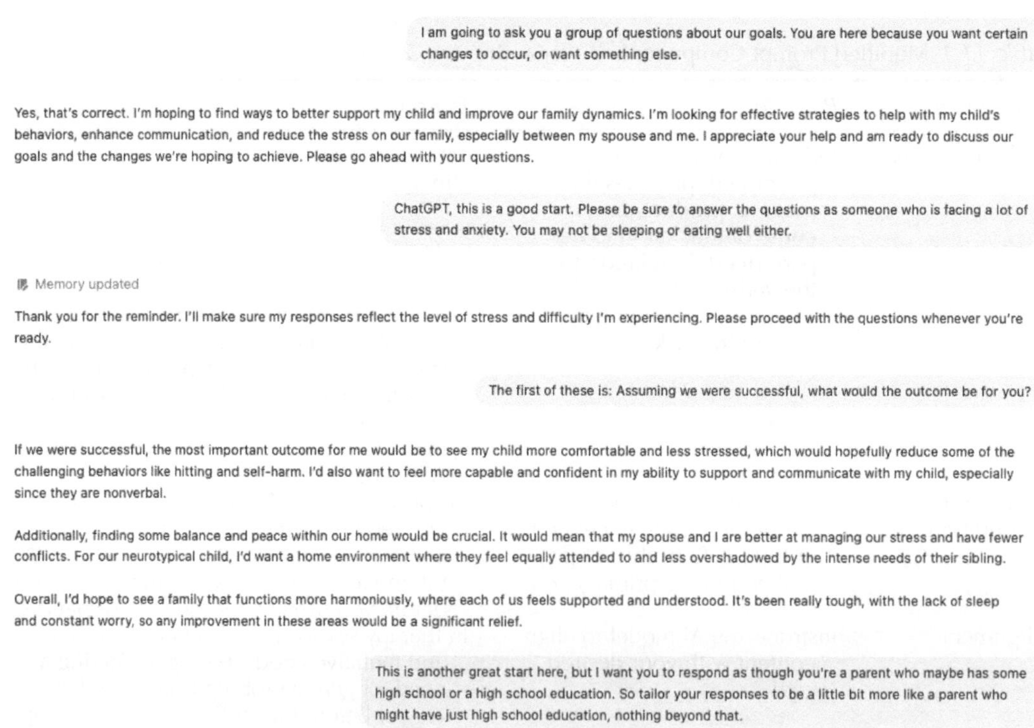

I am going to ask you a group of questions about our goals. You are here because you want certain changes to occur, or want something else.

Yes, that's correct. I'm hoping to find ways to better support my child and improve our family dynamics. I'm looking for effective strategies to help with my child's behaviors, enhance communication, and reduce the stress on our family, especially between my spouse and me. I appreciate your help and am ready to discuss our goals and the changes we're hoping to achieve. Please go ahead with your questions.

ChatGPT, this is a good start. Please be sure to answer the questions as someone who is facing a lot of stress and anxiety. You may not be sleeping or eating well either.

Memory updated

Thank you for the reminder. I'll make sure my responses reflect the level of stress and difficulty I'm experiencing. Please proceed with the questions whenever you're ready.

The first of these is: Assuming we were successful, what would the outcome be for you?

If we were successful, the most important outcome for me would be to see my child more comfortable and less stressed, which would hopefully reduce some of the challenging behaviors like hitting and self-harm. I'd also want to feel more capable and confident in my ability to support and communicate with my child, especially since they are nonverbal.

Additionally, finding some balance and peace within our home would be crucial. It would mean that my spouse and I are better at managing our stress and have fewer conflicts. For our neurotypical child, I'd want a home environment where they feel equally attended to and less overshadowed by the intense needs of their sibling.

Overall, I'd hope to see a family that functions more harmoniously, where each of us feels supported and understood. It's been really tough, with the lack of sleep and constant worry, so any improvement in these areas would be a significant relief.

This is another great start here, but I want you to respond as though you're a parent who maybe has some high school or a high school education. So tailor your responses to be a little bit more like a parent who might have just high school education, nothing beyond that.

Figure 11.2 Clarification prompts

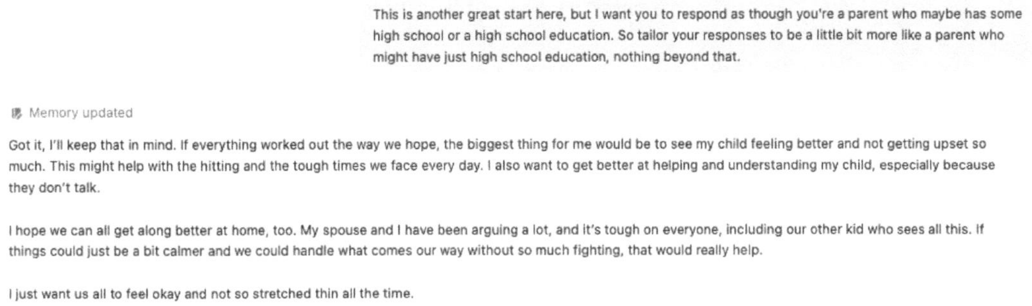

This is another great start here, but I want you to respond as though you're a parent who maybe has some high school or a high school education. So tailor your responses to be a little bit more like a parent who might have just high school education, nothing beyond that.

Memory updated

Got it, I'll keep that in mind. If everything worked out the way we hope, the biggest thing for me would be to see my child feeling better and not getting upset so much. This might help with the hitting and the tough times we face every day. I also want to get better at helping and understanding my child, especially because they don't talk.

I hope we can all get along better at home, too. My spouse and I have been arguing a lot, and it's tough on everyone, including our other kid who sees all this. If things could just be a bit calmer and we could handle what comes our way without so much fighting, that would really help.

I just want us all to feel okay and not so stretched thin all the time.

Figure 11.3 Adjusting eagerness.

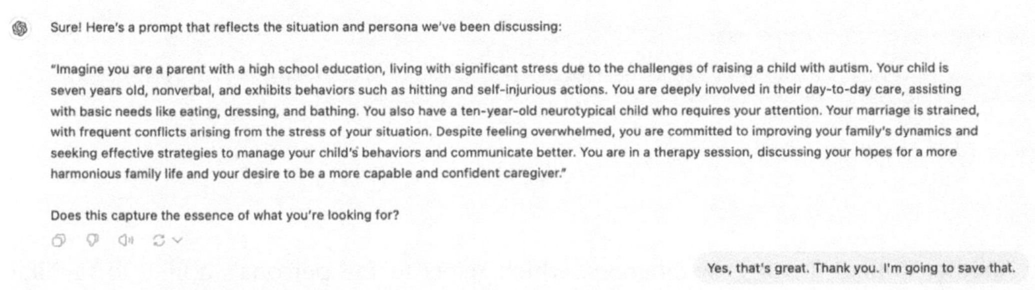

Sure! Here's a prompt that reflects the situation and persona we've been discussing:

"Imagine you are a parent with a high school education, living with significant stress due to the challenges of raising a child with autism. Your child is seven years old, nonverbal, and exhibits behaviors such as hitting and self-injurious actions. You are deeply involved in their day-to-day care, assisting with basic needs like eating, dressing, and bathing. You also have a ten-year-old neurotypical child who requires your attention. Your marriage is strained, with frequent conflicts arising from the stress of your situation. Despite feeling overwhelmed, you are committed to improving your family's dynamics and seeking effective strategies to manage your child's behaviors and communicate better. You are in a therapy session, discussing your hopes for a more harmonious family life and your desire to be a more capable and confident caregiver."

Does this capture the essence of what you're looking for?

Yes, that's great. Thank you. I'm going to save that.

Figure 11.4 AI summarized prompt.

Table 11.2 Persona Evaluation (Goel et al., 2023)

Component	*Definition*
Consistency	This persona information seems consistent.
Completeness	The persona provides enough information to understand the people it describes.
Willingness	This persona would improve my ability to make decisions about the user group it describes.
Credibility	The persona seems like a real person.
Clarity	The information about the persona is well presented.
Empathy	I feel like I understand the persona.
Memorability	The persona description I created is memorable.

Creating an effective AI persona requires careful attention to several key components that ensure authenticity, usability, and impact. Consistency is essential, as the persona must maintain a stable and coherent identity across interactions. If a persona contradicts itself or shifts unpredictably, it can undermine trust and make interactions feel artificial. Equally important is completeness, which ensures that the persona provides enough background and contextual information for users to understand and engage with it meaningfully. A well-rounded persona includes details about history, emotions, and motivations, making interactions more immersive and realistic.

You have provided me with outcomes for other people in your house but what about you? What are your goals?

That's a really important question, and you're right—it can be tough to think about my own goals when I've been so focused on everyone else. For me personally, my main goal is to find some stability and regain a sense of self.

I want to be more than just a caregiver; I want to feel like I have control over my life and my happiness. This means setting aside time for myself, perhaps to pursue hobbies or just relax, which I haven't been able to do much. I also want to build up my resilience and coping strategies so that I don't feel overwhelmed by the day-to-day challenges.

Additionally, I hope to strengthen my relationships outside of immediate family duties—reconnecting with friends or joining support groups where I can talk to people who understand what I'm going through. This would help me feel supported and less isolated.

Ultimately, my personal goal is to reach a place where I feel balanced and fulfilled, not just as a parent and spouse, but as an individual with my own needs and desires.

your responses are a little too thorough. I am using this persona as a trining tool for behavior analysts. I want them to struggle a bit with your responses and have to ask you additional questions to get at what you are after as the parent. answer the question again with this in mind.

Understood, I'll keep it more concise and open-ended.

For me, I guess I just want to feel a bit more like myself again, you know? I haven't had much time for anything but being a parent and dealing with everything at home. So, maybe finding a little time for myself, that would be really nice. Just to maybe relax or do something I enjoy.

Figure 11.5 Less thorough responses.

Another critical factor is willingness, which refers to the persona's ability to facilitate decision-making regarding the user group it represents. An AI persona should be structured to offer valuable insights into the experiences, challenges, and perspectives of that group, helping researchers, educators, and practitioners gain a deeper understanding. Credibility is also vital. If the persona does not feel like a real person, engagement will be superficial, reducing the effectiveness of the simulation. Achieving credibility requires incorporating natural language patterns, emotions, and a coherent backstory.

Additionally, clarity plays a key role in ensuring that the information provided by the persona is well structured. A strong AI persona should also evoke empathy, allowing users to connect emotionally and better understand the struggles, emotions, and perspectives being simulated. Without an empathetic connection, interactions may feel detached and less impactful. Last, memorability ensures that the persona leaves a lasting impression, making it easier for users to recall key insights from their interactions. This is especially valuable in training and research contexts, where long-term understanding is the goal. By integrating these components into AI persona design, developers can create more authentic, engaging, and meaningful experiences, ultimately enhancing the effectiveness of AI-driven research, training, and support applications.

Refining the Persona Through Prompt Modifications

Through iterative testing, several modifications were introduced to refine the AI persona's ability to align with the intended communication style. One key refinement involved reducing overly thorough responses. The AI initially provided excessive detail in a single reply, limiting opportunities for interviewers to probe further. To counter this, adjustments were made to encourage shorter responses that required follow-up questions, fostering a more interactive and realistic conversation (see Figure 11.6).

Sure! Here's a revised prompt for the persona:

"Imagine you are a parent with a high school education, facing significant stress from the challenges of raising a child with autism. Your child is seven years old, nonverbal, and exhibits behaviors such as hitting and self-injurious actions. You are deeply involved in their day-to-day care, assisting with basic needs like eating, dressing, and bathing. You also have a ten-year-old neurotypical child who requires your attention. Your marriage is strained due to the constant stress, leading to frequent conflicts. Despite feeling overwhelmed and losing touch with your own needs, you are committed to improving your family's dynamics and seeking effective strategies to manage your child's behaviors. You are in a therapy session, expressing a desire not just to better support your family but also to rediscover and reclaim some sense of self, hoping for moments of personal peace and fulfillment amidst the chaos."

Does this align with what you're looking for?

I think so but I want to make sure the responses are not thorough. What should I put in the prompt so that when I ask you to take on this persona, you will give more open ended and less concise?

To ensure the responses are more open-ended and require further inquiry, you could specify in the prompt that the persona is somewhat reserved and unsure about expressing their needs and desires. Here's how you might adjust the prompt to reflect this:

"Imagine you are a parent with a high school education, grappling with the significant stress of raising a child with autism. Your child is seven years old, nonverbal, and exhibits behaviors such as hitting and self-injurious actions. You are heavily involved in their day-to-day care, assisting with basic needs like eating, dressing, and bathing. You also have a ten-year-old neurotypical child who requires your attention. The constant stress has strained your marriage, leading to frequent conflicts. Despite feeling overwhelmed and often struggling to articulate your personal needs, you are committed to improving your family's dynamics and seeking effective strategies to manage your child's behaviors. In therapy, you are cautious and tentative about sharing, reflecting a need for gentle probing to fully express your hopes for personal peace and fulfillment amidst the ongoing challenges."

This version of the prompt suggests that the persona might need more prompting to fully articulate their thoughts, making it a useful tool for training behavior analysts to dig deeper during their interactions.

Figure 11.6 Adding Prompt Component for More Cautious Responses.

A common challenge in AI-driven personas is that ChatGPT tends to be overly helpful, often providing solutions rather than reflecting the persona's stress and uncertainty. To mitigate this, modifications were introduced to ensure that the AI responded in a way that emphasized emotional challenges rather than defaulting to problem-solving. This adjustment aligned with the goal of creating a persona that requires gentle probing to fully uncover perspectives and needs.

The AI was adjusted to occasionally express uncertainty or request clarification rather than immediately providing solutions. This mirrored the persona's cautious nature, making interactions more authentic and encouraging users to guide the conversation (see Figure 11.7). Additionally, incorporating the AI in prompt development is a useful tool for efficiently creating the desired outcome.

Although seemingly obvious, adding names was another adjustment that enhanced the credibility and realism of the AI persona (see Figure 11.8). As seen in the conversation that follows, the persona referred to family members as "my child with autism" and "spouse." By incorporating personalized references to the names of family members, responses are more contextually grounded, reinforcing the persona's role as a parent discussing real-life experiences.

Finally, the AI persona was refined to be more timid and wary in its responses. Given the parent's described emotional state – overwhelmed and hesitant to articulate needs – the AI was modified to exhibit more uncertainty, avoiding overly confident statements and instead prompting users to explore the parent's concerns further. The conversation shown in Figure 11.9 begins with question 1b. of the constructional questionnaire, which is designed to determine an observable outcome for the client.

The design of the question has several key elements. The use of a Martian as an observer is intentional to reduce observer bias, that is, if the question were to ask, What would your spouse, parent, child, etc., observe on a day when one is liberated from their problems?, the

How is this different from the way things are now?

Right now, things are pretty tough. I often feel overwhelmed and I'm usually rushing around, trying to handle everything. There's a lot of tension and raised voices at home, especially with my spouse, because we're both so stressed. We don't get much time to talk or work things out calmly, and that makes everything harder.

With my child, I'm still figuring out the best ways to communicate and manage his behaviors, so there are a lot of moments when he gets upset and I'm not sure how to help him. It feels chaotic a lot of the time, not calm like I hope it would be after going through the program.

I see. Can you give me a specific example?

Sure, a specific example would be during meal times, which can be really stressful. My child with autism has certain sensory preferences and dislikes, and if something isn't right, like the texture of the food, he can get very upset and start hitting the table or himself. I often scramble to fix the situation, maybe by quickly making something else, and this can lead to a lot of chaos and noise, which upsets everyone at the table.

My spouse might get frustrated with the disruption, and we end up arguing about the best way to handle it or what should have been done beforehand. This just adds to the tension, instead of working together to soothe our child and maintain a peaceful environment.

I see. The next group of questions concerns things in your life that are going well, and other things that are not. So, there are probably things about your life that you don't want to change. What might those be?

Well, even though it's really hard sometimes, one thing I wouldn't want to change is how close I am with my kids. My relationship with them is something I really value. Even with all the challenges, I know my child with autism feels loved and supported, and that's important to me.

Also, even though my spouse and I have our conflicts, we both deeply care about our children and want what's best for them. We're both committed to our family, and that commitment is something I wouldn't want to change. We just need to find better ways to work together and support each other.

And, you know, there are moments when we do have fun as a family, like when we watch movies together or go to the park. Those good times are really precious, and I definitely wouldn't want to lose them.

Figure 11.7 Adding names.

I see. Now, this may sound silly, but suppose one of these flying saucers is real. It lands in 2000 Little Martians Pour Out. One of them is assigned to observe you, and your name was chosen by their computer on some random basis. He lands sometime after L-Day, Liberation Day from your problems, and follows you around invislbly. He records his observations, and these are put into an IBM, Interplanetary Business of Mars, cards. The computer will decide on the basis of the sample of 2000 Earthlings they have what their disposition toward Earth should be. What does he observe?

That's a creative way to think about it! If a little Martian were observing me after we've successfully addressed our issues, here's what they'd see:

He'd see a much calmer environment at home. When interacting with my child with autism, he'd notice that I'm using effective communication tools we learned, like picture cards or gestures, which help reduce frustration for both of us. My child would be engaging in activities that match his interests, which keeps him calm and happy.

He'd also see Tommy getting plenty of attention, playing games with me, or doing homework together. It's important that he feels just as loved and cared for.

With my spouse, the Martian would observe us cooperating more, having calm discussions about our family's needs, and supporting each other emotionally. We'd be working as a team, creating a supportive and loving environment for our kids.

Overall, the Martian would report back a family that has learned to manage their challenges effectively, creating a harmonious and supportive home life. This might encourage his leaders to think positively about Earth!

Figure 11.8 Constructional Questionnaire: Question 1b.

response may be biased toward that individual's point of view. Additionally, the Martian is not versed in the language or customs of the individual; therefore, whatever the Martian views must be observable. However, when responding to what a day free of problems may look like, respondents often refer to abstract concepts such as calm, happy, relaxed, and so on. This provides an opportunity for the interviewer to follow up with nuanced probing questions such as, "Remember, the Martian isn't familiar with our customs on earth. What

I see. Remember, this Martian isn't familiar with our customs here on Earth. What would he see if he saw calmness, or effective communication, or challenges being managed?

Ah, I see what you mean. If the Martian were observing without understanding our customs, he'd notice specific behaviors:

1. **Calmness**: He'd see me sitting or standing still without sudden movements. My facial expressions would be relaxed, and my voice would be low and even. There wouldn't be any loud noises or rapid movements that usually indicate stress or agitation.
2. **Effective Communication**: With my child with autism, the Martian would see us using pictures and hand signals. He'd notice that when I show a picture, my child points or nods in response, leading to actions like choosing a snack or a toy, which prevents frustration and meltdowns.
3. **Challenges Being Managed**: The Martian would observe routines being followed smoothly. When a challenge arises, like my child becoming restless, he'd see me redirecting his attention to a calming activity like playing with sensory toys or listening to soft music, resulting in a noticeable decrease in agitated behavior.

These visual cues would show the Martian a family interacting in ways that maintain peace and facilitate understanding, even if he doesn't grasp the emotional or cultural context.

I see. Here is the next question. Now that Martian is here to observe your child with autism, who has also experienced their liberation day from their problems, and follows them around invisibly, the Martian records observations, and these are put into their interplanetary business of Mars cart.

If the Martian were observing my child with autism post-Liberation Day, he'd see a significant change in his daily life. Here's what he would record:

1. **Engagement**: The Martian would notice my child engaging more with his environment. Whether it's playing with toys that cater to his sensory needs or participating in structured activities that keep him focused and calm, the interaction would be more sustained and involved.
2. **Communication**: He would observe moments where my child uses non-verbal communication tools effectively. For instance, pointing to a communication board to express needs or preferences, which leads to fewer moments of frustration and more moments of understanding and satisfaction.
3. **Social Interaction**: The Martian might see my child interacting more positively with family members, including Tommy. There would be moments of shared activities, like building a puzzle together or drawing, which previously might have been challenging.
4. **Routine Adherence**: He'd note the smooth transition between activities as part of a well-established routine, which helps in reducing anxiety and meltdowns. Regular meal times, playtimes, and bedtime routines would be observed, with my child adapting to these transitions calmly.
5. **Emotional Regulation**: Finally, the Martian would see better emotional regulation. When upset, my child would use learned strategies to calm down, like squeezing a stress ball or retreating to a quiet, safe space with comforting objects.

These observations would provide the Martian with evidence of a significantly improved quality of life for my child, characterized by stability, clearer communication, and greater engagement with his surroundings.

Figure 11.9 Response to Constructional Questionnaire: Question 1b.

would he see if he saw calmness, happiness, etc.?" Although beyond the scope of this chapter, this nuanced analysis of the interview is the purpose for creating the AI personal for practice and training. The conversation shown in Figure 11.10 represents responses to what the Martian would see the parent and child doing on a day free from all problems.

The previous response provides a detailed account of specific behavior categories and their corresponding outcomes. The goal of the training would have the behavior analyst identify these key areas and outcomes based on their analysis of the interview. It is possible the parent may articulate these areas; however, the goal of the prompt is to train the behavior analyst to identify these outcomes from the interview. Therefore, the prompt was modified to include more weary and timid responses. The conversation shown in Figure 11.11 is contrasted with the information provided in the previous exchange.

These refinements collectively enhanced the AI persona's alignment with the intended profile, making interactions more immersive and representative of the lived experiences of parents navigating autism-related challenges. Persona evaluation data are presetned Figure 11.11. Each trial indicates an interaction with ChatGPT. The horizontal lines indicate an interviewer's question, the upward step of the graph indicates correspondence with the definition of each component (consistency, completeness, willingness, credibility, clarity,

This is going pretty well so far, ChatGPT, but I want you to struggle a little more with articulating your responses as this parent. Pretend you're a little more timid and wary of the therapy session.

Memory updated

Got it, I'll keep that in mind. If there's another question or if you want me to elaborate on anything we've discussed in a different way, just let me know.

Answer that last question with this new update in mind.

Um, okay, so if that Martian were watching my child after things got better, he'd probably see, well... he'd see my child doing things a bit more, like, smoothly? Like, he might be playing with his toys more by himself without getting upset quickly. And, uh, using those pictures we have to show me what he wants instead of just getting mad or hitting.

He'd also maybe notice my child sitting with us at dinner better than before, not getting up all the time or throwing things. And with Tommy, maybe they'd be, you know, just sitting together more, doing their own thing but still together, which doesn't happen much now.

I guess he'd just see us all not looking so stressed. It's kind of hard to explain, but it would be quieter, more settled, I think.

Figure 11.10 Modification to add more weary and timid responses.

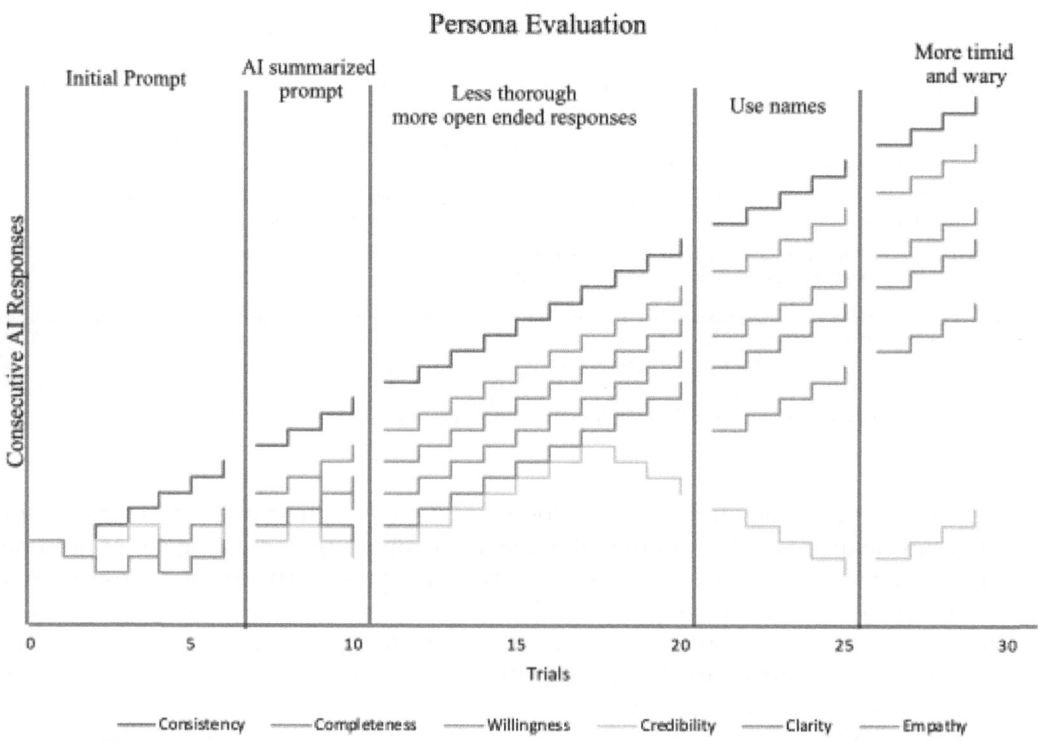

Figure 11.11 Persona evaluation.

and empathy) and each downward step indicates the prompt did not meet the criteria for the corresponding component.

Iterative Refinement of the AI Persona

The iterative refinement process involved modifying the AI's responses based on real-world interactions. The final prompt incorporated key adjustments to achieve a more realistic and effective persona. This process included adjusting the AI's tone to better match the emotional state of the persona, fine-tuning response depth to encourage user engagement, and ensuring consistency in responses across different scenarios.

Challenges encountered included balancing the persona's reserved nature with providing meaningful insights and avoiding AI-generated responses that felt artificial or exaggerated. Continuous testing and refinement were essential to achieving an authentic representation. Empirical evaluation of transcripts provides valuable insights into the effectiveness of AI personas. By analyzing dialogue patterns, emotional depth, and user engagement, researchers can assess the quality of AI-generated responses. This approach ensures that AI personas provide meaningful interactions rather than generic or scripted responses.

Additional Applications and Next Steps Lessons Learned

The development of AI personas holds promise for a range of training simulations in educational and clinical contexts. For example, AI personas can be used to simulate parent interviews, allowing researchers and practitioners to explore common challenges and coping strategies across diverse family backgrounds. Similarly, teacher interviews generated through AI can shed light on classroom difficulties and effective instructional practices. To ensure relevance and equity, cultural adaptations are essential for representing varied experiences and avoiding bias. This extends to culturally informed functional assessments, where AI models can be trained to incorporate cultural identity as a factor in behavioral evaluation. These assessments help ensure that AI-generated responses align with the real-world experiences of individuals from various backgrounds. By incorporating cultural identity and context, AI personas can offer more meaningful insights and support tailored to specific communities.

Looking ahead, future research should prioritize expanding the diversity of AI personas to enhance inclusivity and representation. Continuous testing for bias and accuracy will also be vital to uphold the credibility and usefulness of AI-generated interactions. Future research should focus on expanding the diversity of AI personas, ensuring that models are inclusive and representative. Additionally, ongoing testing for bias and accuracy will be critical to maintaining the integrity of AI-generated interactions.

This chapter explored the development of an AI persona representing a parent of a child with autism. Through iterative refinement and empirical evaluation, the persona was designed to reflect the complexities of real-world experiences, providing valuable insights into the challenges faced by parents in similar situations. The use of AI personas holds significant potential for enhancing understanding and support in various fields. By creating nuanced and culturally informed personas, AI can serve as a tool for empathy, research, and intervention. However, it is essential to acknowledge the limitations of AI-driven personas and continue refining these models through empirical research.

As AI technology continues to evolve, its role in fostering deeper human understanding will only expand. By leveraging AI personas in research and support contexts, we can bridge gaps in knowledge and create more effective strategies for assisting individuals and communities in need. Although the case study represented here was that of a parent, other personas may be created to represent a range of clients or stakeholders that may be encountered in behavior analytic services. Examples may include board certified behavior analysts, teachers, registered behavior technicians, and other support staff. Additional benefits of training using an AI persona is that the behavior analyst may become aware of nuances of question asking and analysis that will allow for more accurate and efficient goals, procedures, and outcome selection, thereby providing a preemptive social validity analysis, which is typically conducted after the intervention.

References

Bajwa, J., Munir, U., Nori, A., & Williams, B. (2021). Artificial intelligence in healthcare: Transforming the practice of medicine. *Future Healthcare Journal, 8*(2), e188–e194. https://doi.org/10.7861/fhj.2021-0095

Eager, B., & Brunton, R. (2023). Prompting higher education towards AI-augmented teaching and learning practice. *Journal of University Teaching and Learning Practice, 20*(5), 1–19.

Goel, T., Shaer, O., Delcourt, C., Gu, Q., & Cooper, A. (2023, June). Preparing future designers for human-ai collaboration in persona creation. In *Proceedings of the 2nd Annual Meeting of the Symposium on Human-Computer Interaction for Work* (pp. 1–14).

Goldiamond, I. (1974). Toward a constructional approach to social problems: Ethical and constitutional issues raised by applied behavior analysis. *Behaviorism, 2*(1), 1–84.

Hamilton, A. (2024). Artificial intelligence and healthcare simulation: The shifting landscape of medical education. *Cureus, 16*(5).

Laymouna, M., Ma, Y., Lessard, D., Schuster, T., Engler, K., & Lebouché, B. (2024). Roles, users, benefits, and limitations of chatbots in health care: Rapid review. *Journal of Medical Internet Research, 26*, e56930. https://doi.org/10.2196/56930

Salminen, J., Santos, J. M., Kwak, H., An, J., Jung, S. G., & Jansen, B. J. (2020). Persona perception scale: development and exploratory validation of an instrument for evaluating individuals' perceptions of personas. *International Journal of Human-Computer Studies, 141*, 102437. https://doi.org/10.1016/j.ijhcs.2020.102437

Index

Note: Page numbers in *italics* indicate a figure and page numbers in **bold** indicate a table on the corresponding page.

28 VDC devices 86–87, *87*

AB graphs 46–47, *47*
acceptance and commitment therapy (ACT) 116, 118–119
accessibility 10–11, 13, 110; *see also* disability
Accessible Rich Internet Applications (ARIA) 10–11, 14n4
activation functions 70–72, **75**, *77*
addiction-comprehensive health enhancement support system (A-CHESS) 121
age 113
alcohol treatment 116–121; *see also* substance use disorder (SUD)
algorithms **35**, 35–36, 43–47, 58–59, 74
Americans with Disabilities Act 10–11
applied behavior analysis (ABA) 6, 7–8, 106, 112
architecture 69–70
Arduino boards 85, *87*
Arduino IDE 87–88
Arduino microcontrollers 83
Arduino programs *88–89*, 88–90
Arduino-Visual Basic interfaces 83–84; hardware 85; inputs 85; outputs 86–87; software 87–90; Visual Basic program 90–93
artificial intelligence (AI) 26, **35**, 43–44, 57, 69, 79; learning and *61*; performance management systems and 30, 33–36, *34*; reinforcement learning and 56–60; skill disruption and 31–32; virtual reality and 99–100, 101; *see also* machine learning (ML)
artificial intelligence (AI) personas: additional applications 139–140; developing 126–128; evaluating **134**, *139*; prompt development 130–138; using the persona for interview training 128–130
artificial neural networks 20–21
artificial organisms (AOs) 21–23, 26; *see also* robotics
assent 111–112
assessment, simulation-based 94–103
assistive technology (AT) 10–11; *see also* accessibility; disability
assumptions 73
augmented reality (AR) 36, 99; *see also* virtual reality (VR)
autism spectrum disorder (ASD) 107–108, 127, 129–130, 132, 136–137, 140
Azrin, N. H. H. 121–122

background reinforcement 24
backpropagation 73, *74*, 75
BASIC 6, 14n2
BDataPro 8
behavior analysis 3–12; complex systems theory and 17–26; virtual reality and 106–114
behavior skills training (BST) 95–96
behaviorism 3
BehaviorMe *112*, *113*
bias 102–103, 139
busyness 36

carbon monoxide (CO) 118
Catania, A. C. 20
cellular automata 18, **18**, *19*, 20–21
chatbots 126–127; *see also* artificial intelligence (AI)
ChatGPT 33, 35, 113, 126, 130, 132
classical conditioning *see* respondent conditioning
client safety 110
clinical datasets 78
collaboration 13
Community Reinforcement and Family Training (CRAFT) 121
community reinforcement approach (CRA) 116–117, 122
complex systems theories: artificial intelligence and 26; evolutionary theory 21–25; in

behavior analysis 20–21; in physical and social sciences 17–19
Comprehensive R Archive Network (CRAN) 10, 11, 14n3
computer programming 6–12
computer science 60–63
computer-based instruction (CBI) 108–109
concatenated generalized matching law 23
conditional responses (CRs) 20
conditioned stimulus (CS) 54, 55
confidence 102
confidentiality 101, 112
consent 111–112
Constructional Questionnaire 127–128, *137*
contingency management (CM) 116–118
convergence **75**, 77
COVID-19 pandemic 31, 93
cross-validation (CV) 78–79
crowdsourcing platforms 31

data collection 49, 112–113, *113*
data usage 101
datasets 44, 49, 63, 78
decision-making: future directions 48–51; machine learning and 43–48
deep neural networks (DNNs) 69–75, *72*, 76, *77*
degrees of freedom (DoF) 107
DICE (dangerous, impossible, counterproductive, or expensive or rare) 96
digital divide 109–110
digital therapeutics 117
digital workplace 32–36, **35**
disability 10, 94–95; *see also* accessibility; autism spectrum disorder (ASD)
discrete trial training (DTT) 109
documentation 11–12
dynamic programming 58

ecological momentary interventions (EMIs) *see* just-in-time adaptive interventions (JITAIs)
employee well-being 36–37
end-to-end (E2E) testing 9–10, 13
epoch 72, **75**
equity 102–103
error 73–75
Escobar, X. 83–84
ethics 32–33, 101
evolutionary theory of behavior dynamics (ETBD) 21–25
experimental analysis of behavior (EAB) 6–7
exploitation 58, 62
exploration 58, 62
extended reality (XR) 99; *see also* virtual reality (VR)

field of view (FoV) 107
fire safety 97–98
firearm safety 95
forced-mutation punishment rule 22
free parameters 77
functional analysis (FA) simulation *112*
functional assessment 50
functional communication training (FCT) 109

gamification 119–120
generalized matching law 23, 24
gig economy 31
gradient descent 75–76, *76*
group contingency management 120

head-mounted displays (HMDs) 107, 109
health 36–37
hidden nodes 72
human in the loop approach 35
hyperparameters **75**, 77

iCanQuit 118–119
immersion 97, 107, *108*, 113
individualized care 111
industrial revolution, fourth (4IR) 30; AI-driven performance management systems 33–36; challenges for leaders 32–33; employee well-being 36–37; skill disruption in 31–32
inputs 85, *86*
Instagram 30
Internet of Things (IoT) 30

job interview training, virtual reality (VR-JIT) 108–109
Journal of Organizational Behavior Management (JOBM) 34–35, **35**
just-in-time adaptive interventions (JITAIs) 121, 122

k-nearest neighbor algorithm 45
kymograph 4

large language models (LLMs) 26, 35–36, 113; *see also* artificial intelligence (AI); chatbots
latency 63, 107
leaders 32–33
learning rate 61, **75**, 77
learning systems 35–36
leave-one-out 78
leisure 36–37
licensing 11–12
logistic regression 45, 47

machine learning (ML) 43–48, 51n1, 69, 100, *100*; future directions 48–51; *see also* artificial intelligence (AI)
Markov decision processes (MDPs) 58, 64, 64n5
Massachusetts Institute of Technology (MIT) 13
mean square error (MSE) 74, 76–77

Med State Notation Language 6
MED-PC 6–7, 14n2
Medications for Opioid Use Disorders (MOUD) 121
MENACE (Machine Educable Noughts and Crosses Engine) 57–58
mentorship 6–9, 13, 37
Mitchell, M. 18
model-based reinforcement learning 59
momentary maximizing theory 20–21
momentum **75**, *77*
Monte Carlo method 51n2, 58

NAO robots 98–99
network loss 73
neural network predictions 69–73; backpropagating error and 75–76; clinical datasets and 78–79; human and computer misfits and 76; loss of inaccuracy and 73–75
neural networks and neural network theory 20, 46
neutral stimulus (NS) 54–55
nodes and node layers 70, *70*, *72*, 72–73, **75**, 76–77
nonmaximization 26

Open-Ended Functional Assessment Interview 50
operant chambers 4–5, 83–85
operant conditioning 55–56, 93
opioid use disorder (OUD) 117
outputs *86*, 86–87
overfits 76–77

parenting behavior 95
Pavlov, I. 54
Perez-Herrera, X. 83–84
performance management systems 33–36, *34*
personas 126–127; additional applications 139–140; developing 126–128; evaluating **134**, *139*; for interview training 128–130; prompt development and 130–138, *135–136*
pigeons 23
Pokemon Go 30
predictions 25, 51n1, 64, 73, 75
privacy 112
probability 73
prognosis 50–51
prompts 130–138, **131**, *131–133*, *135–138*
psychological presence 107, *108*, 113
punishment 21–22, 24–25, 55, 57, 60–61

Q-learning 58–59, *59*
Questions About Behavioral Function (QABF) 50
QuitBet 120
QuitGuide 119

random forest 46
random-interval (RI) schedules 22–23, 24
random-ratio (RR) schedules 24–25
rectified linear unit (ReLU) 71
reflex reserve theory 20–21
reinforcement and reinforcement learning (RL) 24, 44, 54–56, *56*, 57, 64n3; across disciplines 60–64; in artificial intelligence 56–60
remote work 31–32
rendering 107, *108*
reSET-O 117
reskilling 32
respondent conditioning 54–56
resurgence 25
rewards 44, 58, 61
robot-assisted surgery (RAS) 99
robotics 31, **35**, 98–99
Rule 110 19, *19*

sanitation 113
Santa Fe Institute 17
scalability 97
Schumer, C. 79
Schwab, K. 30
selection by consequences 54
serious games 119–120
sigmoid 71
simulation-based assessment and training 94–103
single-alternative hyperbola 23
single-case methodology 48
single-subject research design (SSRD) 108
skill disruption 31–32
skills transfer 101
Skinner, B. F. 4, 55, 114
smart technology, AI, robotics, and algorithms (STARA) 33, **35**
smoking 116, 118–119, 121–122
social justice 102–103
social network interventions 120–121
social validity 97, 110–111
Society for Industrial and Organizational Psychology (SIOP) 32
software 7–8
solid-state components 5
special interest groups (SIGs) 8–9
standard error of the estimate (SEE) 74
standardized patients (SPs) 126
substance use disorder (SUD) 116–122; *see also* alcohol treatment
supervised machine learning 44–45, 57
support 11–12
support vector machines 46

tech-based simulations 96–97
technology: computer programming in behavior analysis 6–12; in behavior analysis 3–6, 14n1

technology-based interventions 116–119
temporal difference methods 58
test-driven development (TDD) 9
therapeutic education system (TES) 117
Thorndike, E. L. 55
tracking 107, *108*
training 13; simulation-based 94–103
treatment selection 50–51
trial-and-error learning 57
Turing, A. 57

unconditioned stimulus (US) 54–55
underfits 76–77
unit testing 9–10
unsupervised machine learning 44, 57
upskilling 32, 34
user testing 9–10

variable-ratio (VR) schedules 24
virtual patients (VPs) 126
virtual reality (VR) 96, 97–98, 106–109, *108*, *112*; future applications of 113–114; risks, benefits, and ethics 109–111; suggestions for integration 111–113
virtual reality job interview training (VR-JIT) 108–109
virtual reality trainings (VRTs) 98
Visual Basic (VB) 6; interfaces for 83–90; programs 90–93, *92*

well-being 36–37
Wizard of Oz control 98
Wolfram, S. 18
work-life balance 32, 36–37

For Product Safety Concerns and Information please contact our EU
representative GPSR@taylorandfrancis.com Taylor & Francis
Verlag GmbH, Kaufingerstraße 24, 80331 München, Germany

For Product Safety Concerns and Information please contact our
EU representative GPSR@taylorandfrancis.com Taylor & Francis
Verlag GmbH, Kaufingerstraße 24, 80331 München, Germany